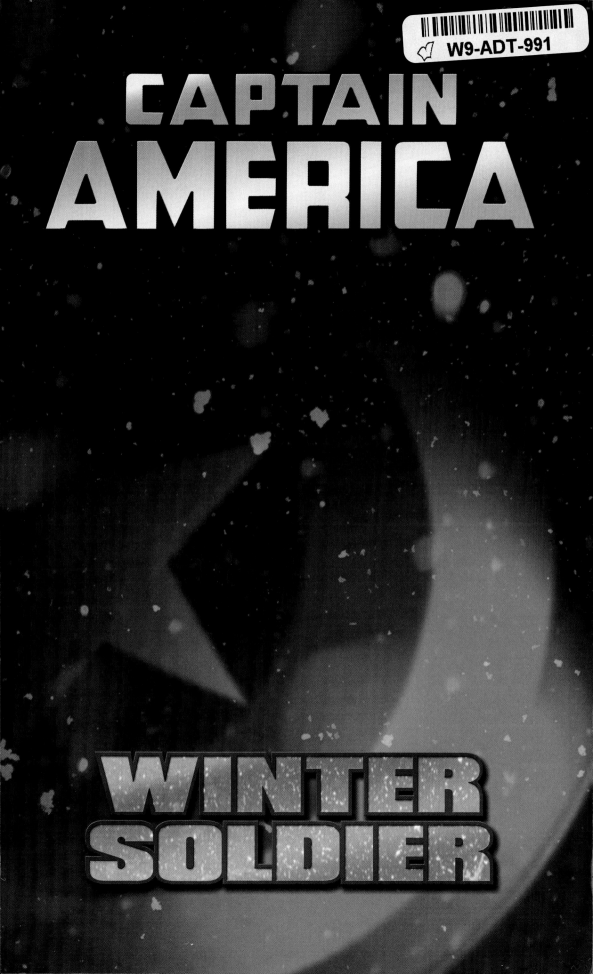

CAPTAIN AMERICA

WINTER SOLDIER

CAPTAIN AMERICA

WINTER SOLDIER

WRITER: Ed Brubaker
ARTIST: Steve Epting
Michael Lark (Flashback Art)
John Paul Leon & Tom Palmer (Issue #7)
COLORIST: Frank D'Armata
LETTERS: Virtual Calligraphy's Randy Gentile
ASSISTANT EDITORS: Nicole Wiley, Molly Lazer
& Andy Schmidt
EDITOR: Tom Brevoort

Captain America created by
Joe Simon & Jack Kirby

COLLECTION EDITOR: Jennifer Grünwald
SENIOR EDITOR, SPECIAL PROJECTS: Jeff Youngquist
DIRECTOR OF SALES: David Gabriel
BOOK DESIGNER: Patrick McGrath
CREATIVE DIRECTOR: Tom Marvelli

EDITOR IN CHIEF: Joe Quesada
PUBLISHER: Dan Buckley

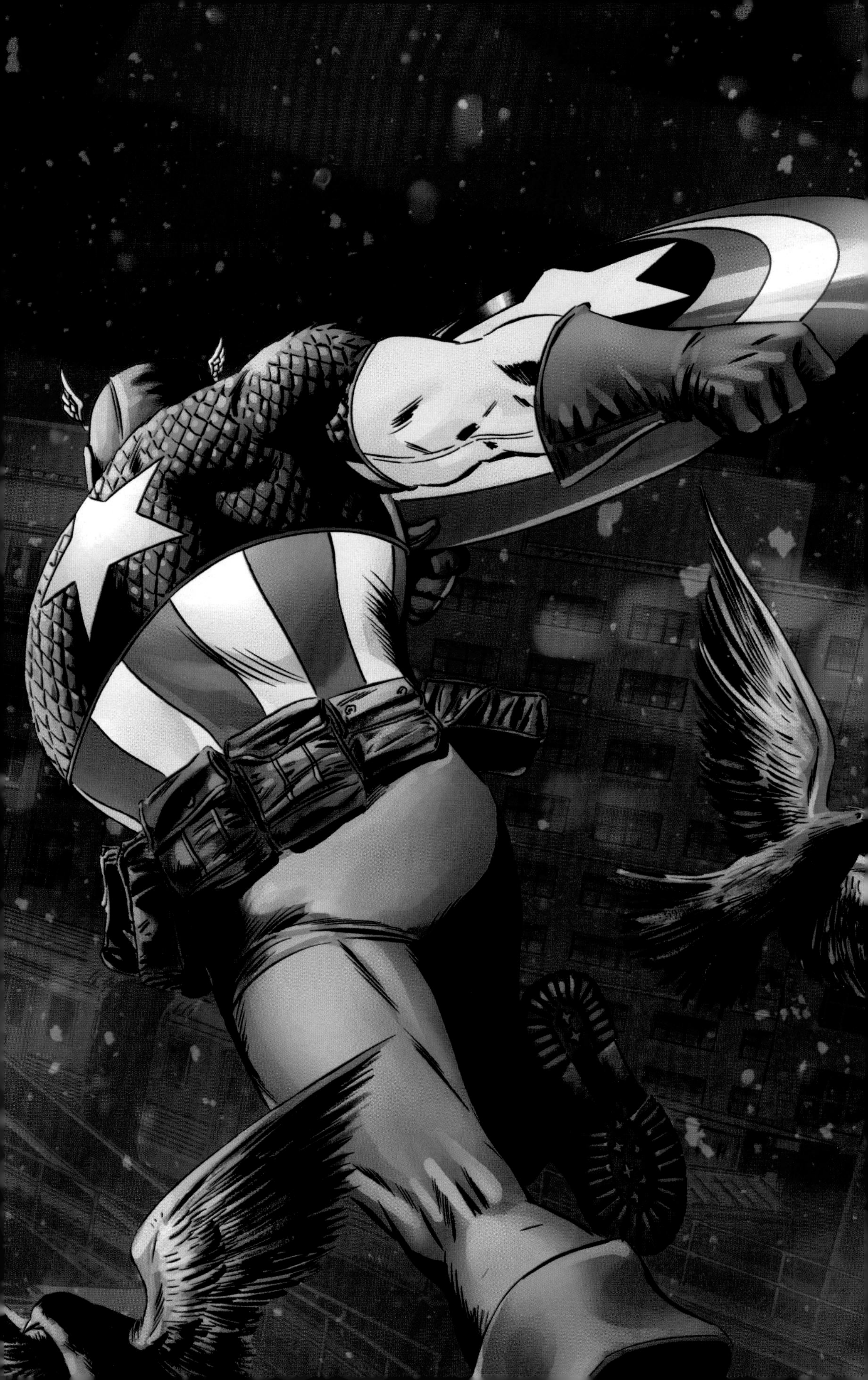

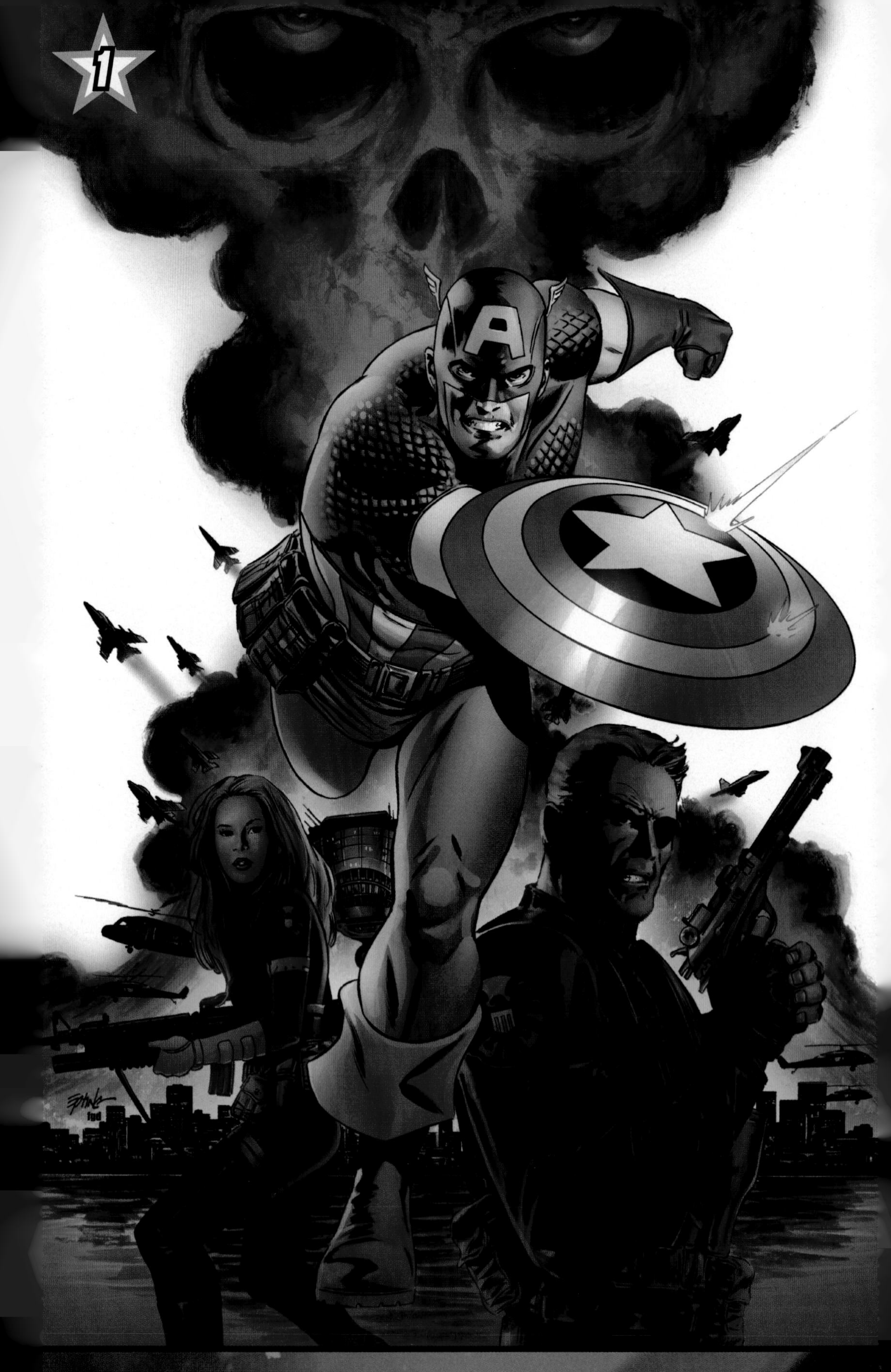
1

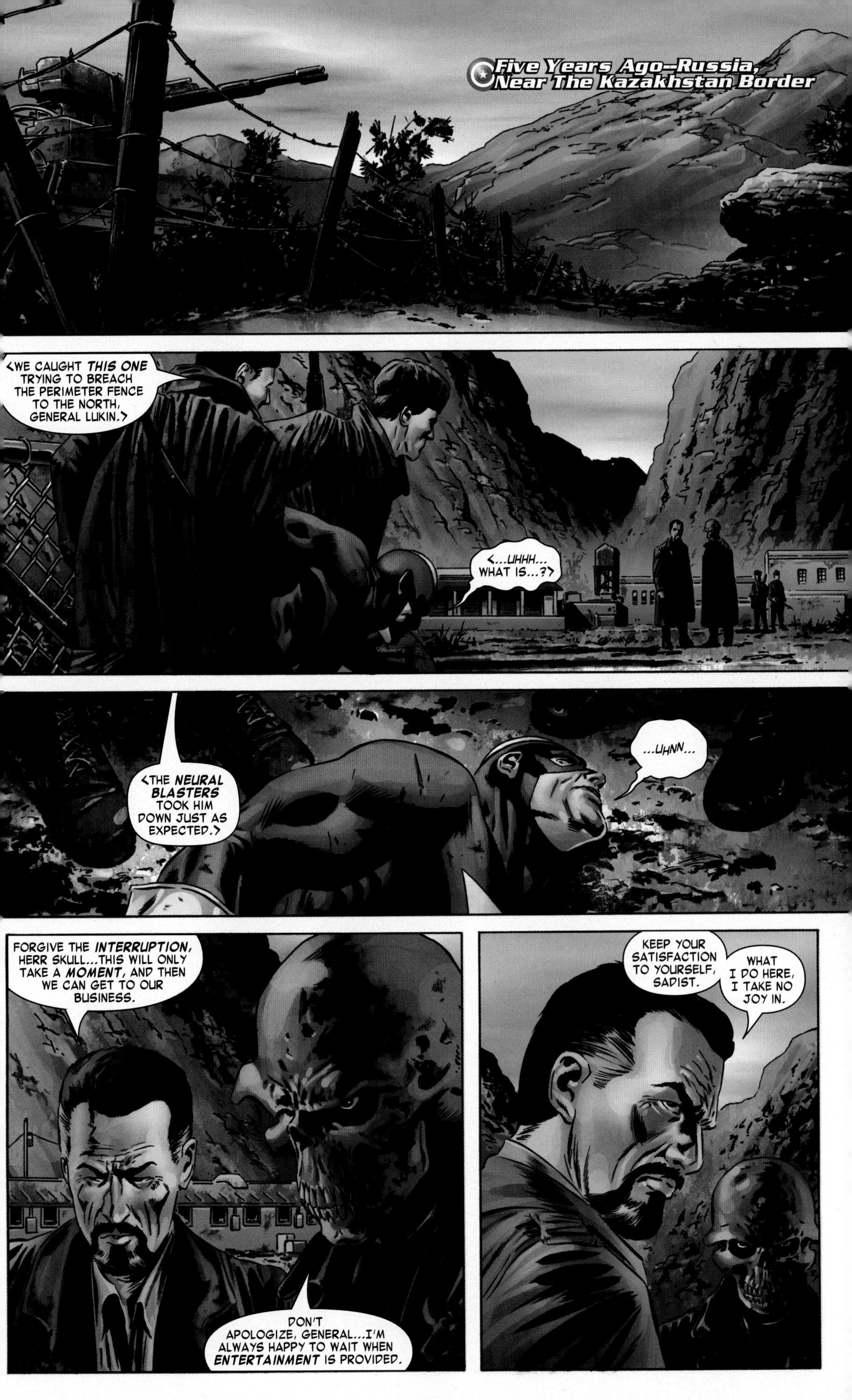
Five Years Ago--Russia, Near The Kazakhstan Border
<WE CAUGHT THIS ONE TRYING TO BREACH THE PERIMETER FENCE TO THE NORTH, GENERAL LUKIN.>
<...UHHH... WHAT IS...?>
<THE NEURAL BLASTERS TOOK HIM DOWN JUST AS EXPECTED.>
...UHNN...
FORGIVE THE INTERRUPTION, HERR SKULL...THIS WILL ONLY TAKE A MOMENT, AND THEN WE CAN GET TO OUR BUSINESS.
DON'T APOLOGIZE, GENERAL...I'M ALWAYS HAPPY TO WAIT WHEN ENTERTAINMENT IS PROVIDED.
KEEP YOUR SATISFACTION TO YOURSELF, SADIST.
WHAT I DO HERE, I TAKE NO JOY IN.

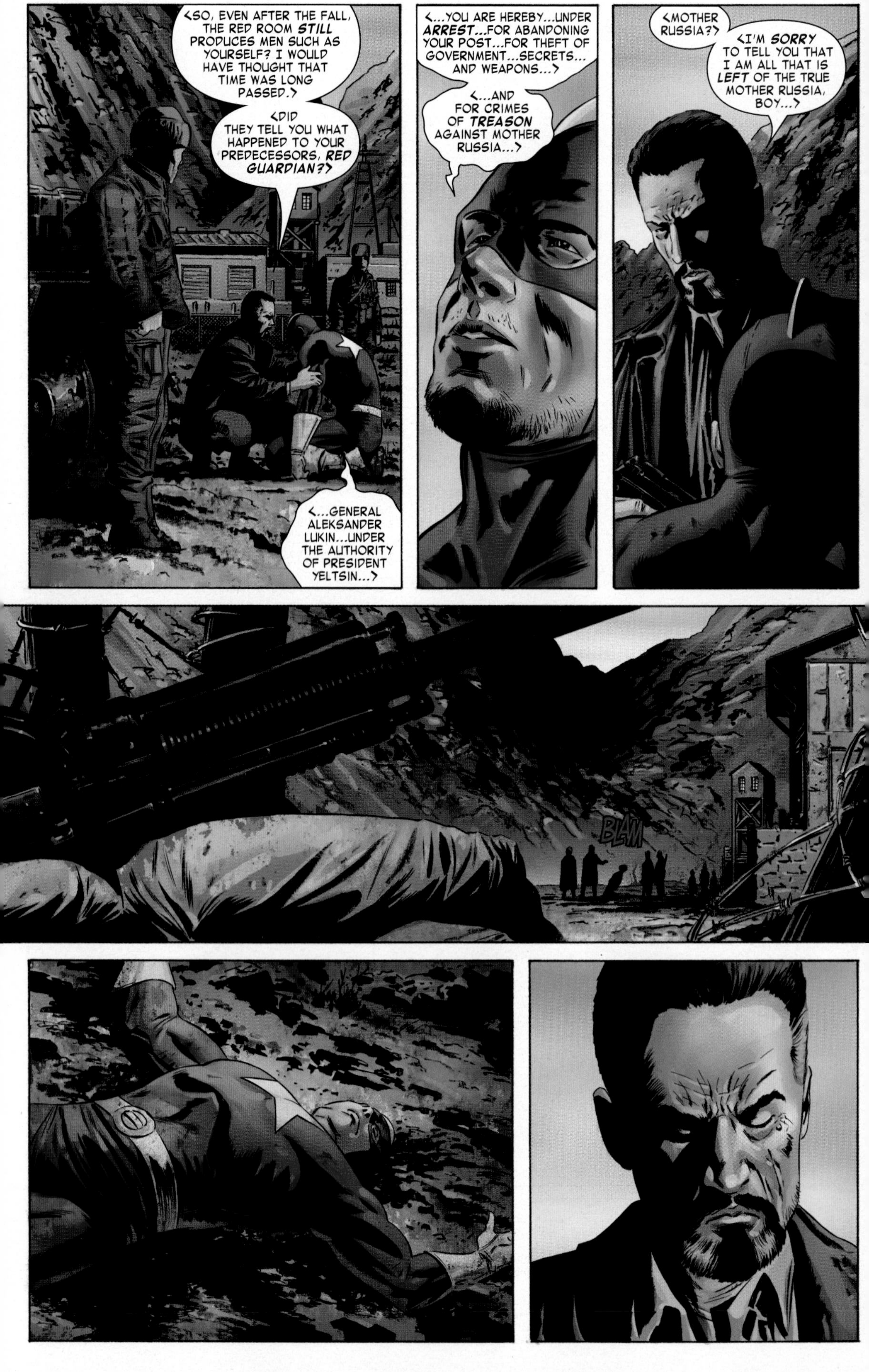

<SO, EVEN AFTER THE FALL, THE RED ROOM STILL PRODUCES MEN SUCH AS YOURSELF? I WOULD HAVE THOUGHT THAT TIME WAS LONG PASSED.>
<DID THEY TELL YOU WHAT HAPPENED TO YOUR PREDECESSORS, RED GUARDIAN?>
<...GENERAL ALEKSANDER LUKIN...UNDER THE AUTHORITY OF PRESIDENT YELTSIN...>
<...YOU ARE HEREBY...UNDER ARREST...FOR ABANDONING YOUR POST...FOR THEFT OF GOVERNMENT...SECRETS... AND WEAPONS...>
<...AND FOR CRIMES OF TREASON AGAINST MOTHER RUSSIA...>
<MOTHER RUSSIA?>
<I'M SORRY TO TELL YOU THAT I AM ALL THAT IS LEFT OF THE TRUE MOTHER RUSSIA, BOY...>
BLAM

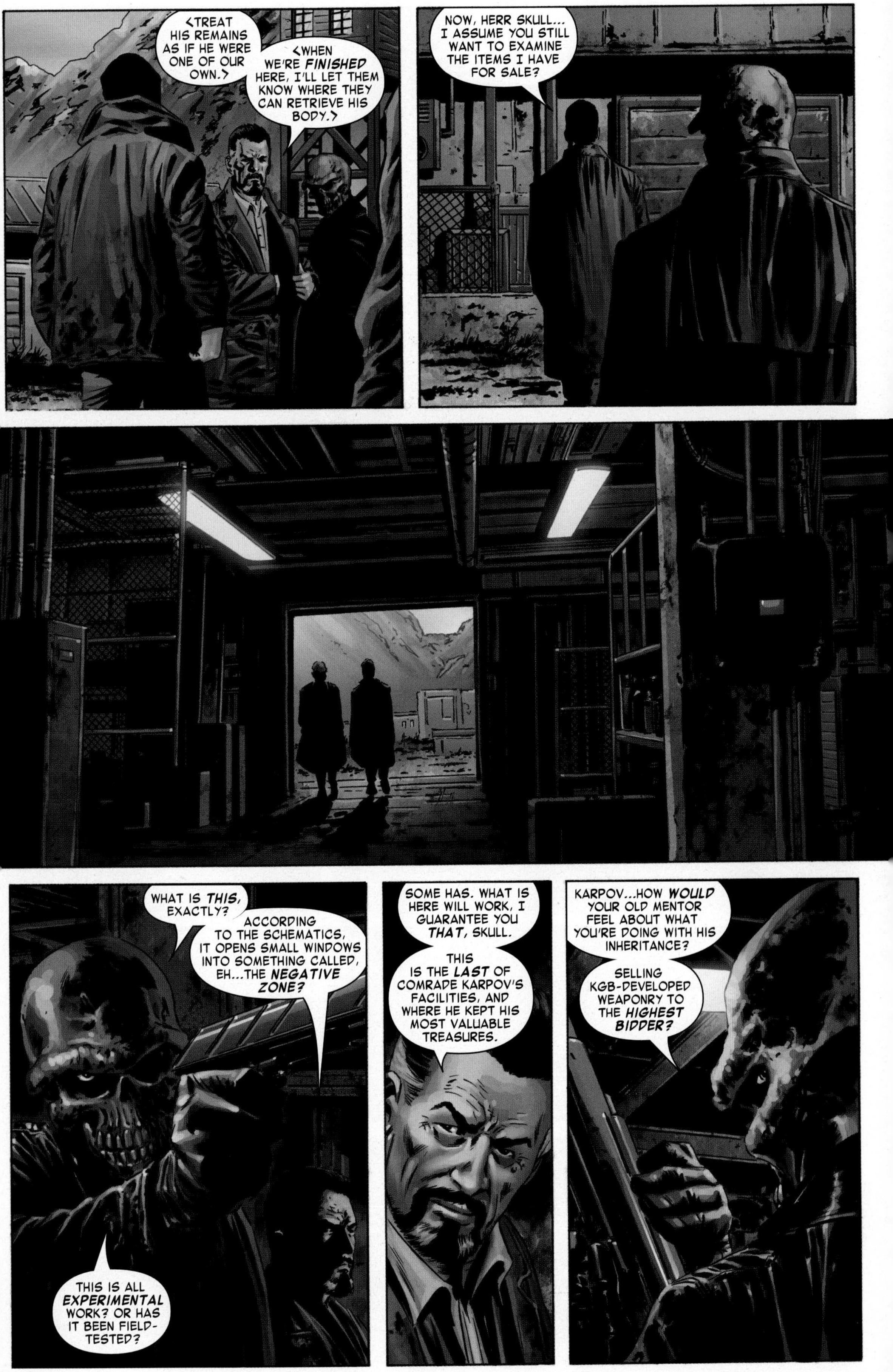

<TREAT HIS REMAINS AS IF HE WERE ONE OF OUR OWN.>
<WHEN WE'RE FINISHED HERE, I'LL LET THEM KNOW WHERE THEY CAN RETRIEVE HIS BODY.>
NOW, HERR SKULL... I ASSUME YOU STILL WANT TO EXAMINE THE ITEMS I HAVE FOR SALE?
WHAT IS THIS, EXACTLY?
ACCORDING TO THE SCHEMATICS, IT OPENS SMALL WINDOWS INTO SOMETHING CALLED, EH...THE NEGATIVE ZONE?
THIS IS ALL EXPERIMENTAL WORK? OR HAS IT BEEN FIELD-TESTED?
SOME HAS. WHAT IS HERE WILL WORK, I GUARANTEE YOU THAT, SKULL.
THIS IS THE LAST OF COMRADE KARPOV'S FACILITIES, AND WHERE HE KEPT HIS MOST VALUABLE TREASURES.
KARPOV...HOW WOULD YOUR OLD MENTOR FEEL ABOUT WHAT YOU'RE DOING WITH HIS INHERITANCE?
SELLING KGB-DEVELOPED WEAPONRY TO THE HIGHEST BIDDER?

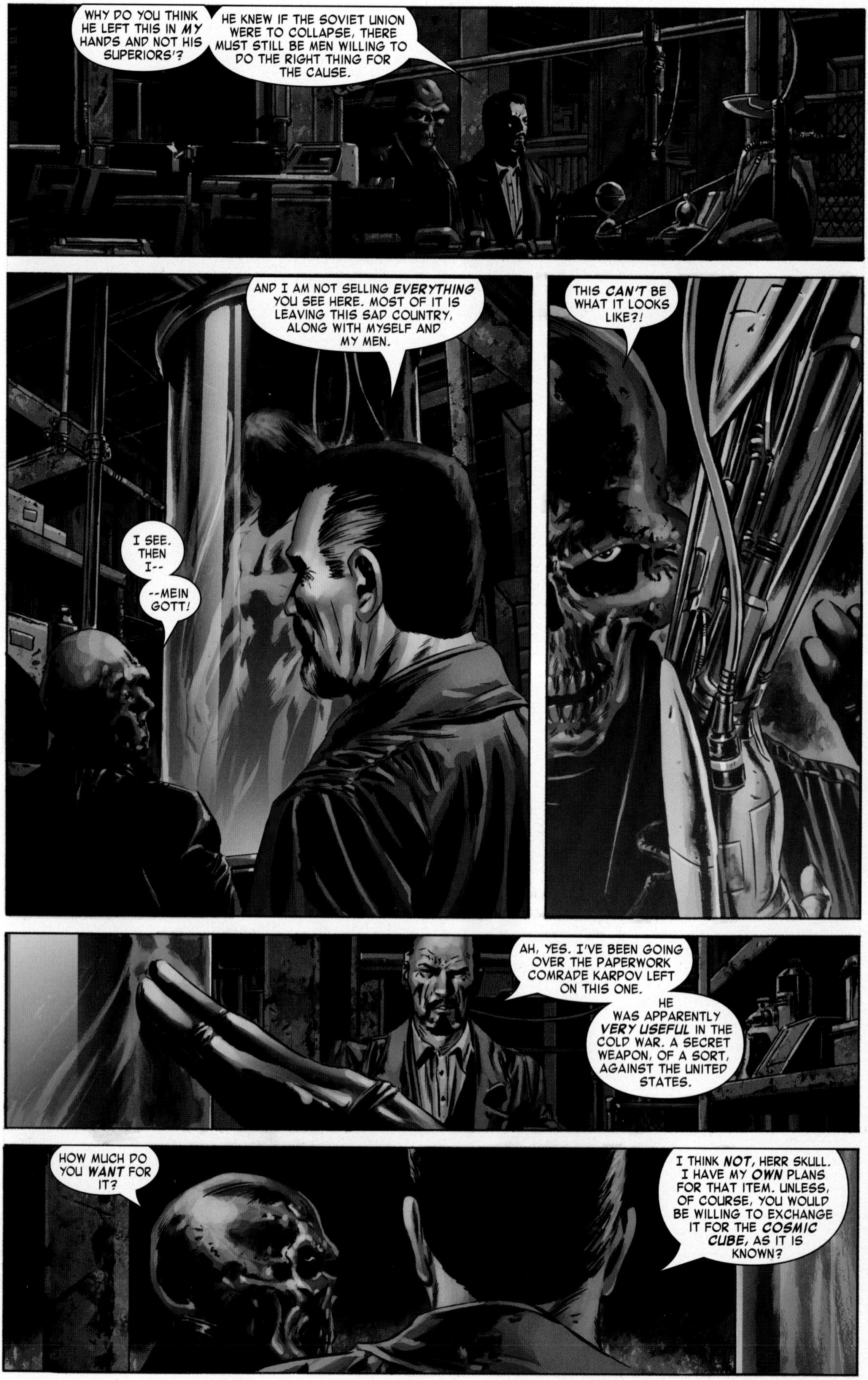
WHY DO YOU THINK HE LEFT THIS IN *MY* HANDS AND NOT HIS SUPERIORS'?
HE KNEW IF THE SOVIET UNION WERE TO COLLAPSE, THERE MUST STILL BE MEN WILLING TO DO THE RIGHT THING FOR THE CAUSE.
AND I AM NOT SELLING **EVERYTHING** YOU SEE HERE. MOST OF IT IS LEAVING THIS SAD COUNTRY, ALONG WITH MYSELF AND MY MEN.
I SEE. THEN I--
--MEIN GOTT!
THIS **CAN'T** BE WHAT IT LOOKS LIKE?!
AH, YES. I'VE BEEN GOING OVER THE PAPERWORK COMRADE KARPOV LEFT ON THIS ONE.
HE WAS APPARENTLY **VERY USEFUL** IN THE COLD WAR. A SECRET WEAPON, OF A SORT, AGAINST THE UNITED STATES.
HOW MUCH DO YOU **WANT** FOR IT?
I THINK **NOT**, HERR SKULL. I HAVE MY **OWN** PLANS FOR THAT ITEM. UNLESS, OF COURSE, YOU WOULD BE WILLING TO EXCHANGE IT FOR THE **COSMIC CUBE**, AS IT IS KNOWN?

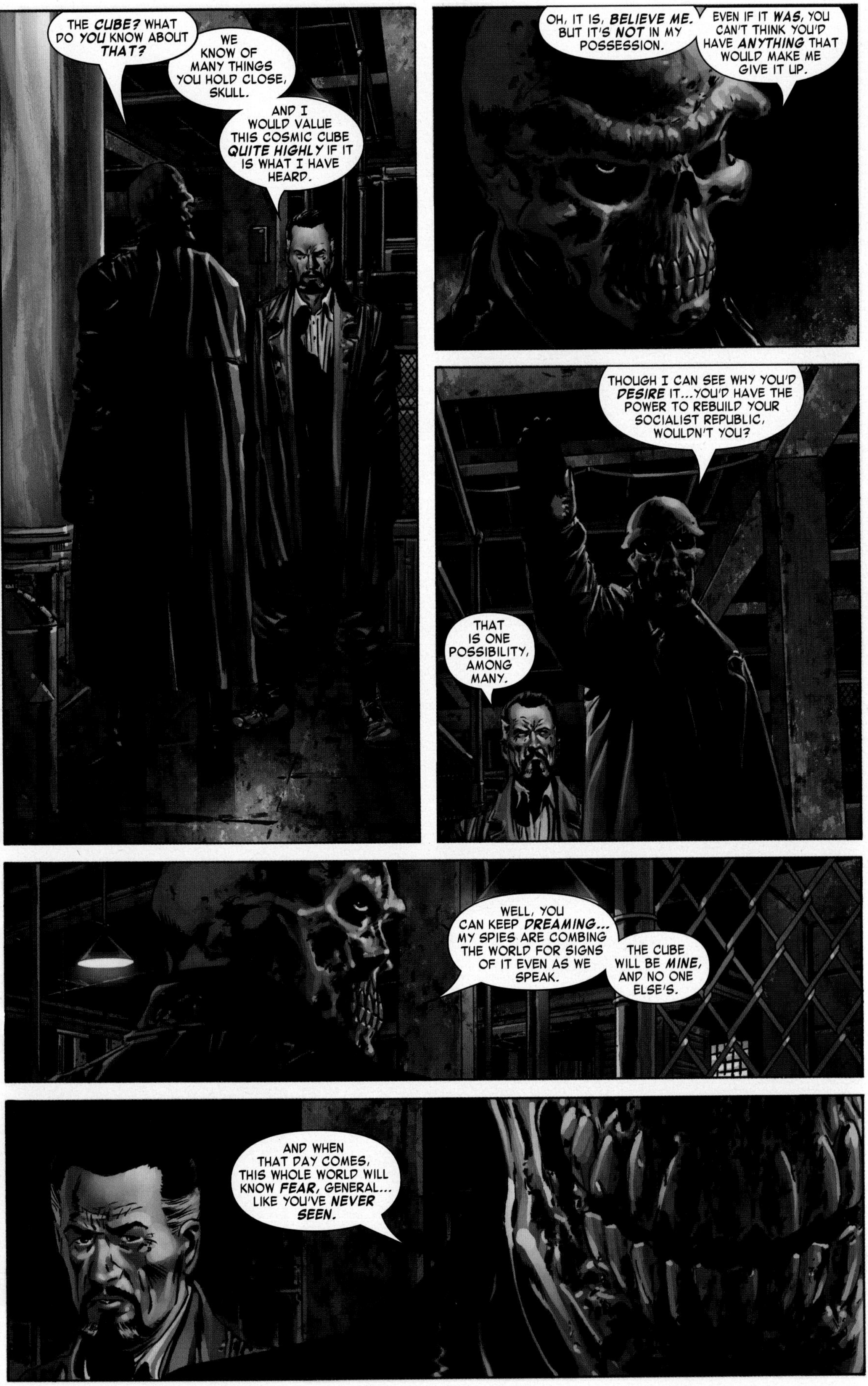
THE CUBE? WHAT DO YOU KNOW ABOUT THAT?
WE KNOW OF MANY THINGS YOU HOLD CLOSE, SKULL.
AND I WOULD VALUE THIS COSMIC CUBE QUITE HIGHLY IF IT IS WHAT I HAVE HEARD.
OH, IT IS, BELIEVE ME. BUT IT'S NOT IN MY POSSESSION.
EVEN IF IT WAS, YOU CAN'T THINK YOU'D HAVE ANYTHING THAT WOULD MAKE ME GIVE IT UP.
THOUGH I CAN SEE WHY YOU'D DESIRE IT...YOU'D HAVE THE POWER TO REBUILD YOUR SOCIALIST REPUBLIC, WOULDN'T YOU?
THAT IS ONE POSSIBILITY, AMONG MANY.
WELL, YOU CAN KEEP DREAMING... MY SPIES ARE COMBING THE WORLD FOR SIGNS OF IT EVEN AS WE SPEAK.
THE CUBE WILL BE MINE, AND NO ONE ELSE'S.
AND WHEN THAT DAY COMES, THIS WHOLE WORLD WILL KNOW FEAR, GENERAL... LIKE YOU'VE NEVER SEEN.

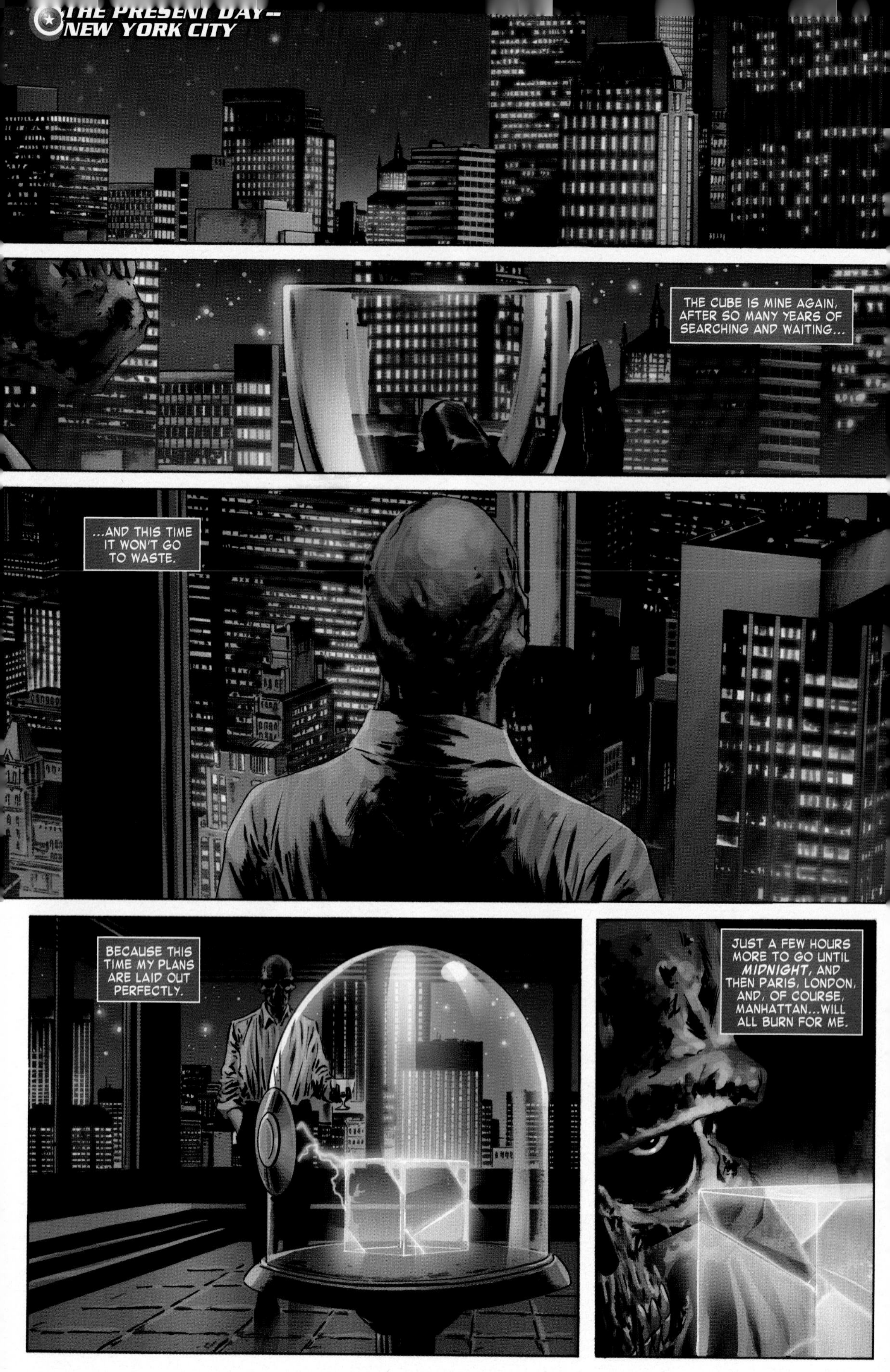
THE PRESENT DAY--
NEW YORK CITY
THE CUBE IS MINE AGAIN, AFTER SO MANY YEARS OF SEARCHING AND WAITING...
...AND THIS TIME IT WON'T GO TO WASTE.
BECAUSE THIS TIME MY PLANS ARE LAID OUT PERFECTLY.
JUST A FEW HOURS MORE TO GO UNTIL *MIDNIGHT*, AND THEN PARIS, LONDON, AND, OF COURSE, MANHATTAN...WILL ALL BURN FOR ME.

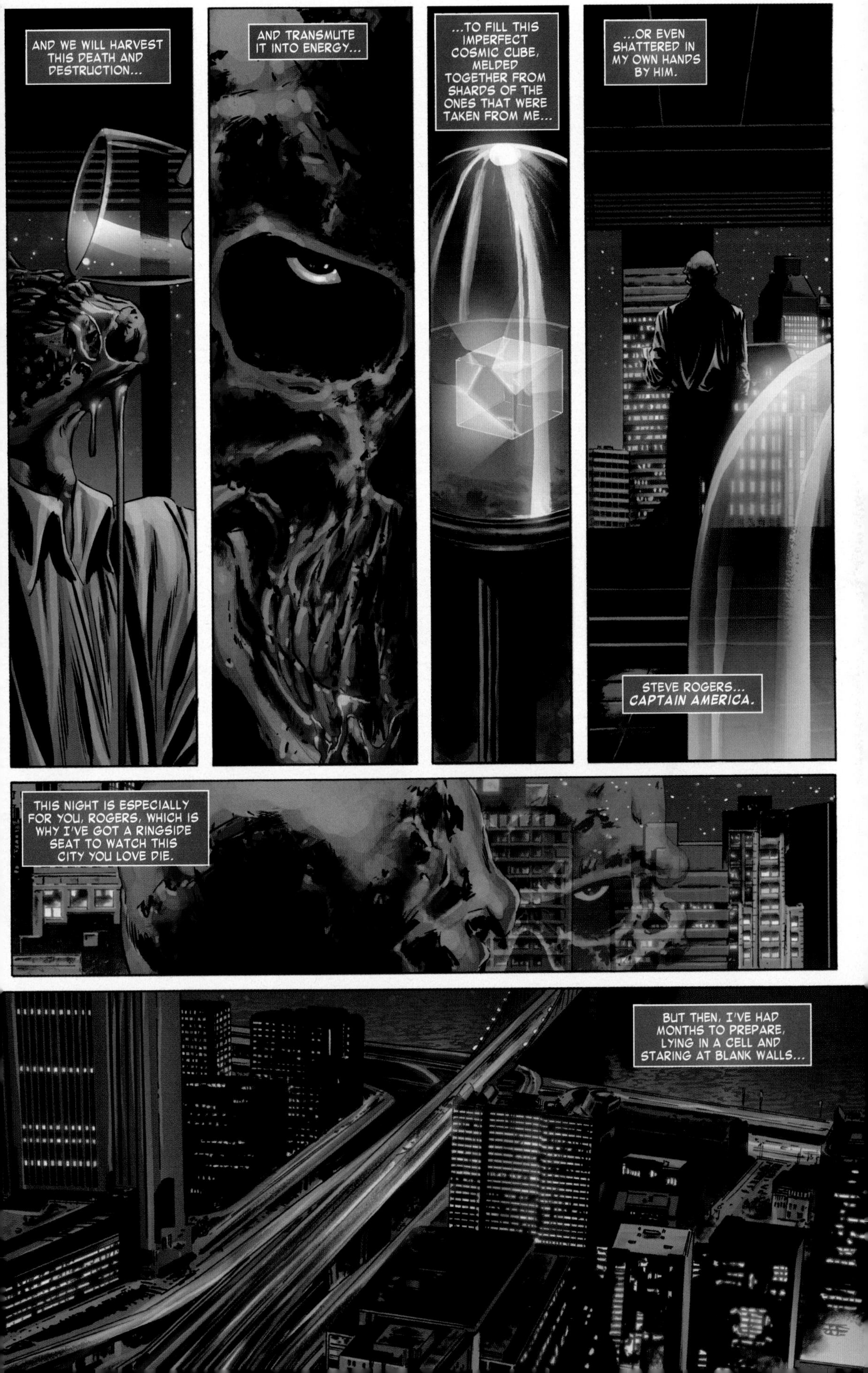
AND WE WILL HARVEST THIS DEATH AND DESTRUCTION...
AND TRANSMUTE IT INTO ENERGY...
...TO FILL THIS IMPERFECT COSMIC CUBE, MELDED TOGETHER FROM SHARDS OF THE ONES THAT WERE TAKEN FROM ME...
...OR EVEN SHATTERED IN MY OWN HANDS BY HIM.
STEVE ROGERS... *CAPTAIN AMERICA.*
THIS NIGHT IS ESPECIALLY FOR YOU, ROGERS, WHICH IS WHY I'VE GOT A RINGSIDE SEAT TO WATCH THIS CITY YOU LOVE DIE.
BUT THEN, I'VE HAD MONTHS TO PREPARE, LYING IN A CELL AND STARING AT BLANK WALLS...

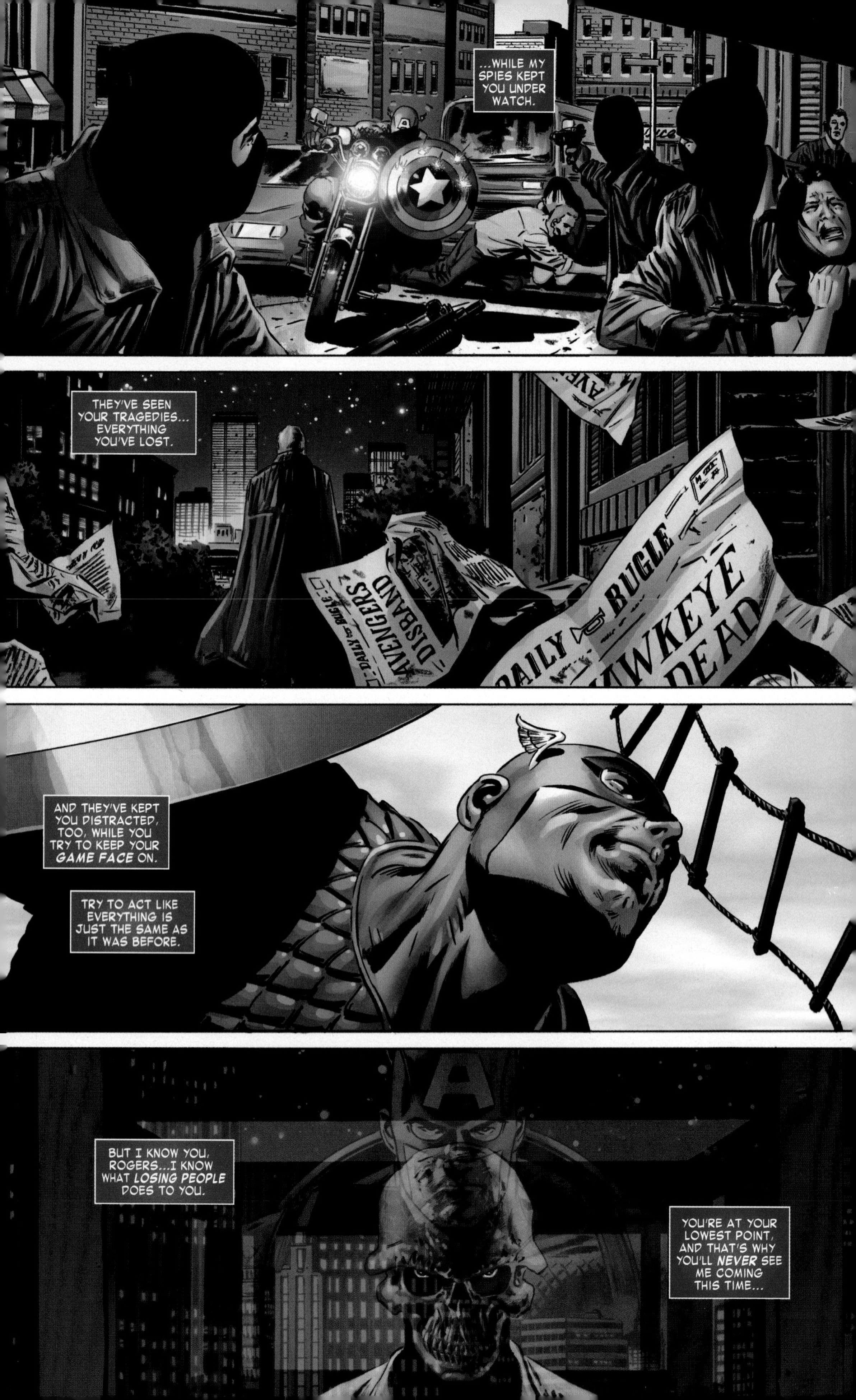

...WHILE MY SPIES KEPT YOU UNDER WATCH.
THEY'VE SEEN YOUR TRAGEDIES... EVERYTHING YOU'VE LOST.
DAILY BUGLE
AVENGERS DISBAND
AND THEY'VE KEPT YOU DISTRACTED, TOO, WHILE YOU TRY TO KEEP YOUR *GAME FACE* ON.
TRY TO ACT LIKE EVERYTHING IS JUST THE SAME AS IT WAS BEFORE.
BUT I KNOW YOU, ROGERS...I KNOW WHAT *LOSING PEOPLE* DOES TO YOU.
YOU'RE AT YOUR LOWEST POINT, AND THAT'S WHY YOU'LL *NEVER* SEE ME COMING THIS TIME...

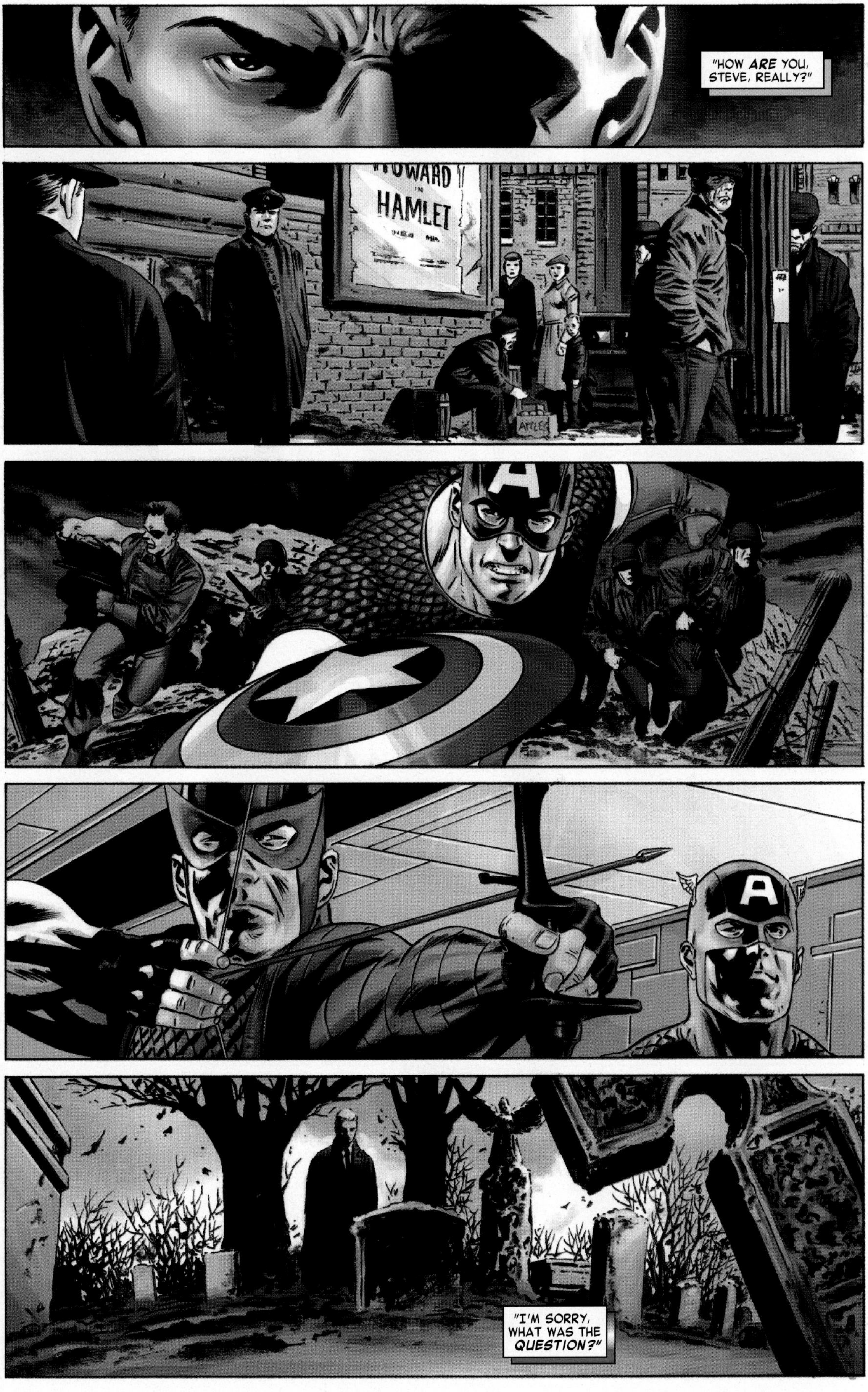
"HOW ARE YOU, STEVE, REALLY?"
HOWARD IN HAMLET
APPLES
"I'M SORRY, WHAT WAS THE QUESTION?"

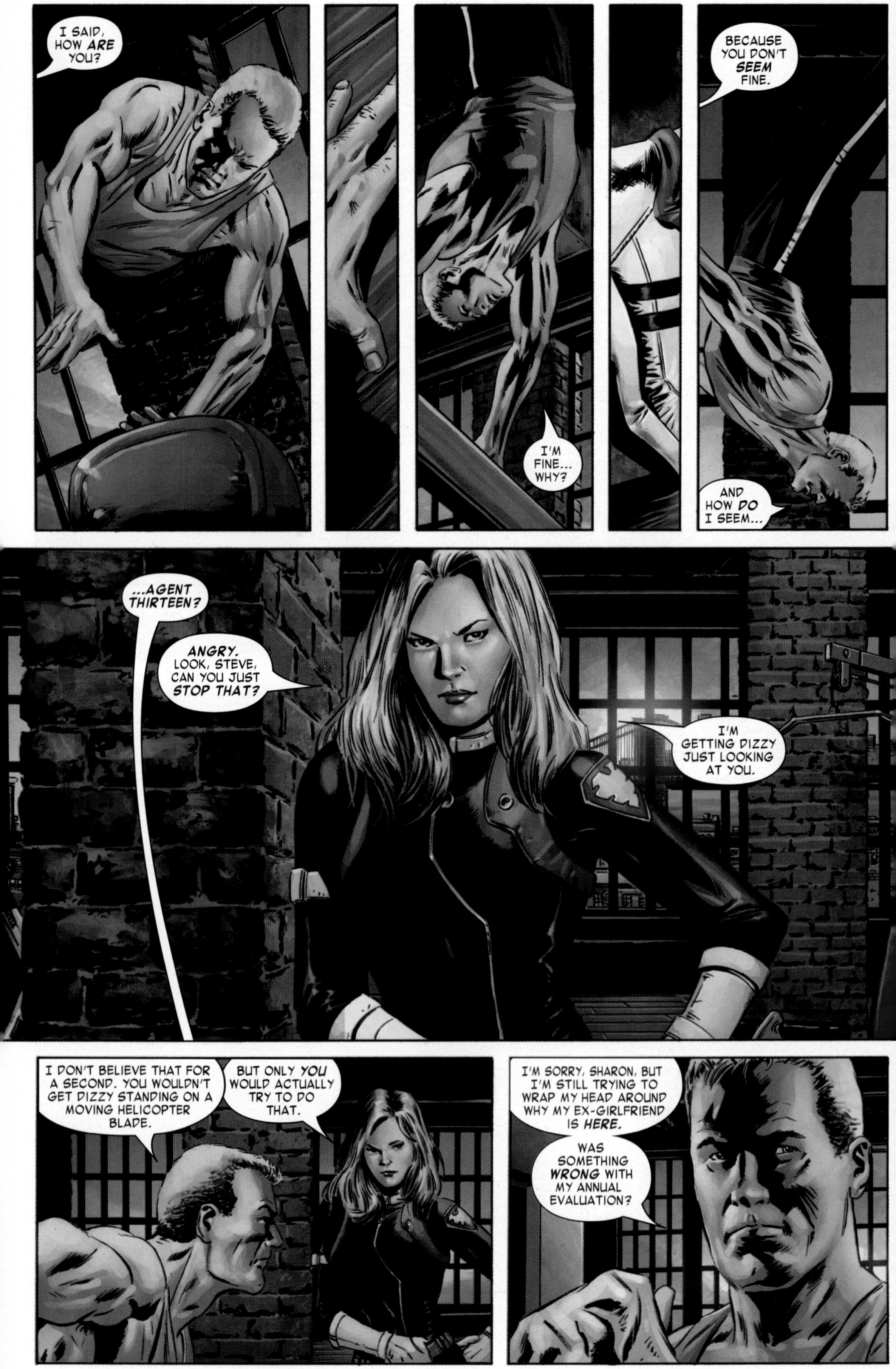

I SAID, HOW ARE YOU?
I'M FINE... WHY?
BECAUSE YOU DON'T SEEM FINE.
AND HOW DO I SEEM...
...AGENT THIRTEEN?
ANGRY. LOOK, STEVE, CAN YOU JUST STOP THAT?
I'M GETTING DIZZY JUST LOOKING AT YOU.
I DON'T BELIEVE THAT FOR A SECOND. YOU WOULDN'T GET DIZZY STANDING ON A MOVING HELICOPTER BLADE.
BUT ONLY YOU WOULD ACTUALLY TRY TO DO THAT.
I'M SORRY, SHARON, BUT I'M STILL TRYING TO WRAP MY HEAD AROUND WHY MY EX-GIRLFRIEND IS HERE.
WAS SOMETHING WRONG WITH MY ANNUAL EVALUATION?

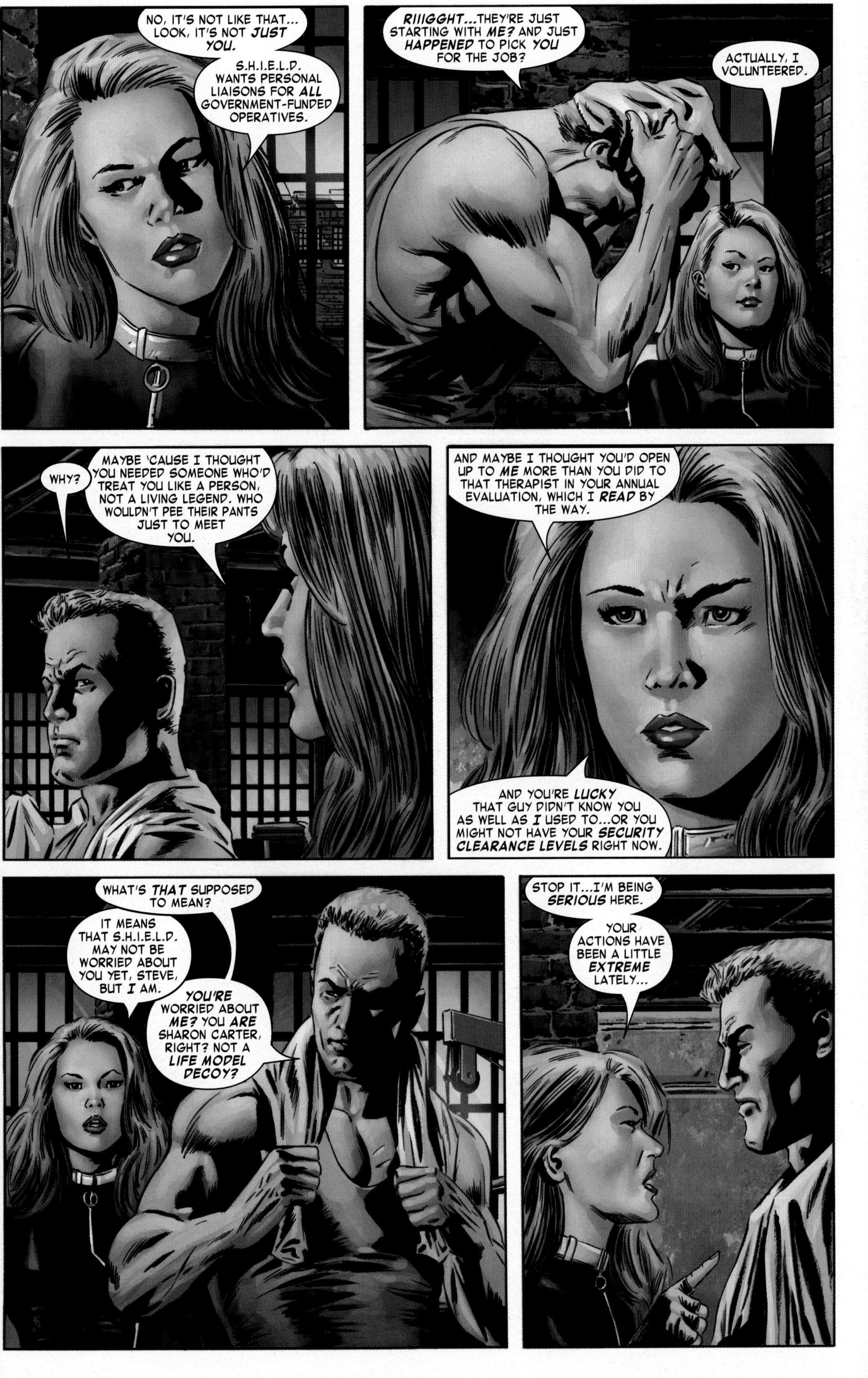
NO, IT'S NOT LIKE THAT... LOOK, IT'S NOT JUST YOU.
S.H.I.E.L.D. WANTS PERSONAL LIAISONS FOR ALL GOVERNMENT-FUNDED OPERATIVES.
RIIIGGHT...THEY'RE JUST STARTING WITH ME? AND JUST HAPPENED TO PICK YOU FOR THE JOB?
ACTUALLY, I VOLUNTEERED.
WHY?
MAYBE 'CAUSE I THOUGHT YOU NEEDED SOMEONE WHO'D TREAT YOU LIKE A PERSON, NOT A LIVING LEGEND. WHO WOULDN'T PEE THEIR PANTS JUST TO MEET YOU.
AND MAYBE I THOUGHT YOU'D OPEN UP TO ME MORE THAN YOU DID TO THAT THERAPIST IN YOUR ANNUAL EVALUATION, WHICH I READ BY THE WAY.
AND YOU'RE LUCKY THAT GUY DIDN'T KNOW YOU AS WELL AS I USED TO...OR YOU MIGHT NOT HAVE YOUR SECURITY CLEARANCE LEVELS RIGHT NOW.
WHAT'S THAT SUPPOSED TO MEAN?
IT MEANS THAT S.H.I.E.L.D. MAY NOT BE WORRIED ABOUT YOU YET, STEVE, BUT I AM.
YOU'RE WORRIED ABOUT ME? YOU ARE SHARON CARTER, RIGHT? NOT A LIFE MODEL DECOY?
STOP IT...I'M BEING SERIOUS HERE.
YOUR ACTIONS HAVE BEEN A LITTLE EXTREME LATELY...

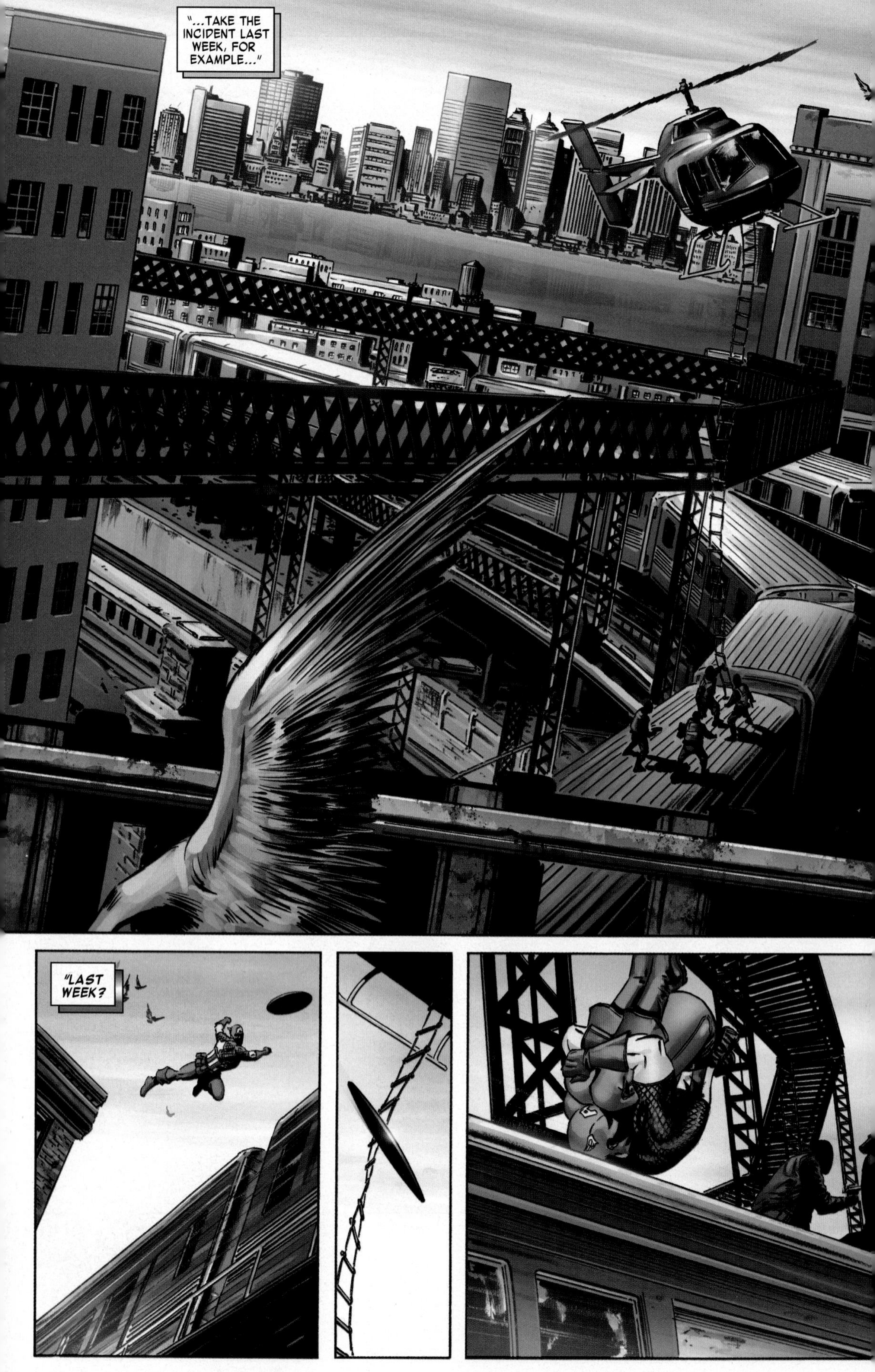
"...TAKE THE INCIDENT LAST WEEK, FOR EXAMPLE..."
"LAST WEEK?

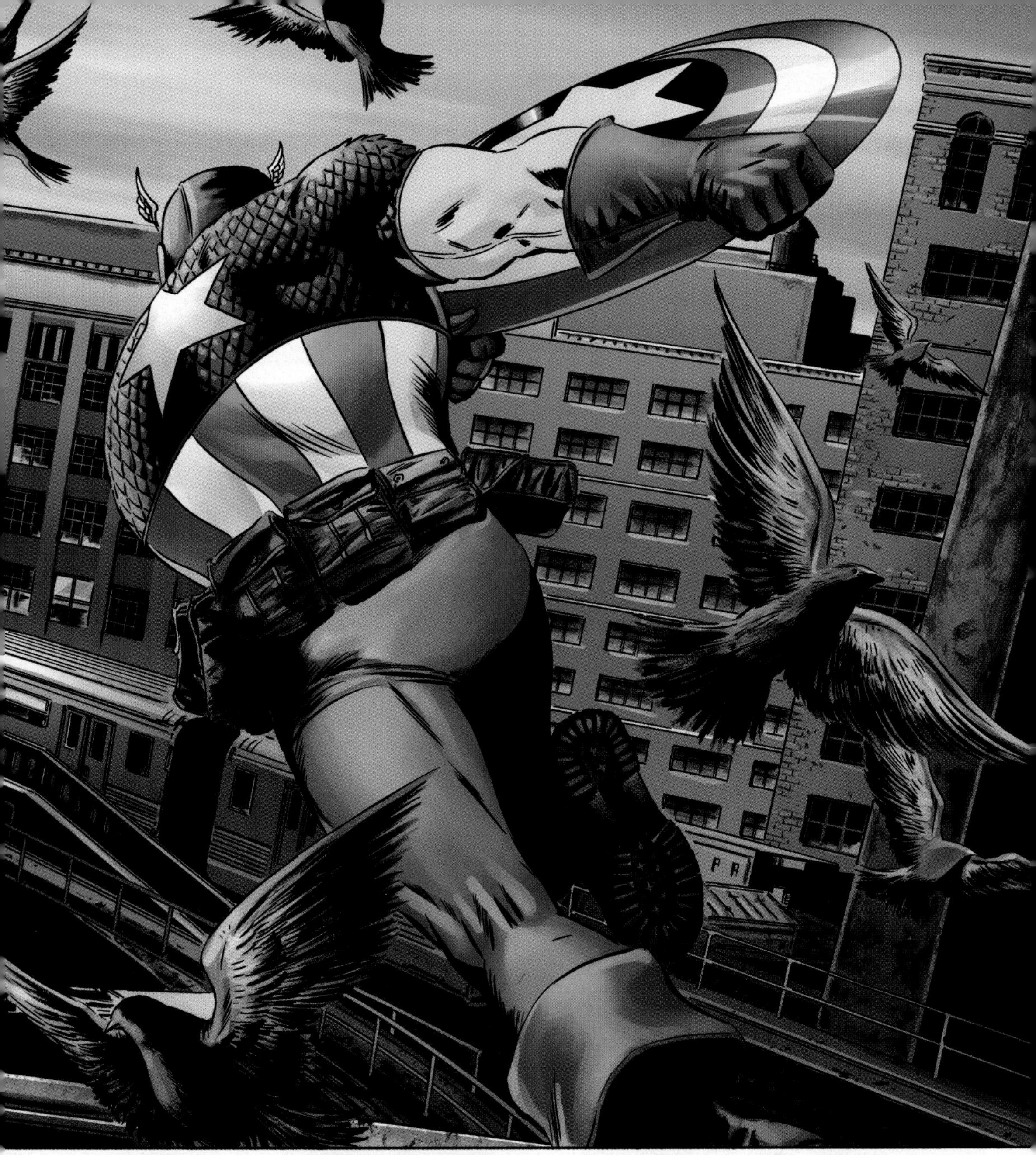

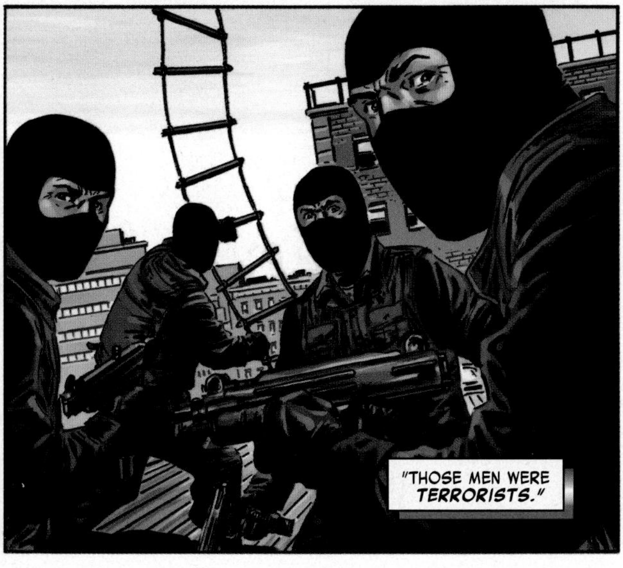
"THOSE MEN WERE TERRORISTS."

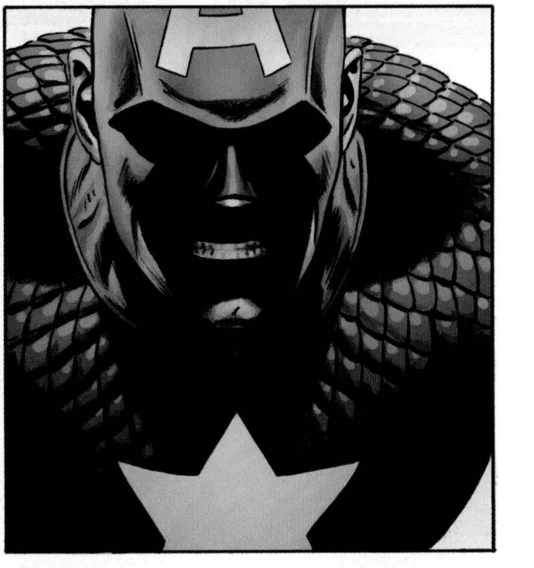

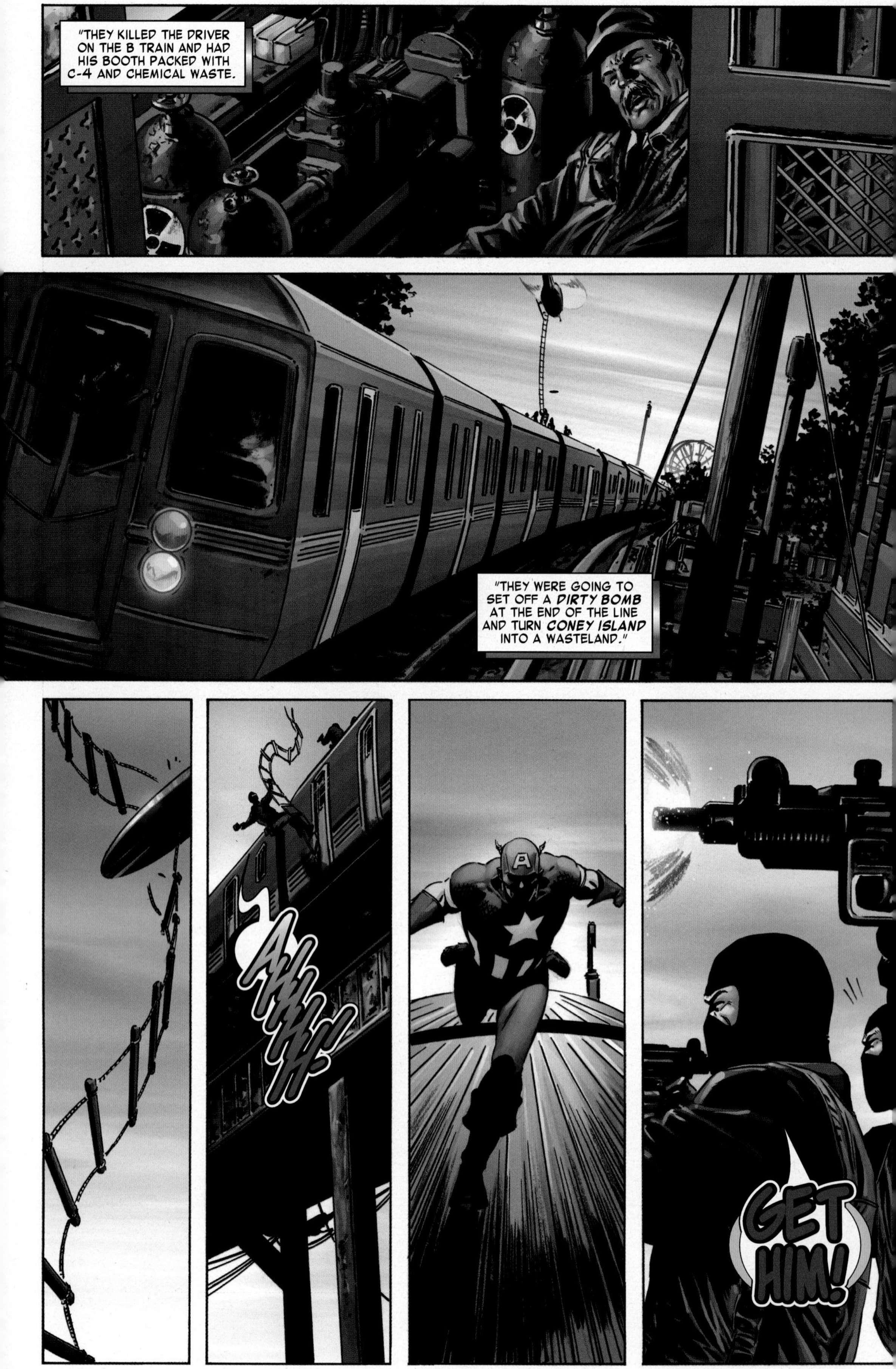
"THEY KILLED THE DRIVER ON THE B TRAIN AND HAD HIS BOOTH PACKED WITH C-4 AND CHEMICAL WASTE.
"THEY WERE GOING TO SET OFF A *DIRTY BOMB* AT THE END OF THE LINE AND TURN *CONEY ISLAND* INTO A WASTELAND."
GET HIM!

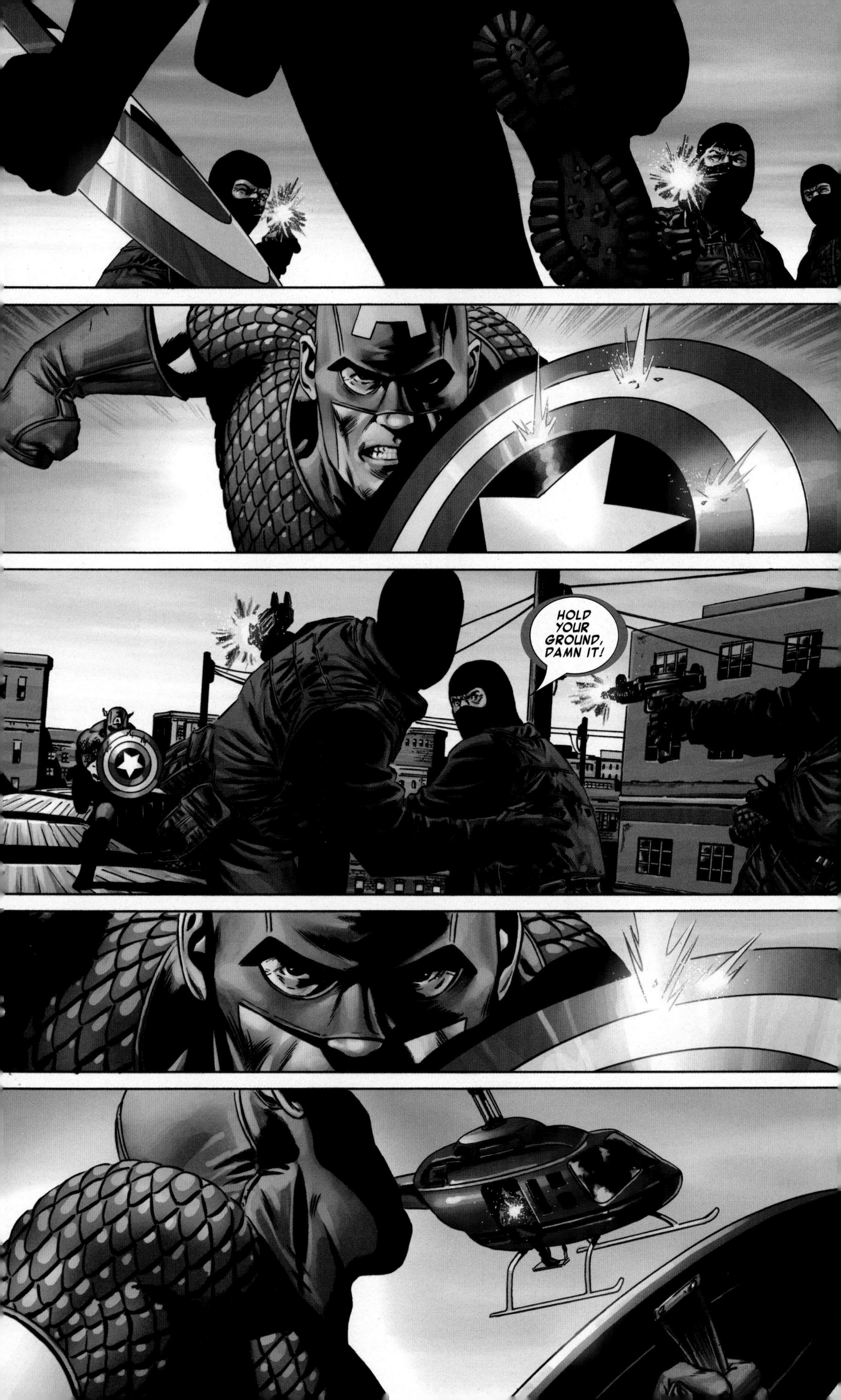
HOLD YOUR GROUND, DAMN IT!

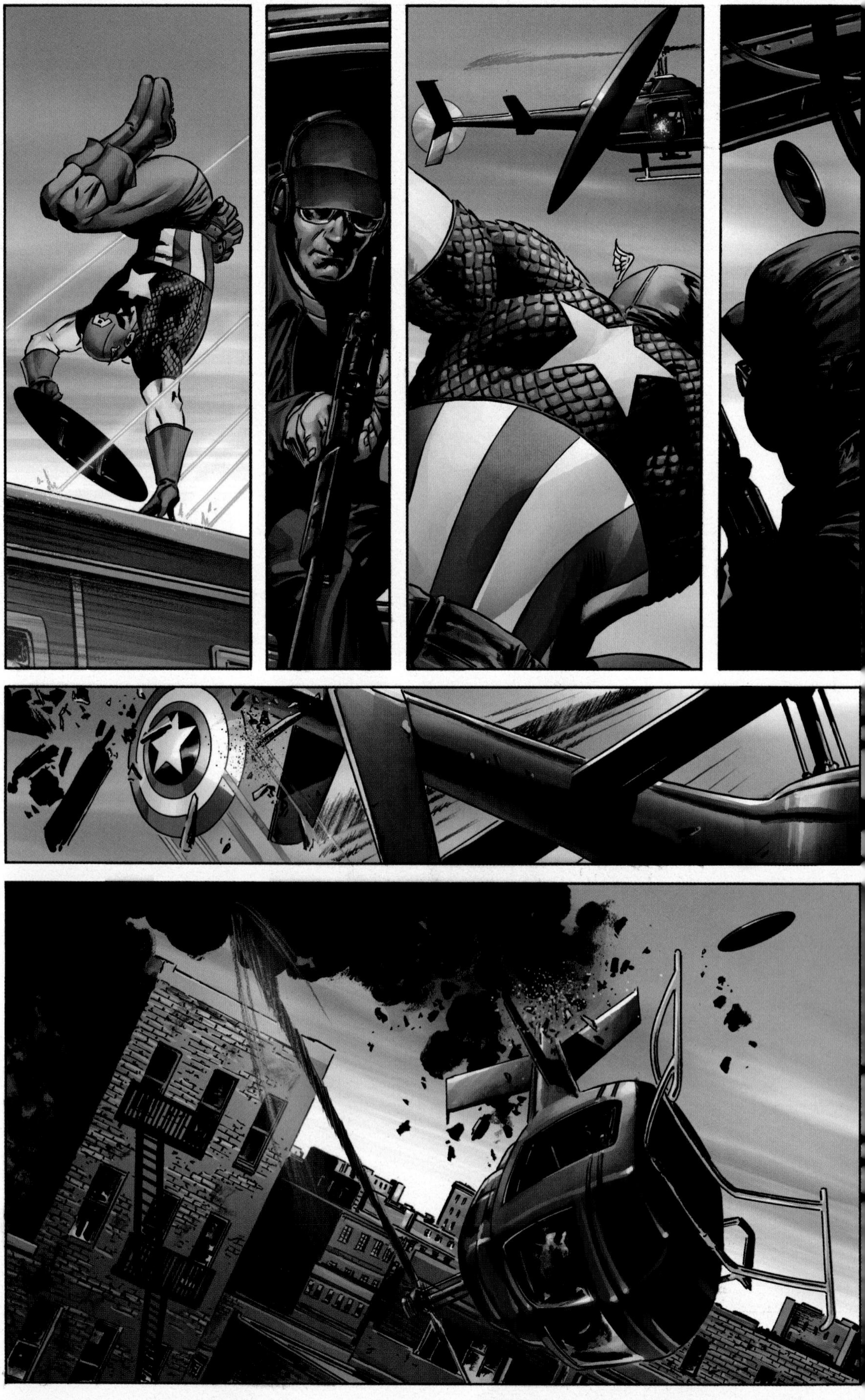

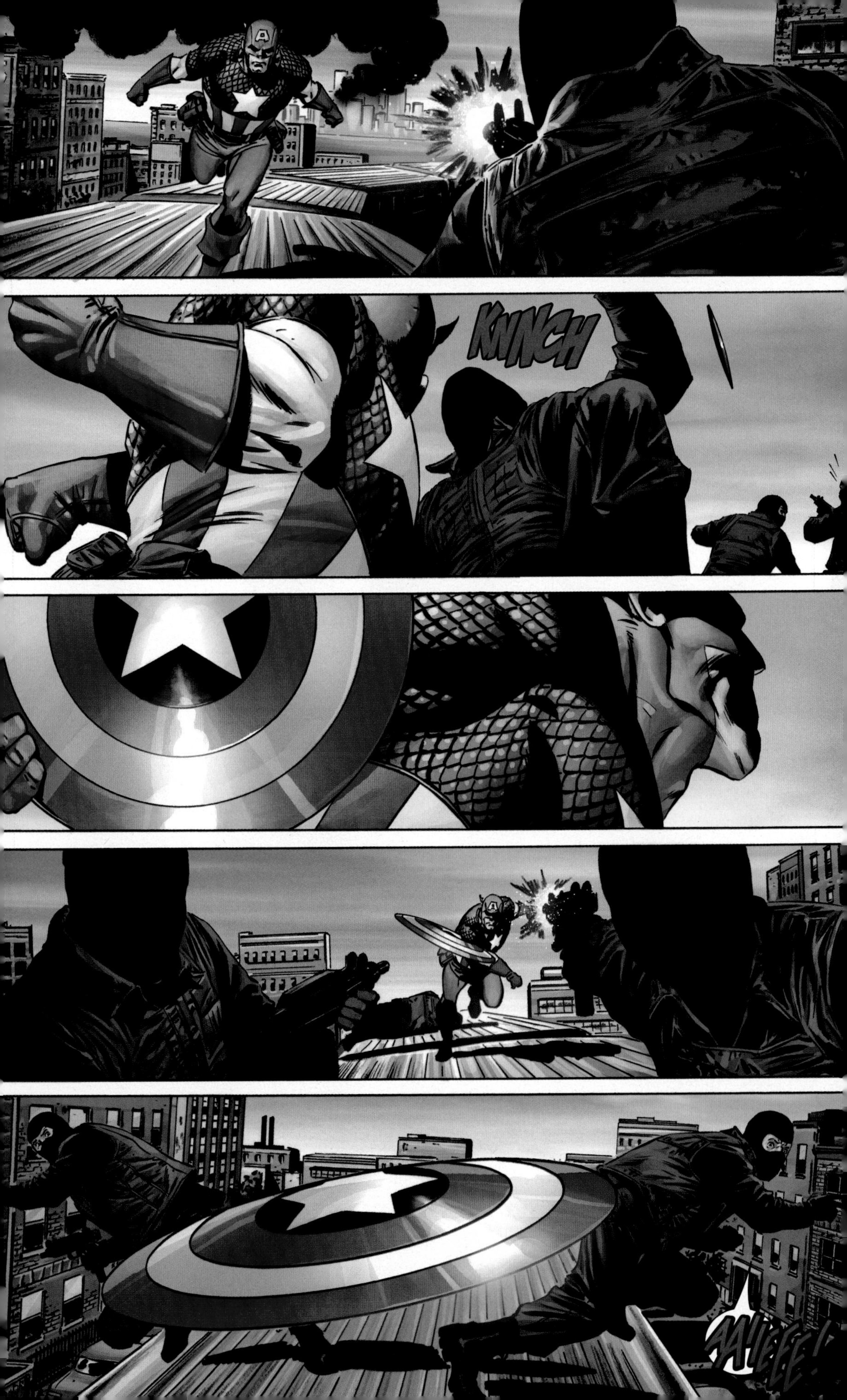
KNNCH
AAHEEEE!

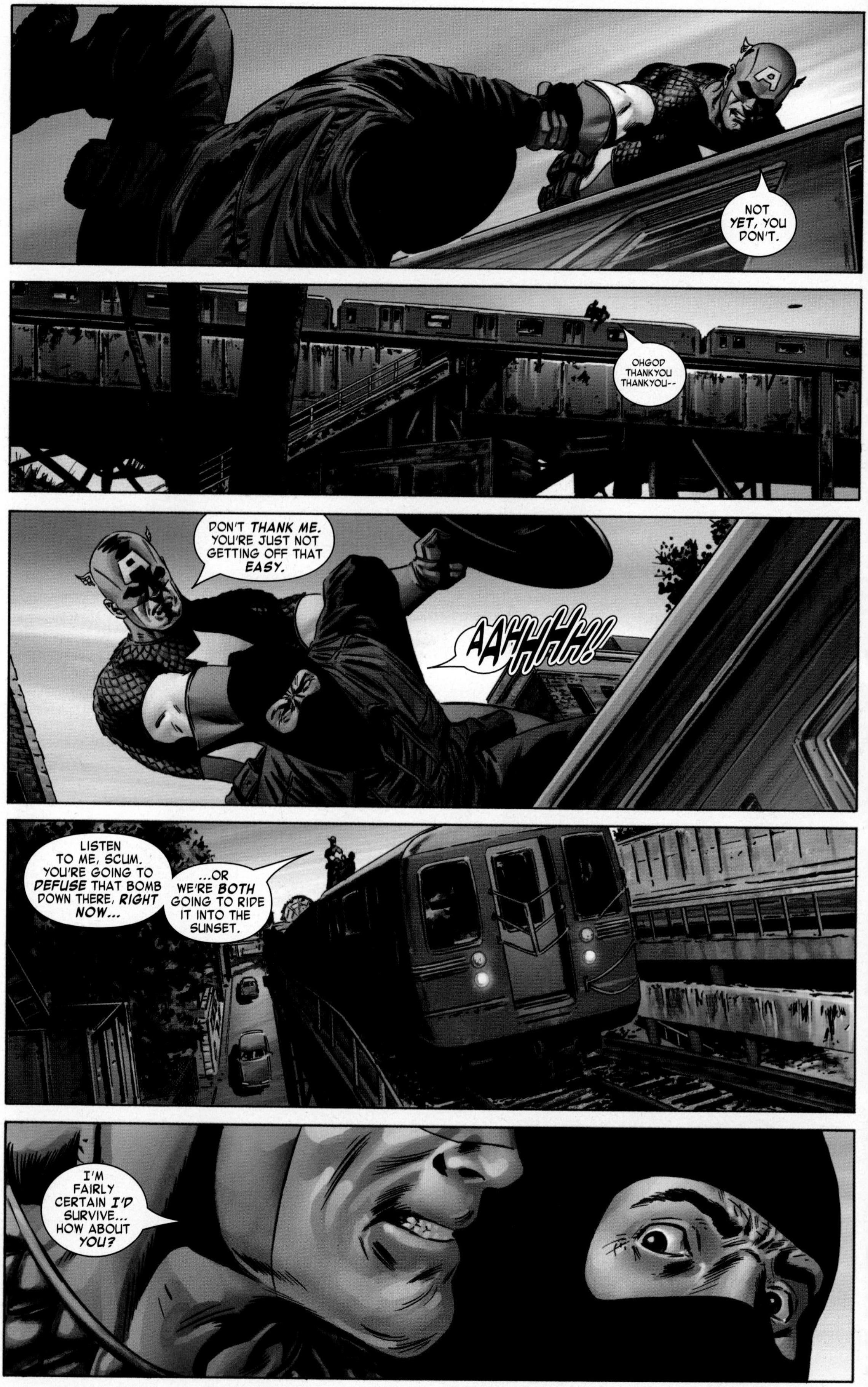
NOT YET, YOU DON'T.
OHGOD THANKYOU THANKYOU--
DON'T THANK ME. YOU'RE JUST NOT GETTING OFF THAT EASY.
AAHHHH!
LISTEN TO ME, SCUM. YOU'RE GOING TO DEFUSE THAT BOMB DOWN THERE, RIGHT NOW...
...OR WE'RE BOTH GOING TO RIDE IT INTO THE SUNSET.
I'M FAIRLY CERTAIN I'D SURVIVE... HOW ABOUT YOU?

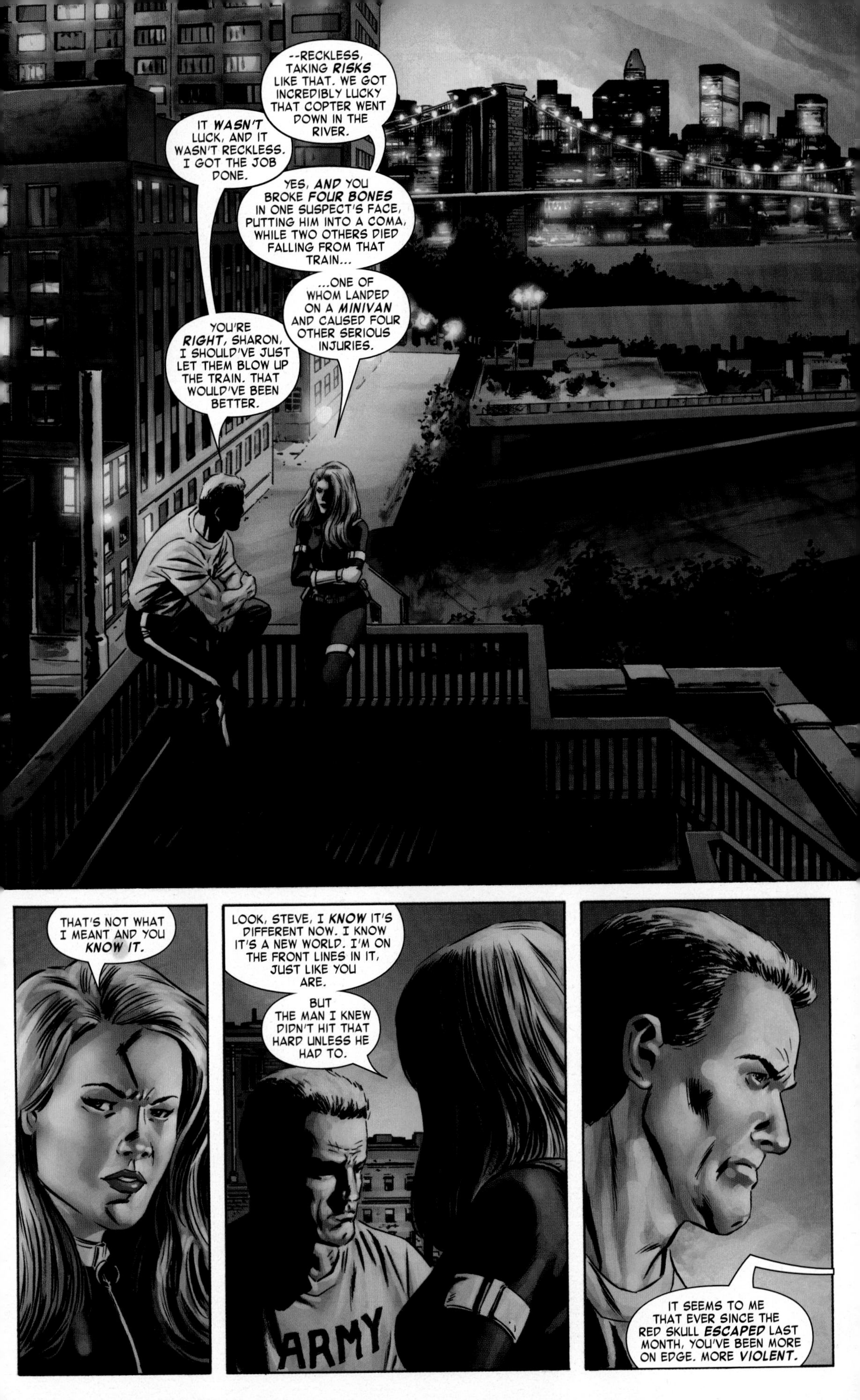
--RECKLESS, TAKING RISKS LIKE THAT. WE GOT INCREDIBLY LUCKY THAT COPTER WENT DOWN IN THE RIVER.
IT WASN'T LUCK, AND IT WASN'T RECKLESS. I GOT THE JOB DONE.
YES, AND YOU BROKE FOUR BONES IN ONE SUSPECT'S FACE, PUTTING HIM INTO A COMA, WHILE TWO OTHERS DIED FALLING FROM THAT TRAIN...
...ONE OF WHOM LANDED ON A MINIVAN AND CAUSED FOUR OTHER SERIOUS INJURIES.
YOU'RE RIGHT, SHARON, I SHOULD'VE JUST LET THEM BLOW UP THE TRAIN. THAT WOULD'VE BEEN BETTER.
THAT'S NOT WHAT I MEANT AND YOU KNOW IT.
LOOK, STEVE, I KNOW IT'S DIFFERENT NOW. I KNOW IT'S A NEW WORLD. I'M ON THE FRONT LINES IN IT, JUST LIKE YOU ARE.
BUT THE MAN I KNEW DIDN'T HIT THAT HARD UNLESS HE HAD TO.
ARMY
IT SEEMS TO ME THAT EVER SINCE THE RED SKULL ESCAPED LAST MONTH, YOU'VE BEEN MORE ON EDGE. MORE VIOLENT.

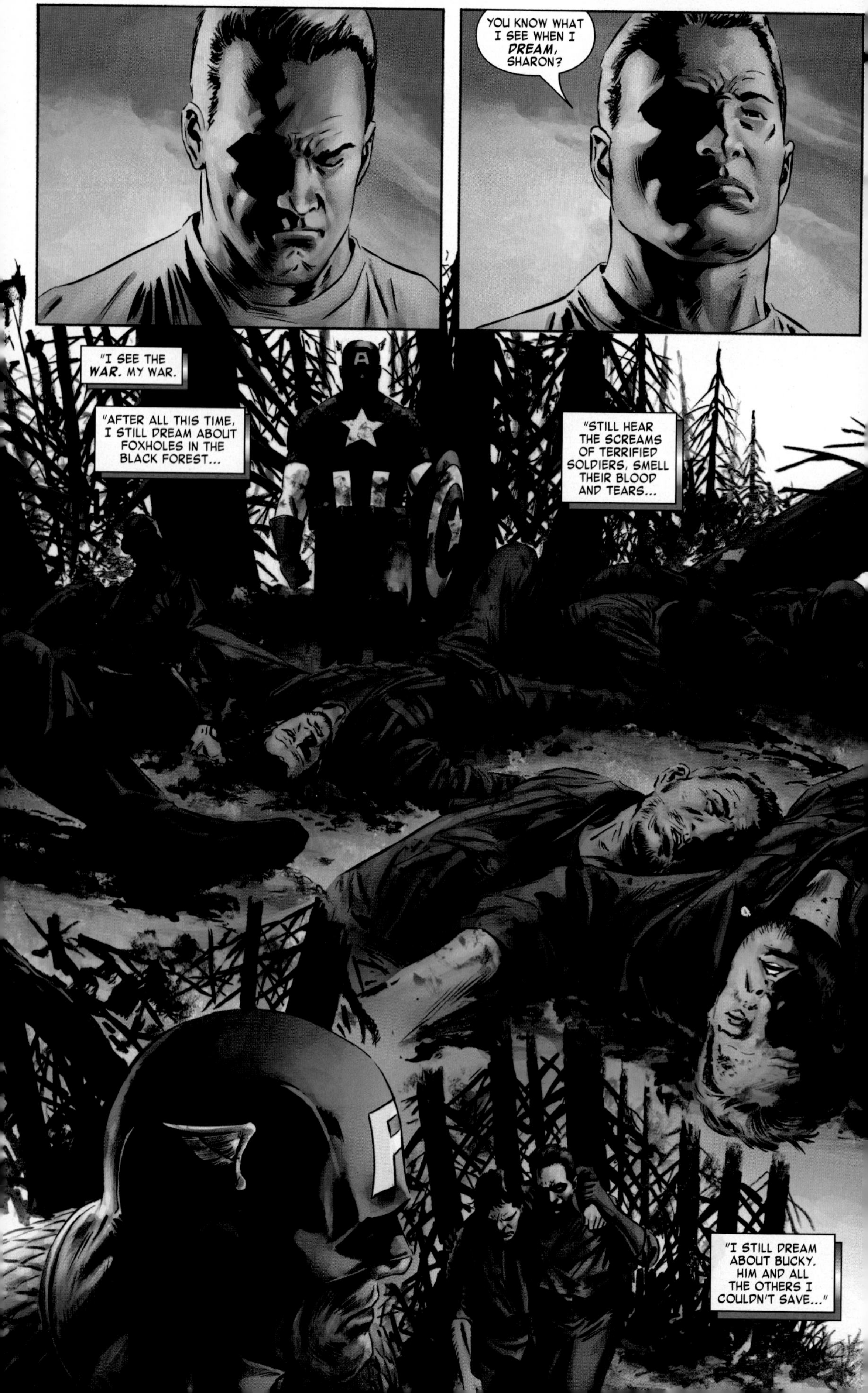
YOU KNOW WHAT I SEE WHEN I DREAM, SHARON?
"I SEE THE WAR. MY WAR.
"AFTER ALL THIS TIME, I STILL DREAM ABOUT FOXHOLES IN THE BLACK FOREST...
"STILL HEAR THE SCREAMS OF TERRIFIED SOLDIERS, SMELL THEIR BLOOD AND TEARS...
"I STILL DREAM ABOUT BUCKY. HIM AND ALL THE OTHERS I COULDN'T SAVE..."

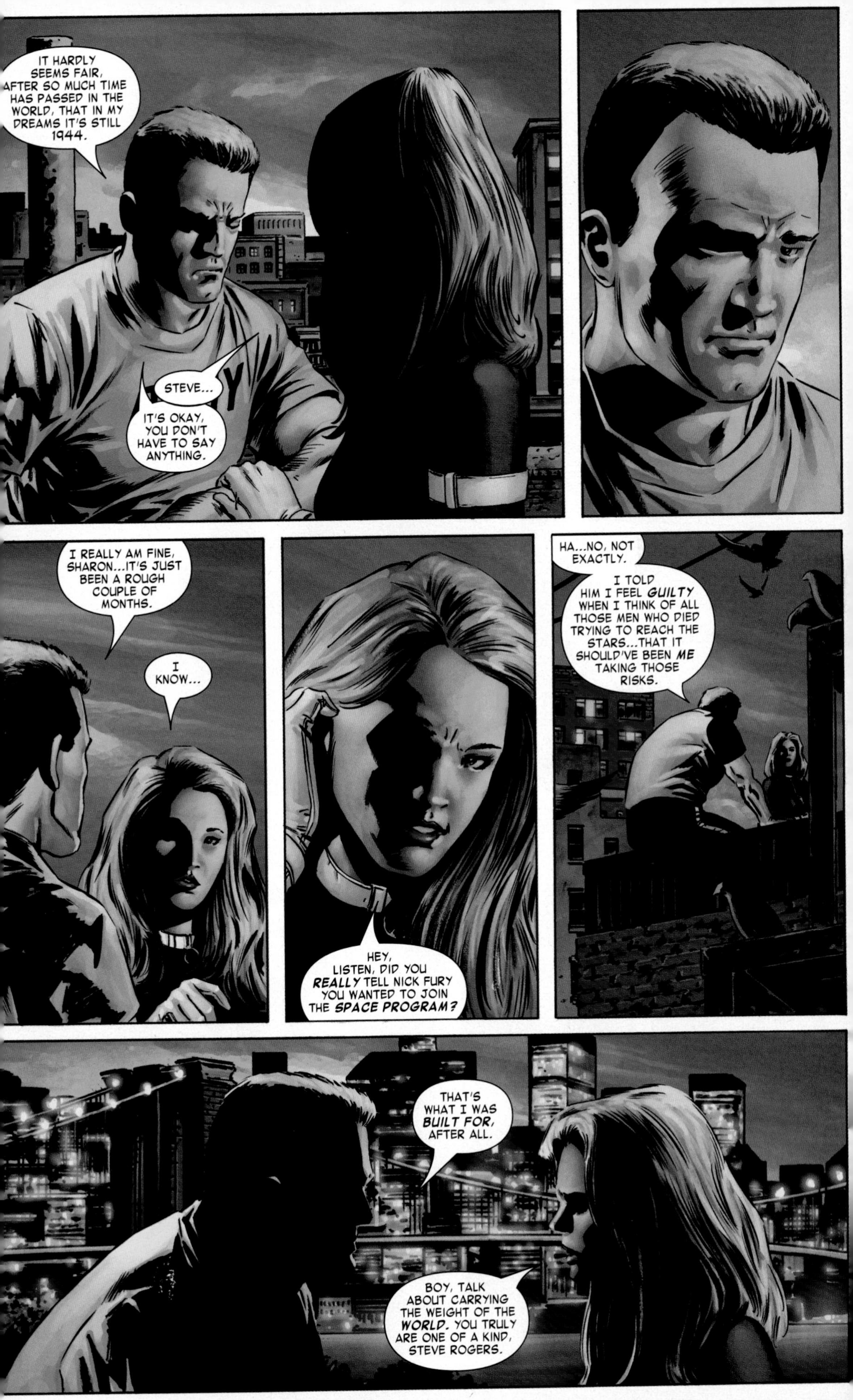
IT HARDLY SEEMS FAIR, AFTER SO MUCH TIME HAS PASSED IN THE WORLD, THAT IN MY DREAMS IT'S STILL 1944.
STEVE...
IT'S OKAY, YOU DON'T HAVE TO SAY ANYTHING.
I REALLY AM FINE, SHARON...IT'S JUST BEEN A ROUGH COUPLE OF MONTHS.
I KNOW...
HEY, LISTEN, DID YOU REALLY TELL NICK FURY YOU WANTED TO JOIN THE SPACE PROGRAM?
HA...NO, NOT EXACTLY.
I TOLD HIM I FEEL GUILTY WHEN I THINK OF ALL THOSE MEN WHO DIED TRYING TO REACH THE STARS...THAT IT SHOULD'VE BEEN ME TAKING THOSE RISKS.
THAT'S WHAT I WAS BUILT FOR, AFTER ALL.
BOY, TALK ABOUT CARRYING THE WEIGHT OF THE WORLD. YOU TRULY ARE ONE OF A KIND, STEVE ROGERS.

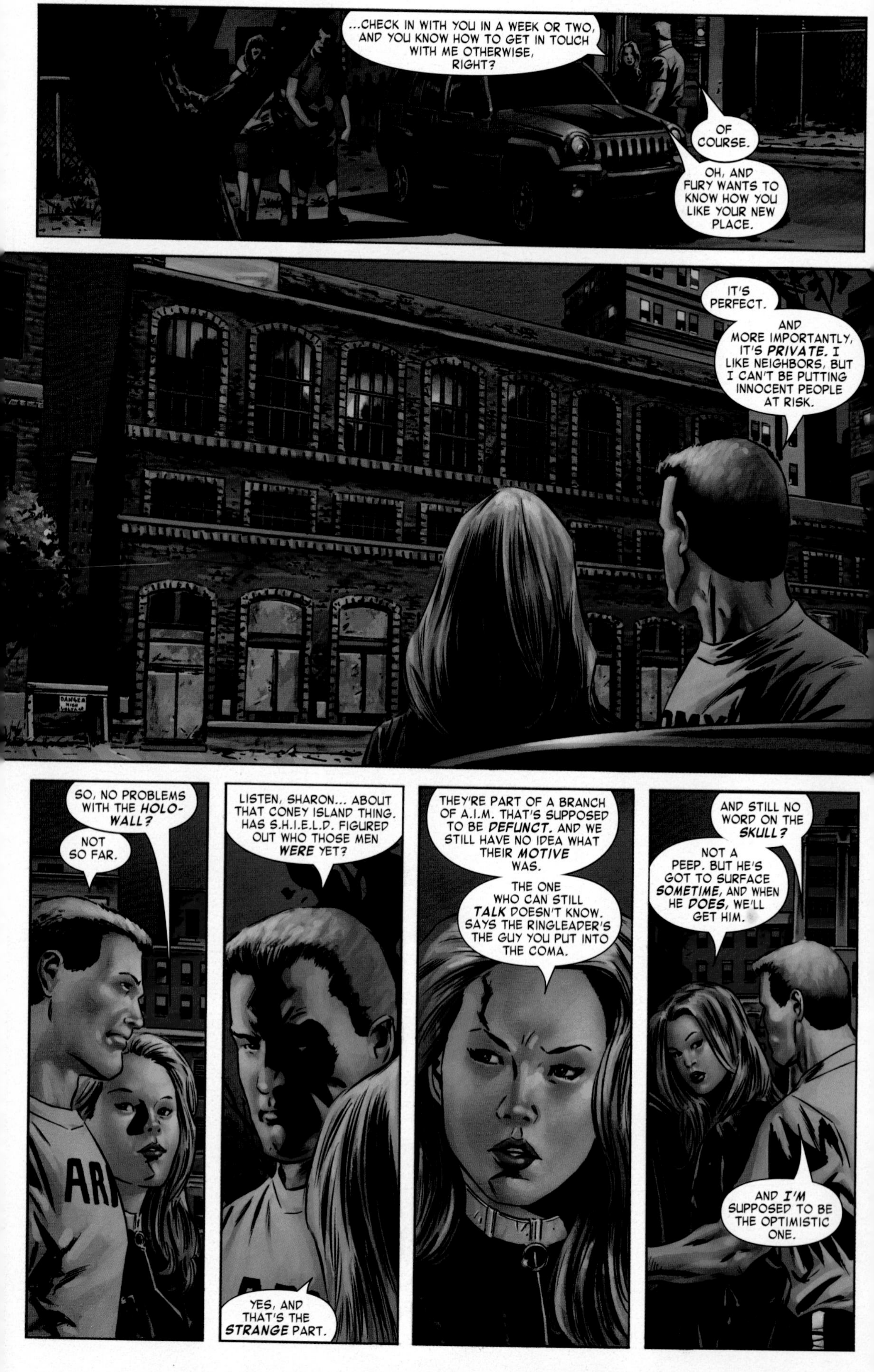
...CHECK IN WITH YOU IN A WEEK OR TWO, AND YOU KNOW HOW TO GET IN TOUCH WITH ME OTHERWISE, RIGHT?
OF COURSE.
OH, AND FURY WANTS TO KNOW HOW YOU LIKE YOUR NEW PLACE.
IT'S PERFECT.
AND MORE IMPORTANTLY, IT'S PRIVATE. I LIKE NEIGHBORS, BUT I CAN'T BE PUTTING INNOCENT PEOPLE AT RISK.
SO, NO PROBLEMS WITH THE HOLO-WALL?
NOT SO FAR.
LISTEN, SHARON... ABOUT THAT CONEY ISLAND THING. HAS S.H.I.E.L.D. FIGURED OUT WHO THOSE MEN WERE YET?
YES, AND THAT'S THE STRANGE PART.
THEY'RE PART OF A BRANCH OF A.I.M. THAT'S SUPPOSED TO BE DEFUNCT. AND WE STILL HAVE NO IDEA WHAT THEIR MOTIVE WAS.
THE ONE WHO CAN STILL TALK DOESN'T KNOW. SAYS THE RINGLEADER'S THE GUY YOU PUT INTO THE COMA.
AND STILL NO WORD ON THE SKULL?
NOT A PEEP. BUT HE'S GOT TO SURFACE SOMETIME, AND WHEN HE DOES, WE'LL GET HIM.
AND I'M SUPPOSED TO BE THE OPTIMISTIC ONE.

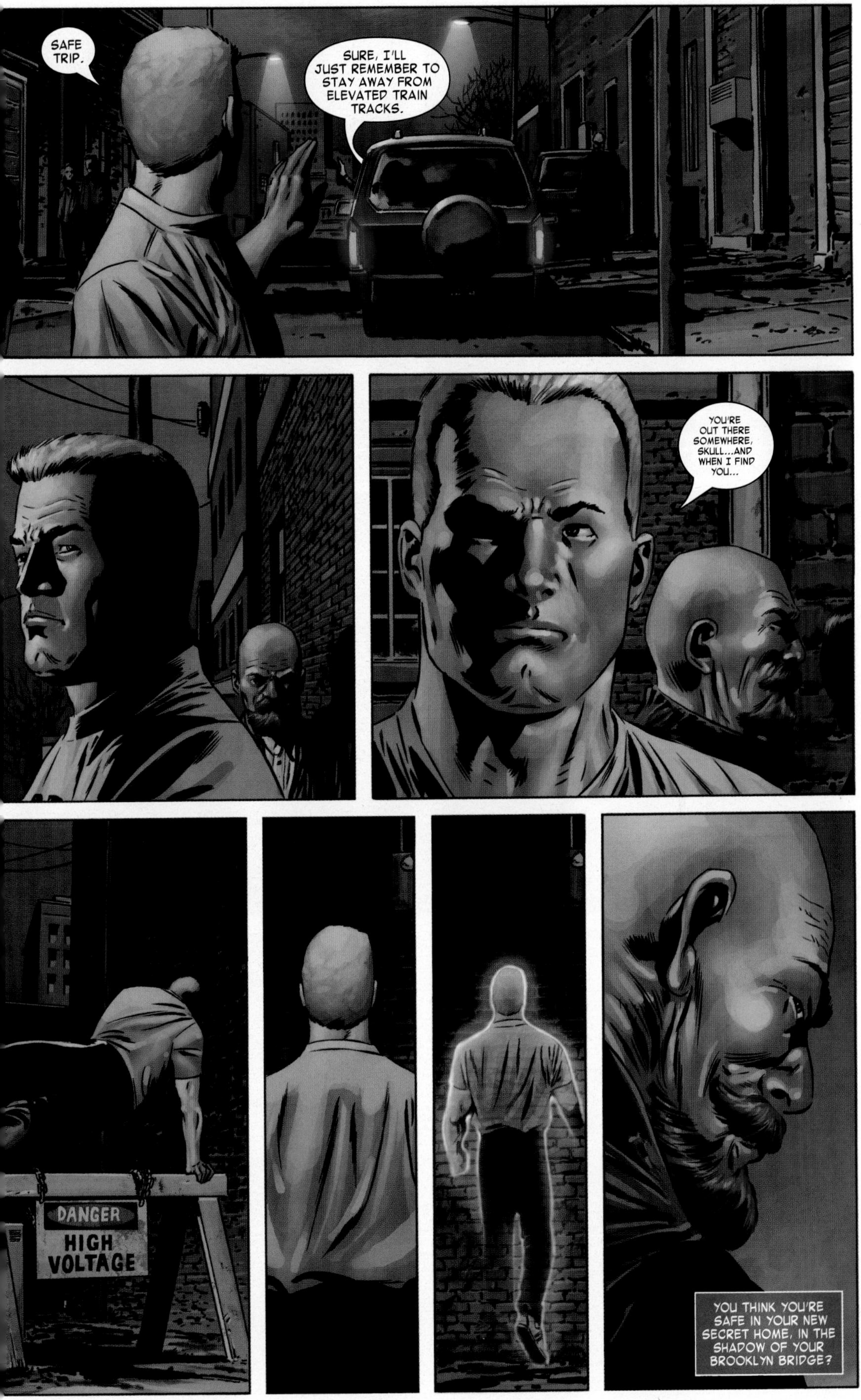
SAFE TRIP.
SURE, I'LL JUST REMEMBER TO STAY AWAY FROM ELEVATED TRAIN TRACKS.
YOU'RE OUT THERE SOMEWHERE, SKULL...AND WHEN I FIND YOU...
DANGER
HIGH VOLTAGE
YOU THINK YOU'RE SAFE IN YOUR NEW SECRET HOME, IN THE SHADOW OF YOUR BROOKLYN BRIDGE?

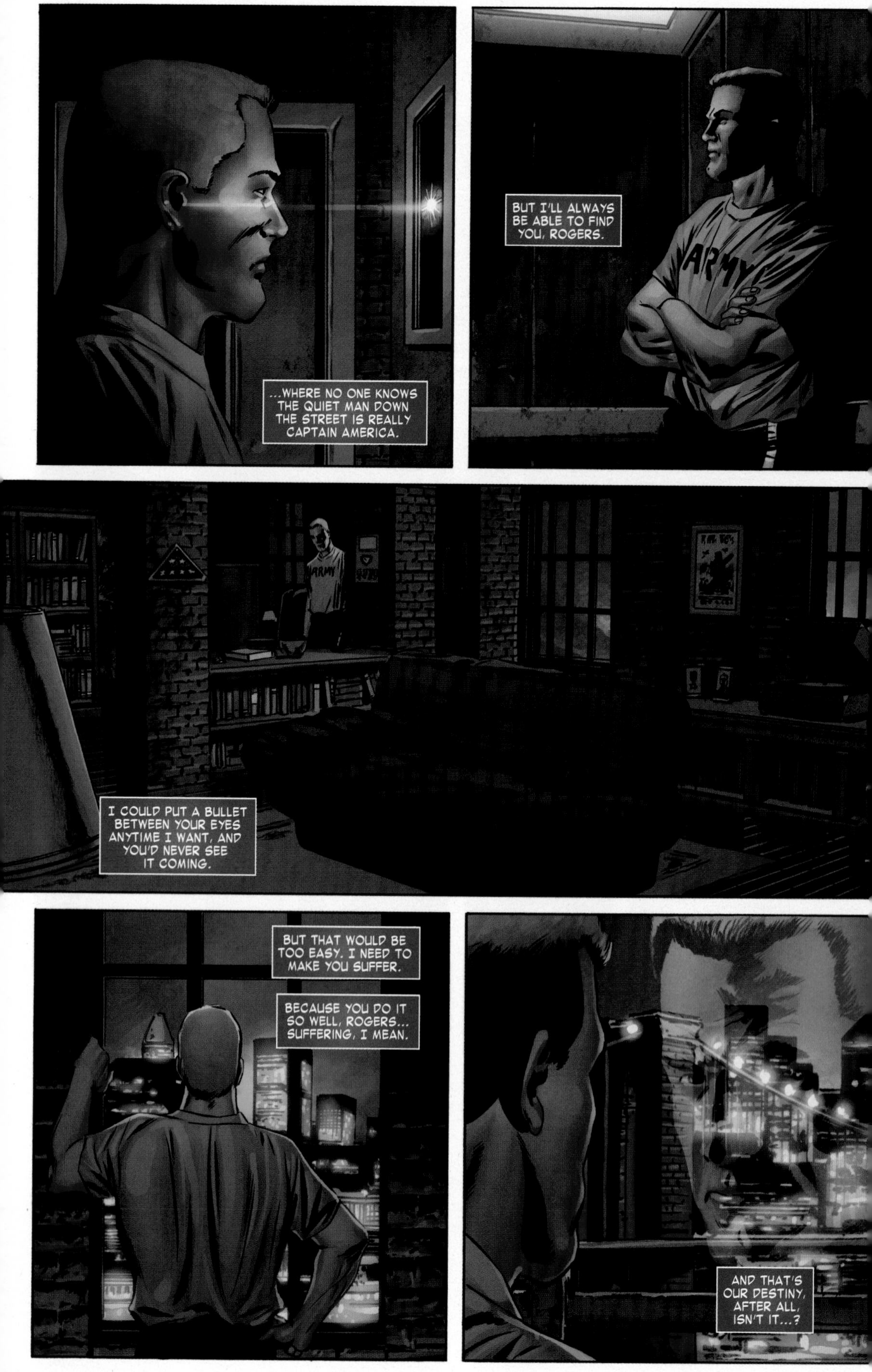
...WHERE NO ONE KNOWS THE QUIET MAN DOWN THE STREET IS REALLY CAPTAIN AMERICA.
BUT I'LL ALWAYS BE ABLE TO FIND YOU, ROGERS.
ARMY
I COULD PUT A BULLET BETWEEN YOUR EYES ANYTIME I WANT, AND YOU'D NEVER SEE IT COMING.
BUT THAT WOULD BE TOO EASY. I NEED TO MAKE YOU SUFFER.
BECAUSE YOU DO IT SO WELL, ROGERS... SUFFERING, I MEAN.
AND THAT'S OUR DESTINY, AFTER ALL, ISN'T IT...?

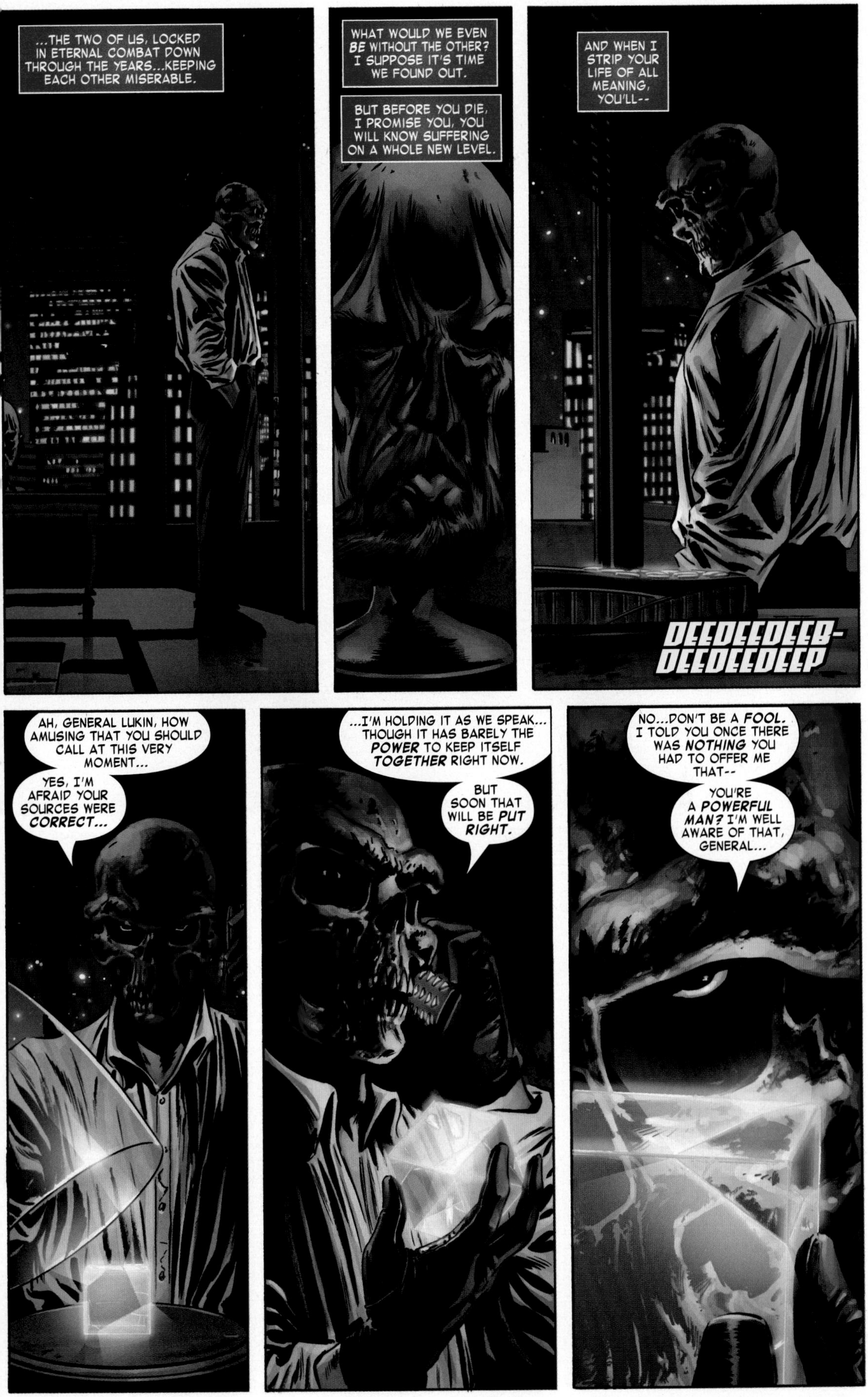
...THE TWO OF US, LOCKED IN ETERNAL COMBAT DOWN THROUGH THE YEARS...KEEPING EACH OTHER MISERABLE.
WHAT WOULD WE EVEN BE WITHOUT THE OTHER? I SUPPOSE IT'S TIME WE FOUND OUT.
BUT BEFORE YOU DIE, I PROMISE YOU, YOU WILL KNOW SUFFERING ON A WHOLE NEW LEVEL.
AND WHEN I STRIP YOUR LIFE OF ALL MEANING, YOU'LL--
DEEDEEDEEB-DEEDEEDEEP
AH, GENERAL LUKIN, HOW AMUSING THAT YOU SHOULD CALL AT THIS VERY MOMENT...
YES, I'M AFRAID YOUR SOURCES WERE CORRECT...
...I'M HOLDING IT AS WE SPEAK... THOUGH IT HAS BARELY THE POWER TO KEEP ITSELF TOGETHER RIGHT NOW.
BUT SOON THAT WILL BE PUT RIGHT.
NO...DON'T BE A FOOL. I TOLD YOU ONCE THERE WAS NOTHING YOU HAD TO OFFER ME THAT--
YOU'RE A POWERFUL MAN? I'M WELL AWARE OF THAT, GENERAL...

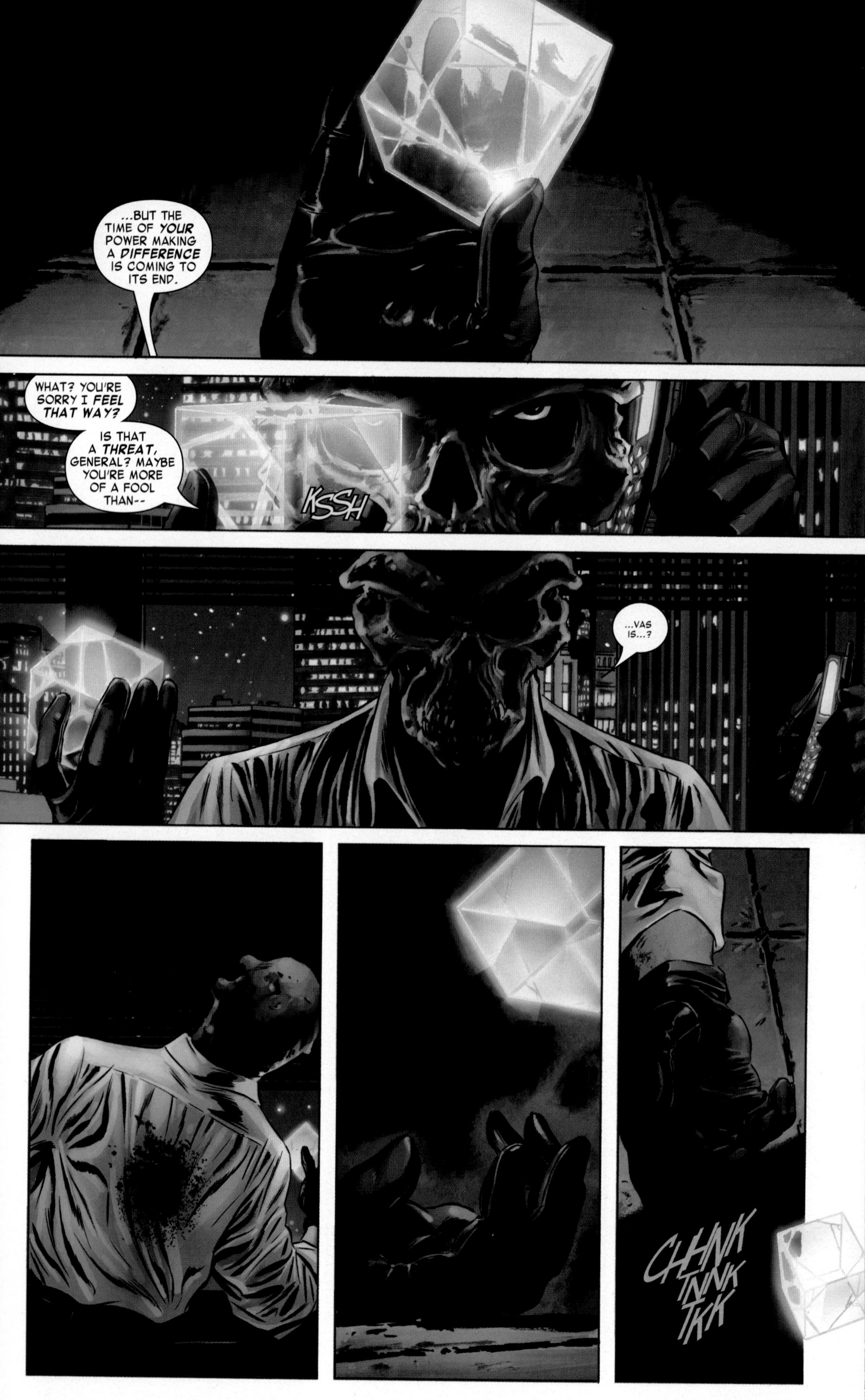
...BUT THE TIME OF YOUR POWER MAKING A DIFFERENCE IS COMING TO ITS END.
WHAT? YOU'RE SORRY I FEEL THAT WAY?
IS THAT A THREAT, GENERAL? MAYBE YOU'RE MORE OF A FOOL THAN--
KSSH
...VAS IS...?
CHINK TINK TK/K

MISSION ACCOMPLISHED, GENERAL...THE CUBE IS YOURS.
THE RED SKULL? NO, NO TROUBLE AT ALL, SIR...

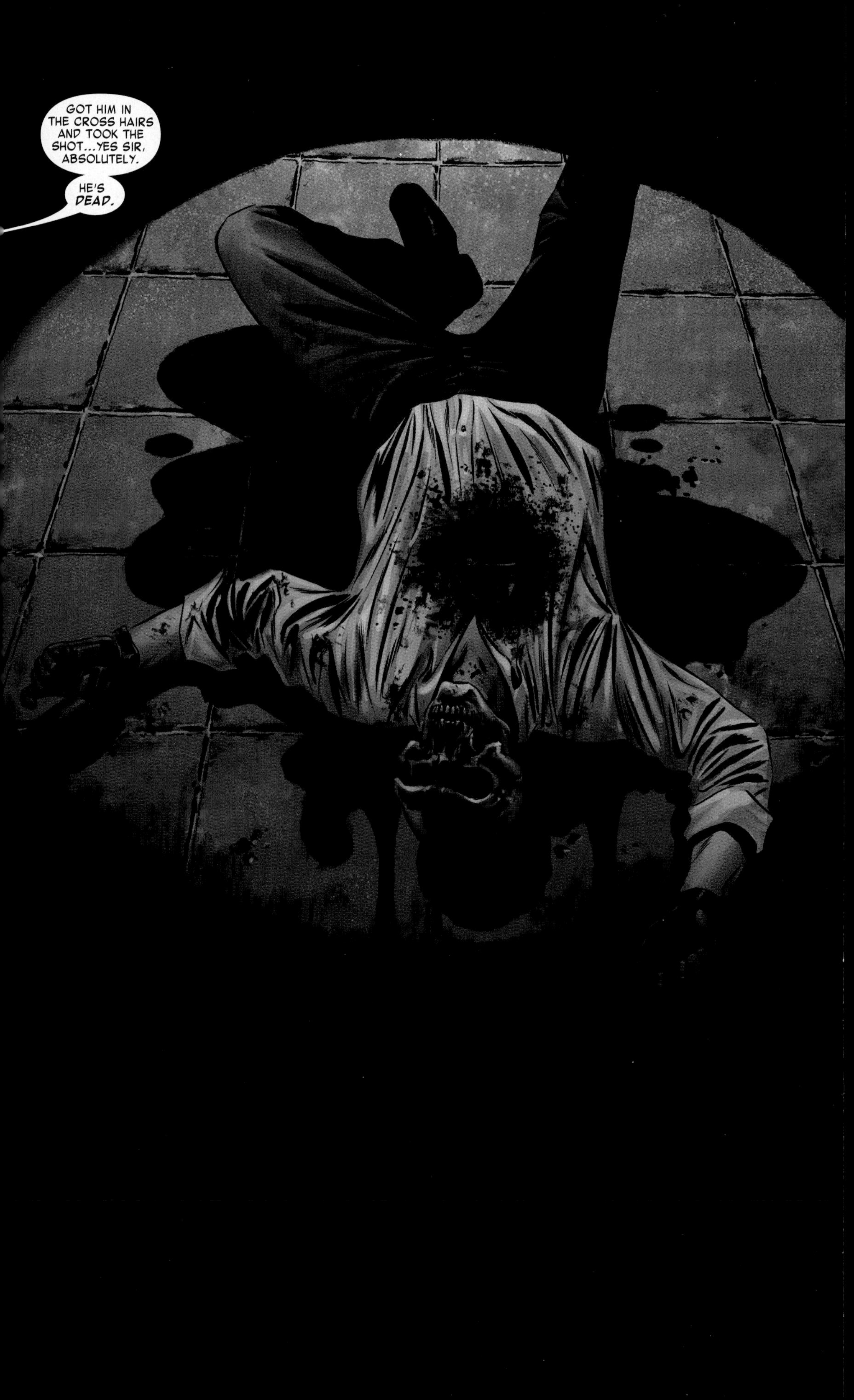
GOT HIM IN THE CROSS HAIRS AND TOOK THE SHOT...YES SIR, ABSOLUTELY.
HE'S *DEAD.*

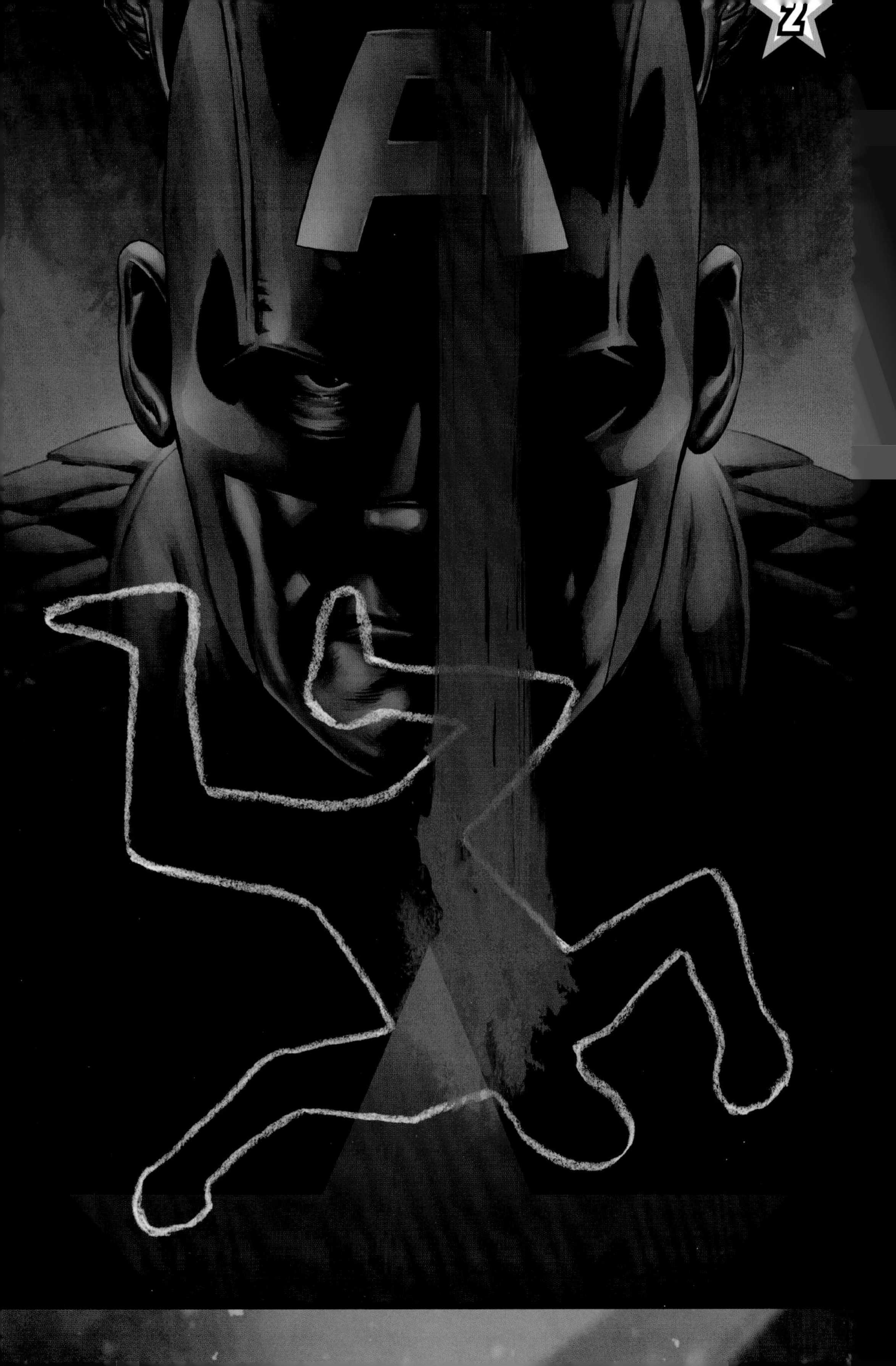
2

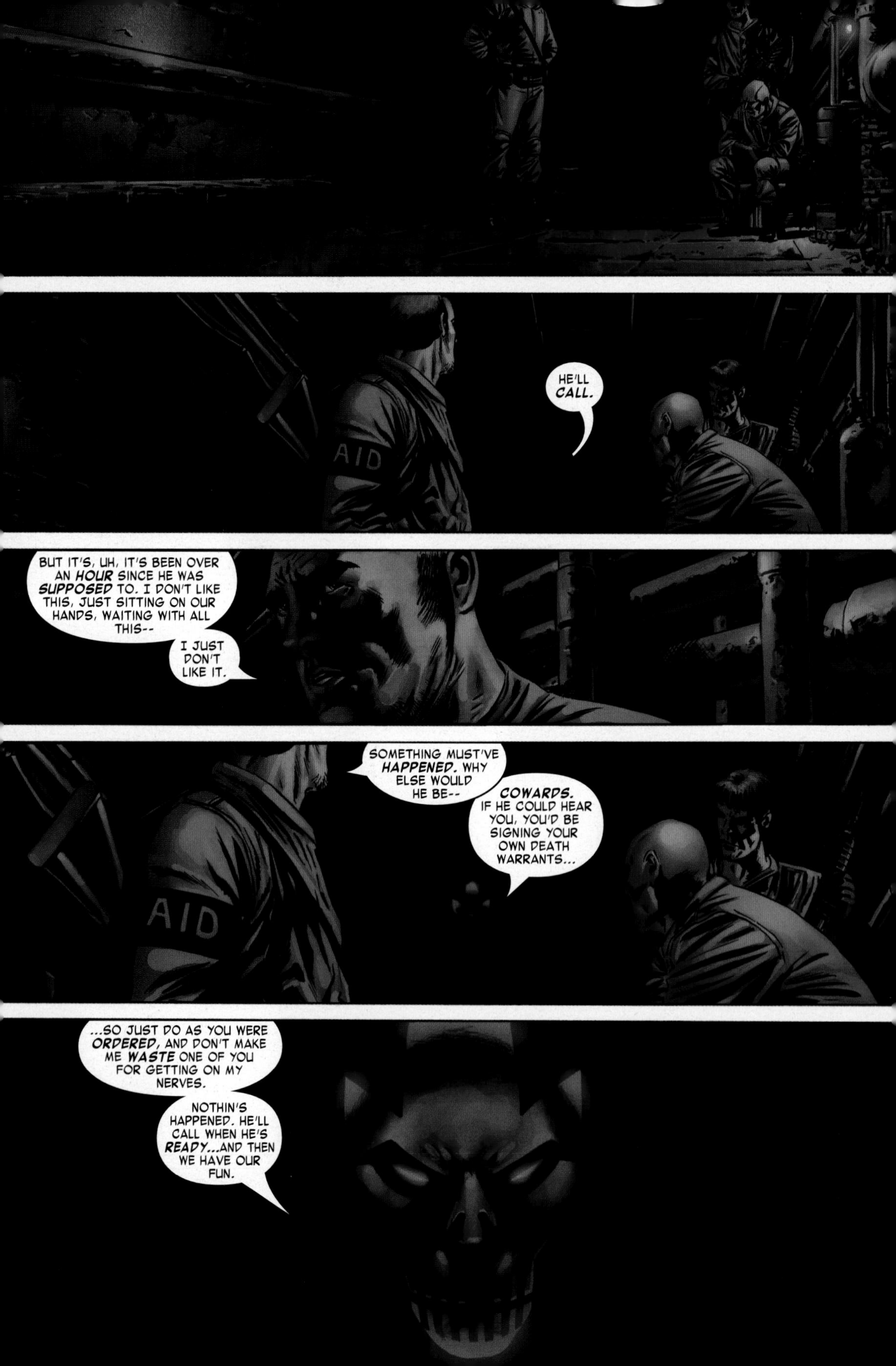
HE'LL CALL.
BUT IT'S, UH, IT'S BEEN OVER AN HOUR SINCE HE WAS SUPPOSED TO. I DON'T LIKE THIS, JUST SITTING ON OUR HANDS, WAITING WITH ALL THIS--
I JUST DON'T LIKE IT.
SOMETHING MUST'VE HAPPENED. WHY ELSE WOULD HE BE--
COWARDS. IF HE COULD HEAR YOU, YOU'D BE SIGNING YOUR OWN DEATH WARRANTS...
...SO JUST DO AS YOU WERE ORDERED, AND DON'T MAKE ME WASTE ONE OF YOU FOR GETTING ON MY NERVES.
NOTHIN'S HAPPENED. HE'LL CALL WHEN HE'S READY...AND THEN WE HAVE OUR FUN.

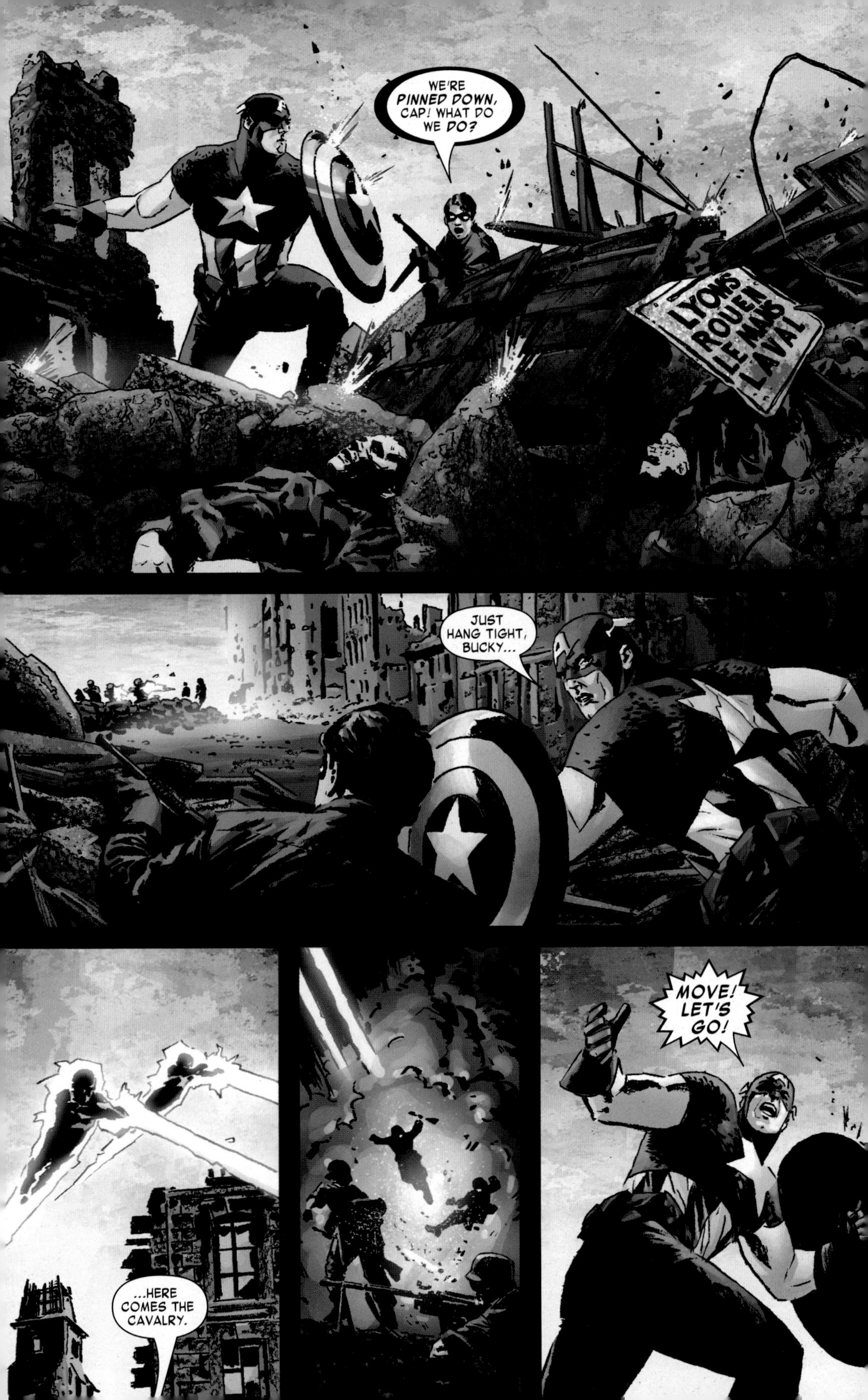
WE'RE PINNED DOWN, CAP! WHAT DO WE DO?
LYONS
ROUEN
LE MANS
LAVAL
JUST HANG TIGHT, BUCKY...
...HERE COMES THE CAVALRY.
MOVE! LET'S GO!

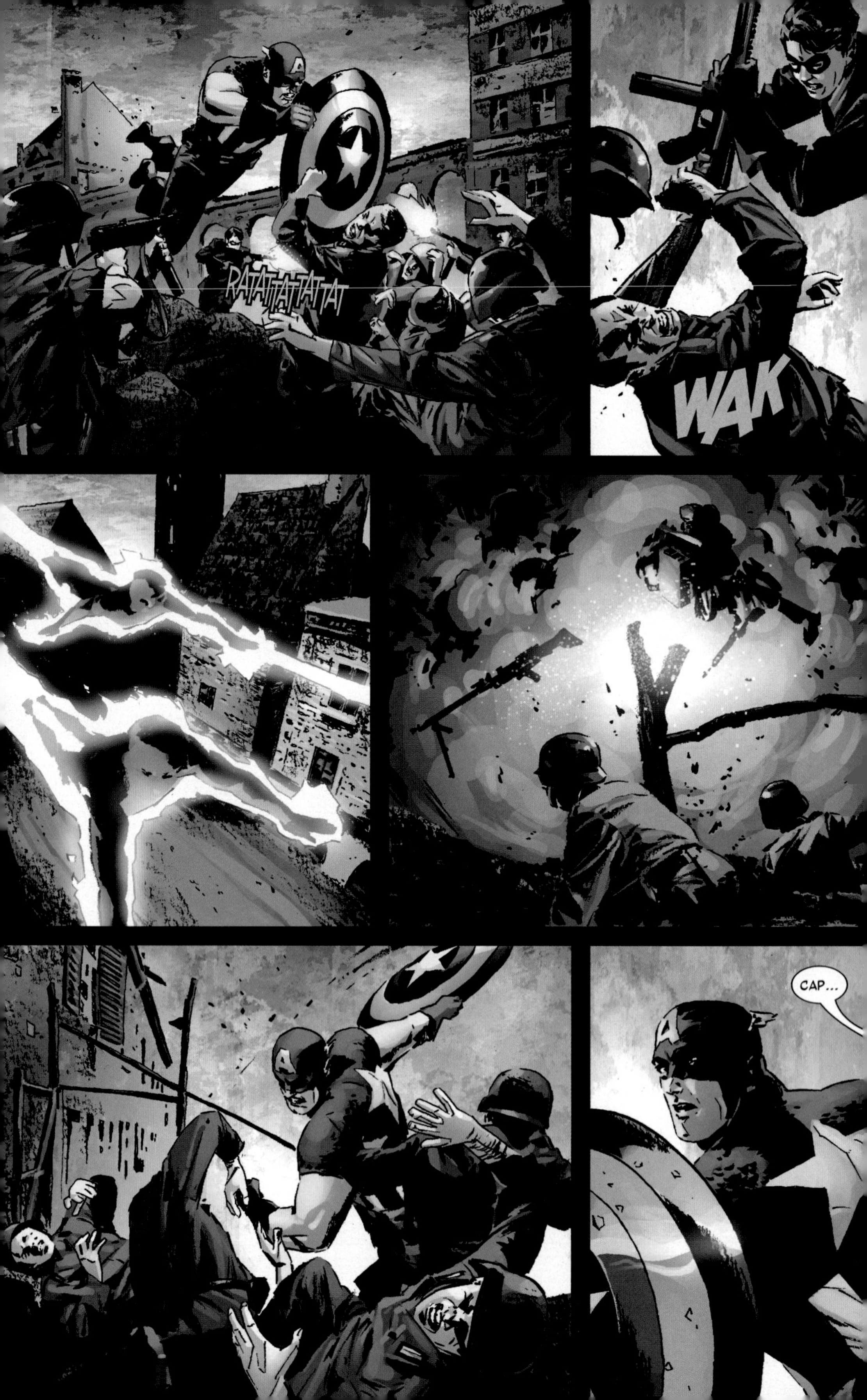
RATATTATTATTAT
WAK
CAP...

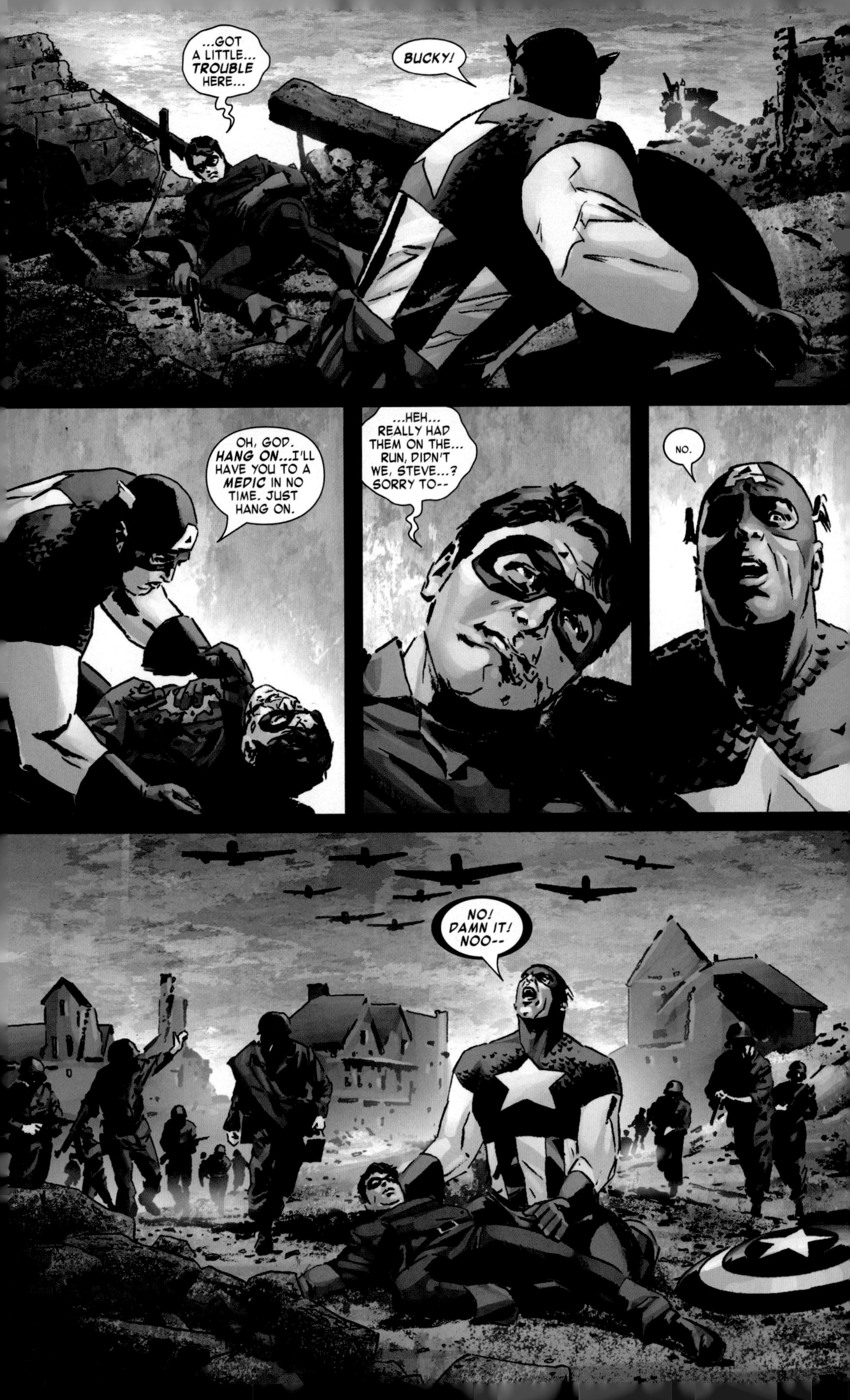
...GOT A LITTLE... TROUBLE HERE...
BUCKY!
OH, GOD. HANG ON...I'LL HAVE YOU TO A MEDIC IN NO TIME. JUST HANG ON.
...HEH... REALLY HAD THEM ON THE... RUN, DIDN'T WE, STEVE...? SORRY TO--
NO.
NO! DAMN IT! NOO--

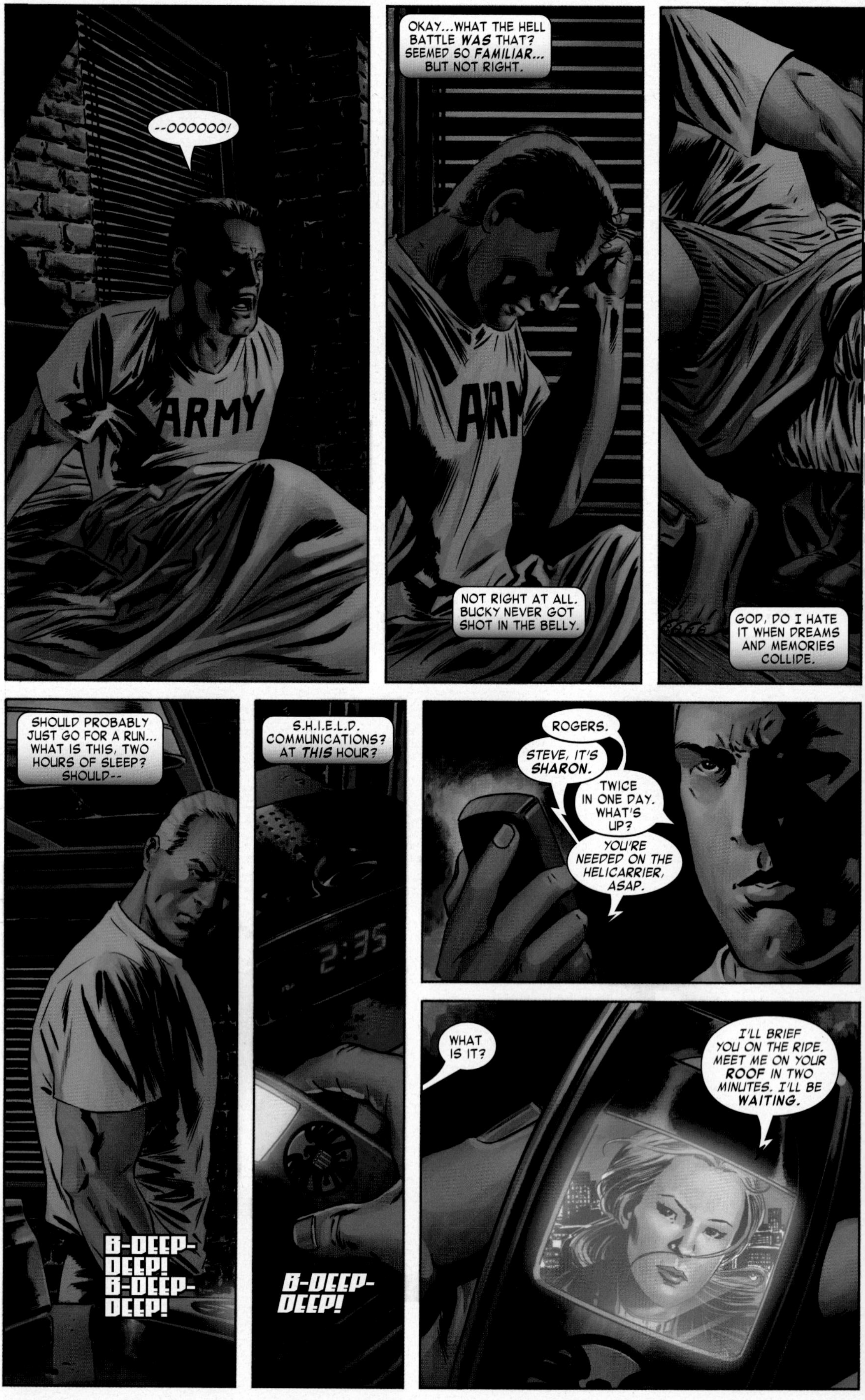
--OOOOOO!
OKAY...WHAT THE HELL BATTLE WAS THAT? SEEMED SO FAMILIAR... BUT NOT RIGHT.
NOT RIGHT AT ALL. BUCKY NEVER GOT SHOT IN THE BELLY.
GOD, DO I HATE IT WHEN DREAMS AND MEMORIES COLLIDE.
SHOULD PROBABLY JUST GO FOR A RUN... WHAT IS THIS, TWO HOURS OF SLEEP? SHOULD--
B-DEEP-DEEP! B-DEEP-DEEP!
S.H.I.E.L.D. COMMUNICATIONS? AT THIS HOUR?
2:35
B-DEEP-DEEP!
ROGERS.
STEVE, IT'S SHARON.
TWICE IN ONE DAY. WHAT'S UP?
YOU'RE NEEDED ON THE HELICARRIER, ASAP.
WHAT IS IT?
I'LL BRIEF YOU ON THE RIDE. MEET ME ON YOUR ROOF IN TWO MINUTES. I'LL BE WAITING.

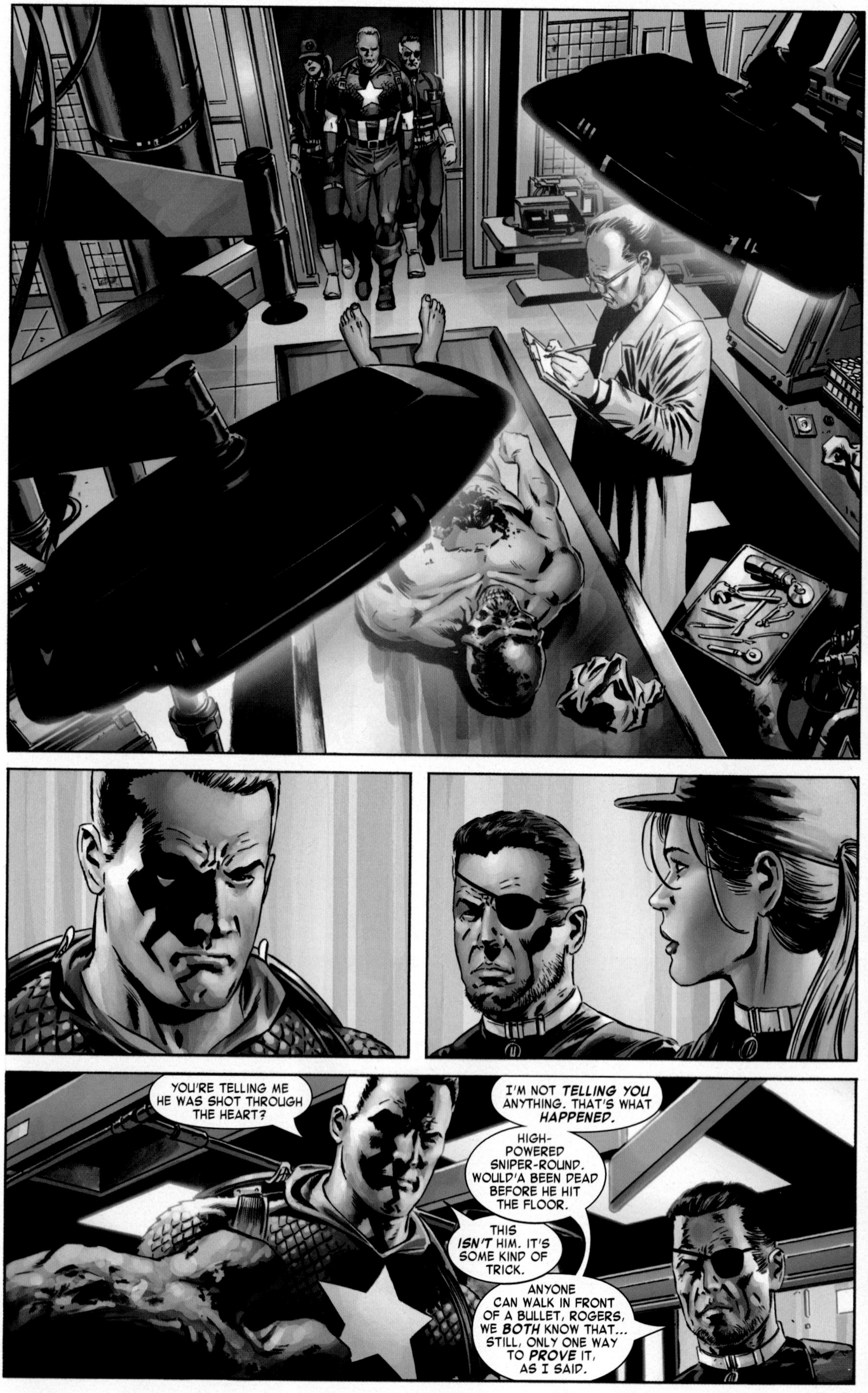
YOU'RE TELLING ME HE WAS SHOT THROUGH THE HEART?
I'M NOT TELLING YOU ANYTHING. THAT'S WHAT HAPPENED.
HIGH-POWERED SNIPER-ROUND. WOULD'A BEEN DEAD BEFORE HE HIT THE FLOOR.
THIS ISN'T HIM. IT'S SOME KIND OF TRICK.
ANYONE CAN WALK IN FRONT OF A BULLET, ROGERS, WE BOTH KNOW THAT... STILL, ONLY ONE WAY TO PROVE IT, AS I SAID.

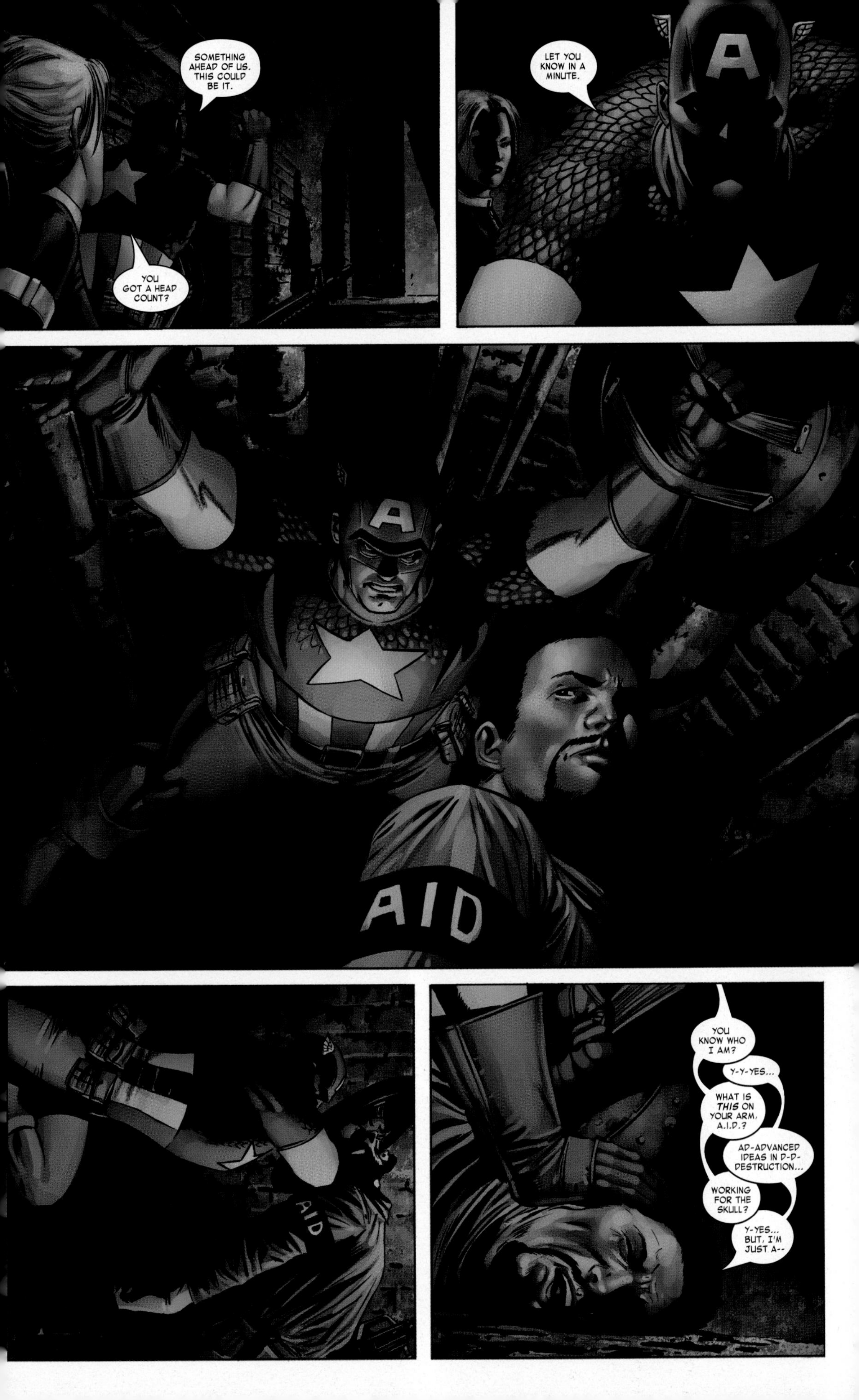
SOMETHING AHEAD OF US. THIS COULD BE IT.
YOU GOT A HEAD COUNT?
LET YOU KNOW IN A MINUTE.
AID
AID
YOU KNOW WHO I AM?
Y-Y-YES...
WHAT IS *THIS* ON YOUR ARM, A.I.D.?
AD-ADVANCED IDEAS IN D-D-DESTRUCTION...
WORKING FOR THE SKULL?
Y-YES... BUT, I'M JUST A--

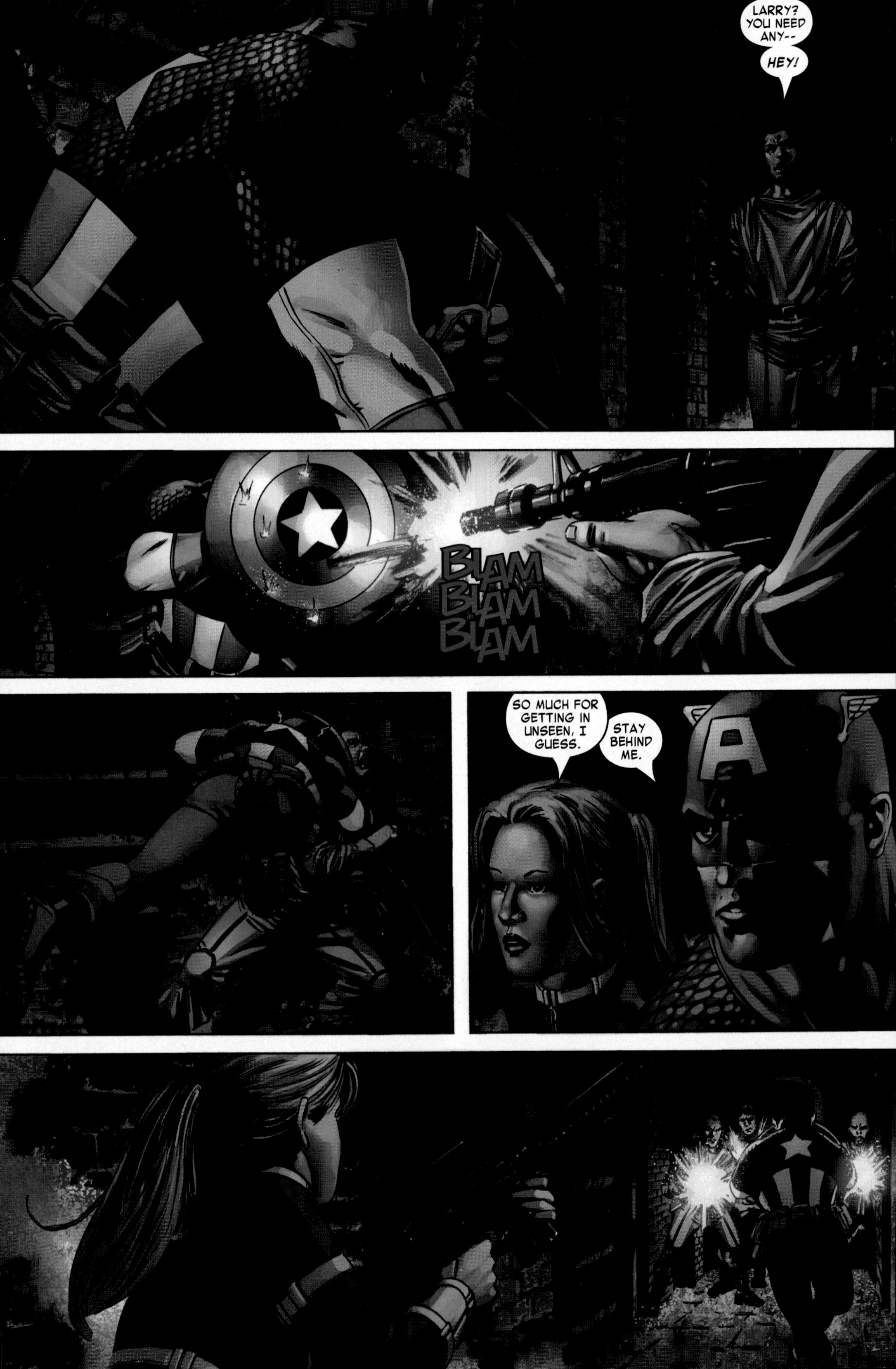

LARRY? YOU NEED ANY--
HEY!
BLAM BLAM BLAM
SO MUCH FOR GETTING IN UNSEEN, I GUESS.
STAY BEHIND ME.

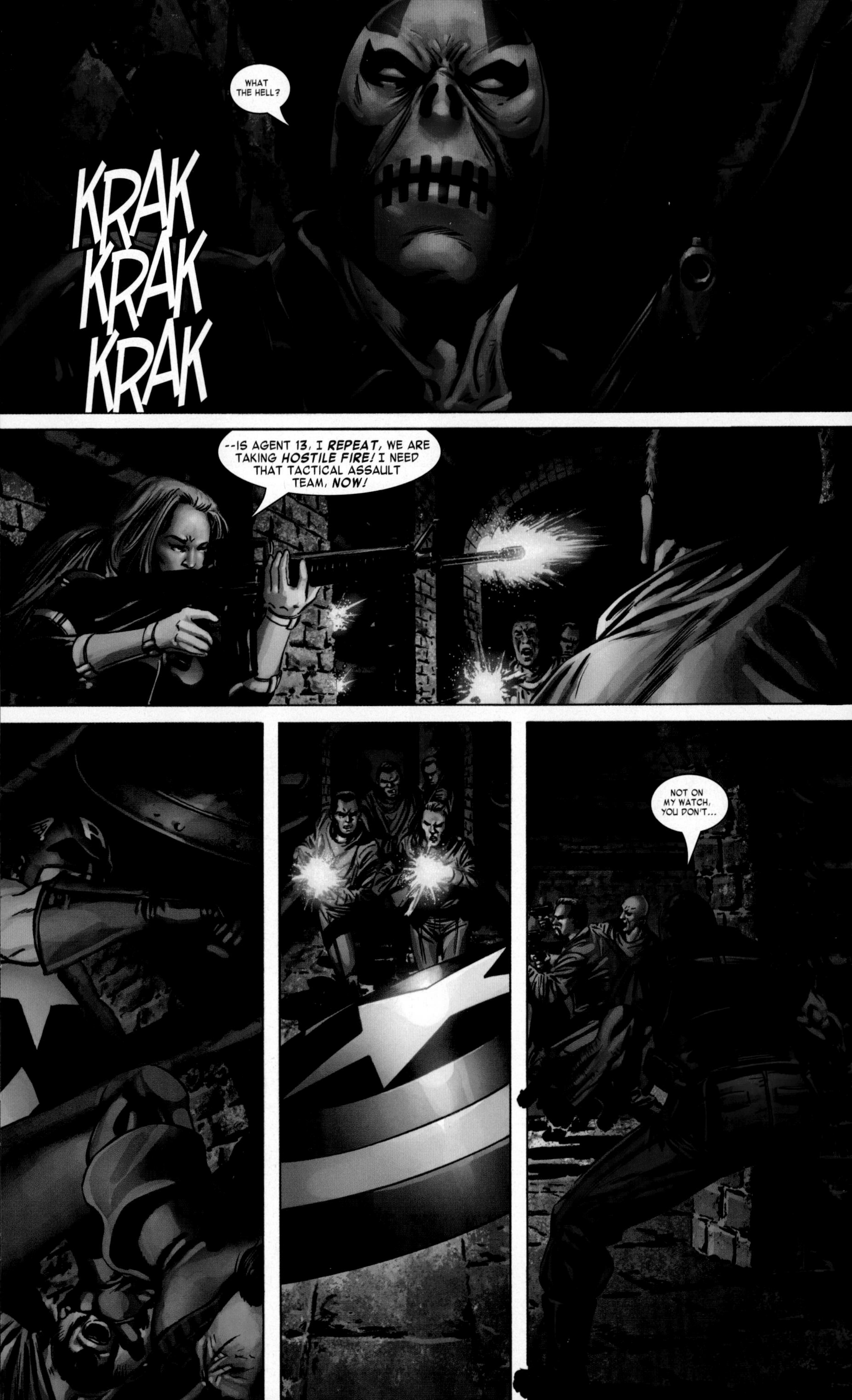
WHAT THE HELL?
KRAK KRAK KRAK
--IS AGENT 13, I REPEAT, WE ARE TAKING HOSTILE FIRE! I NEED THAT TACTICAL ASSAULT TEAM, NOW!
NOT ON MY WATCH, YOU DON'T...

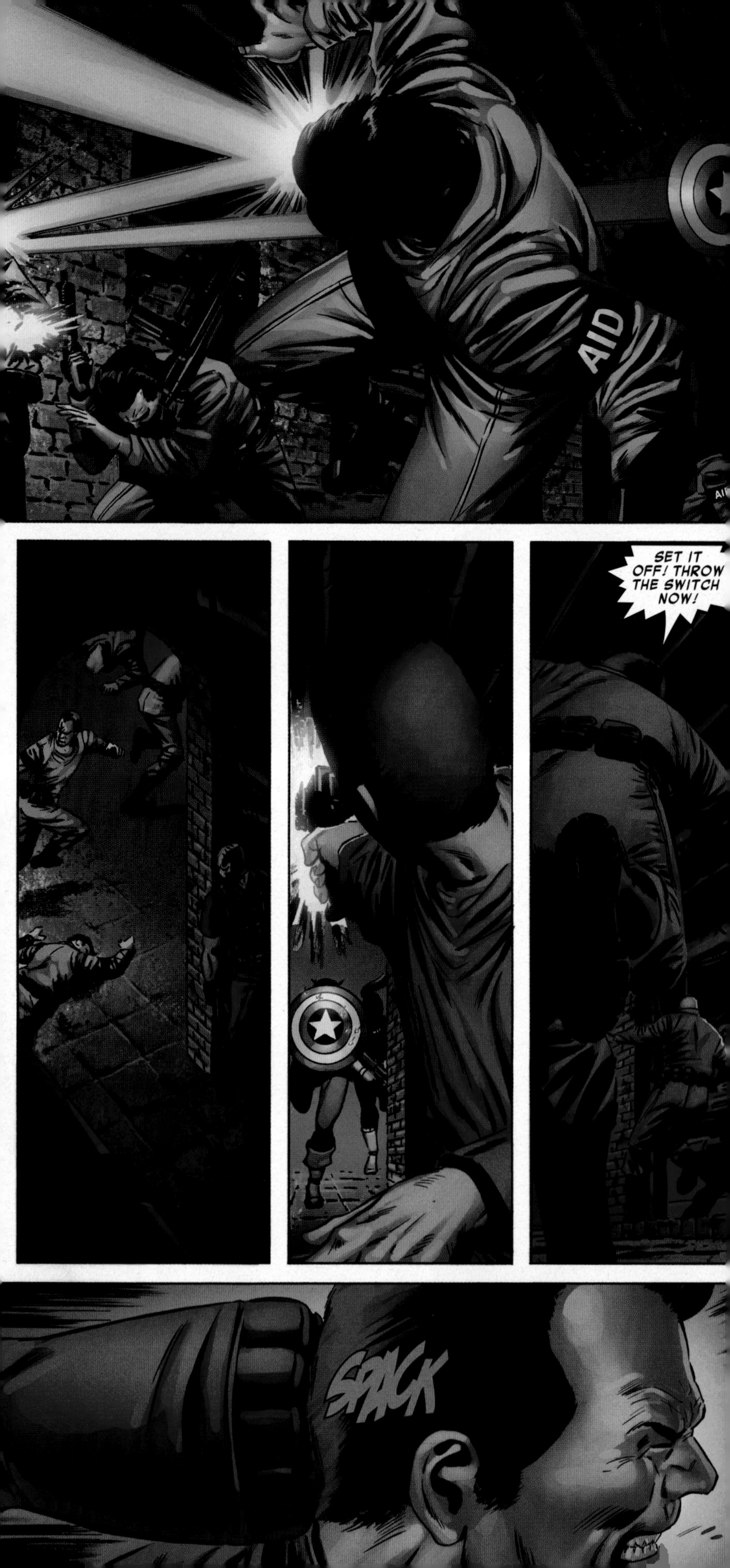
AID
SET IT OFF! THROW THE SWITCH NOW!
SPACK

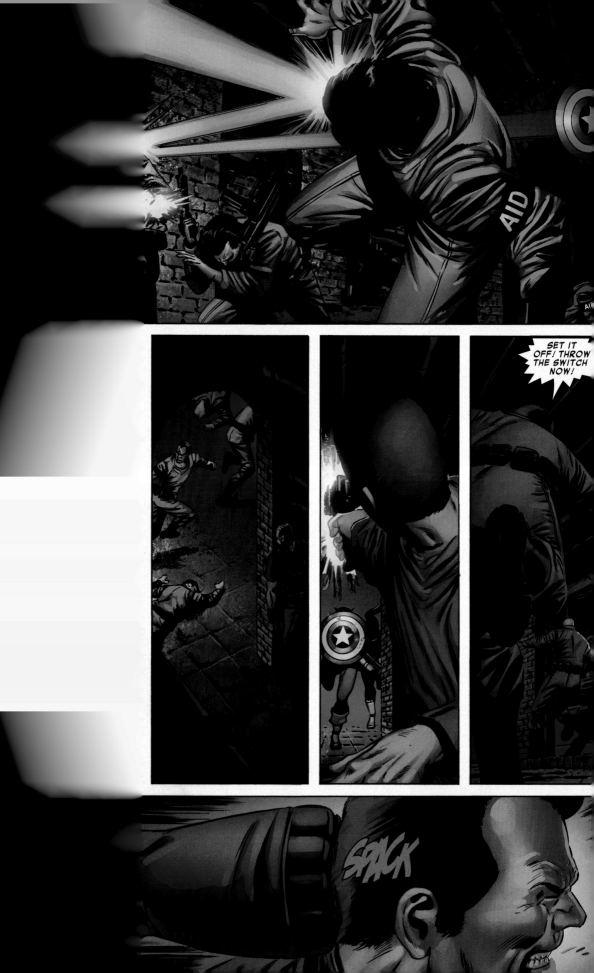

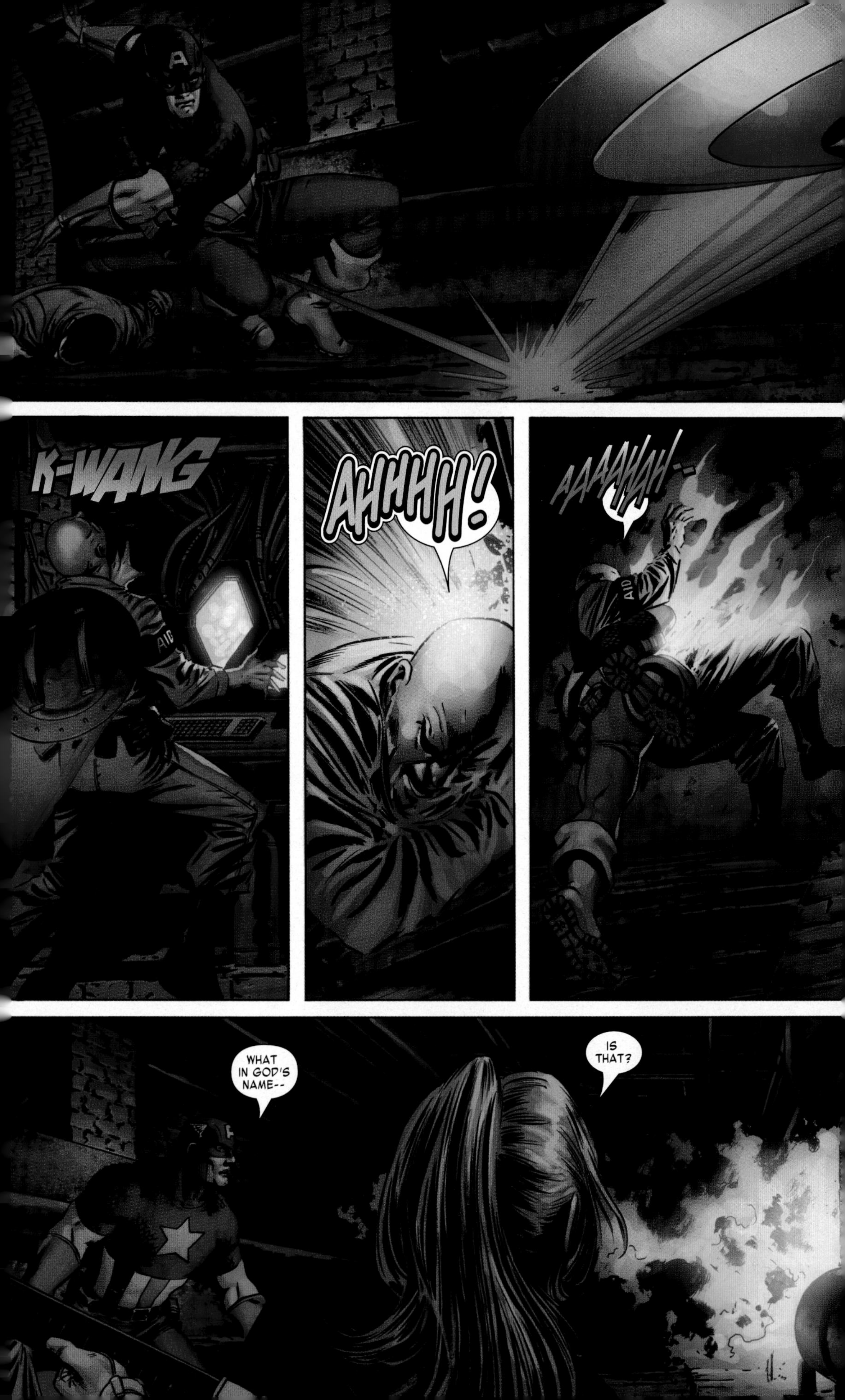
K-WANG
AHHHH!
AAAAAAH--
WHAT IN GOD'S NAME--
IS THAT?

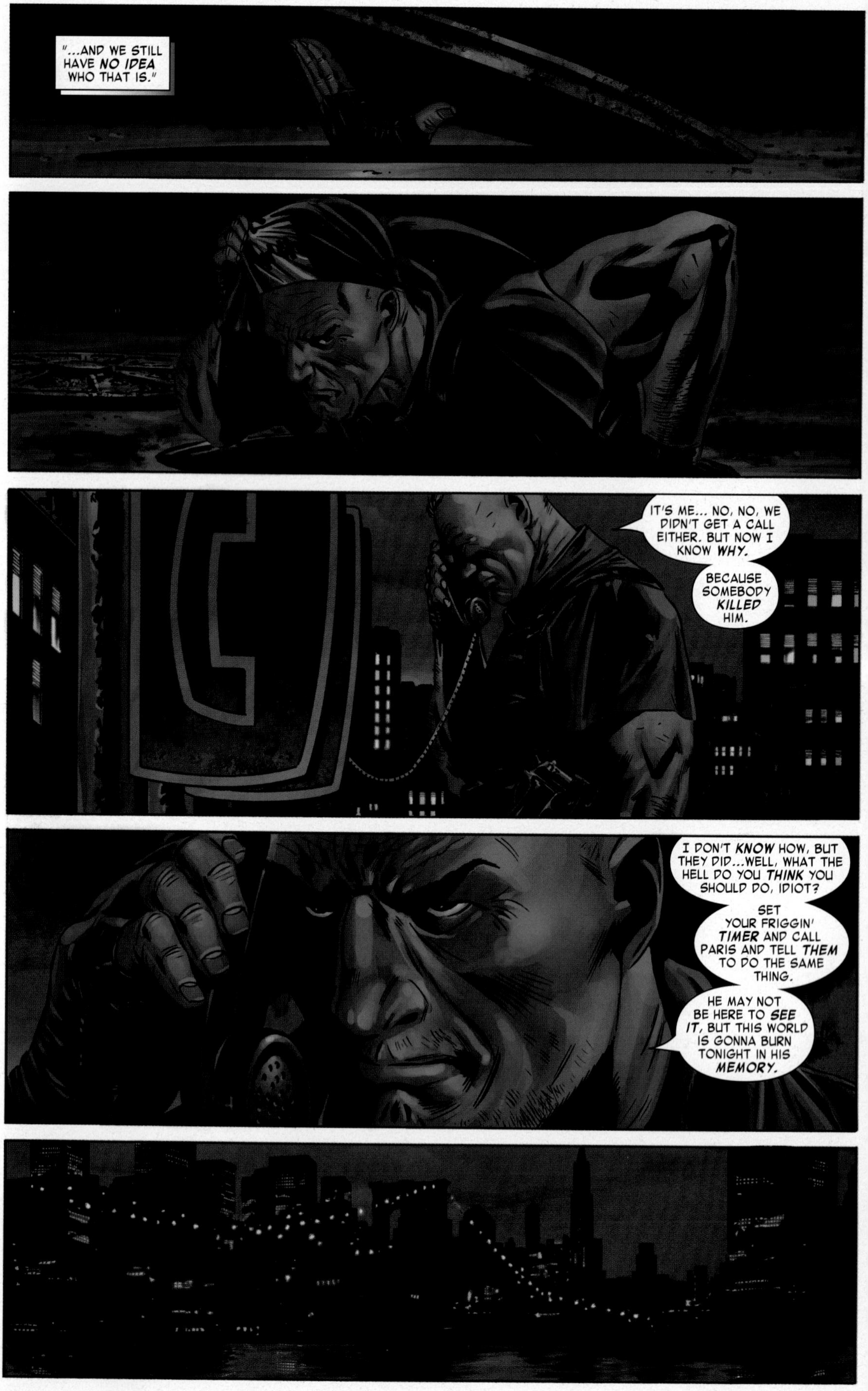
"...AND WE STILL HAVE NO IDEA WHO THAT IS."
IT'S ME... NO, NO, WE DIDN'T GET A CALL EITHER. BUT NOW I KNOW WHY.
BECAUSE SOMEBODY KILLED HIM.
I DON'T KNOW HOW, BUT THEY DID...WELL, WHAT THE HELL DO YOU THINK YOU SHOULD DO, IDIOT?
SET YOUR FRIGGIN' TIMER AND CALL PARIS AND TELL THEM TO DO THE SAME THING.
HE MAY NOT BE HERE TO SEE IT, BUT THIS WORLD IS GONNA BURN TONIGHT IN HIS MEMORY.

3

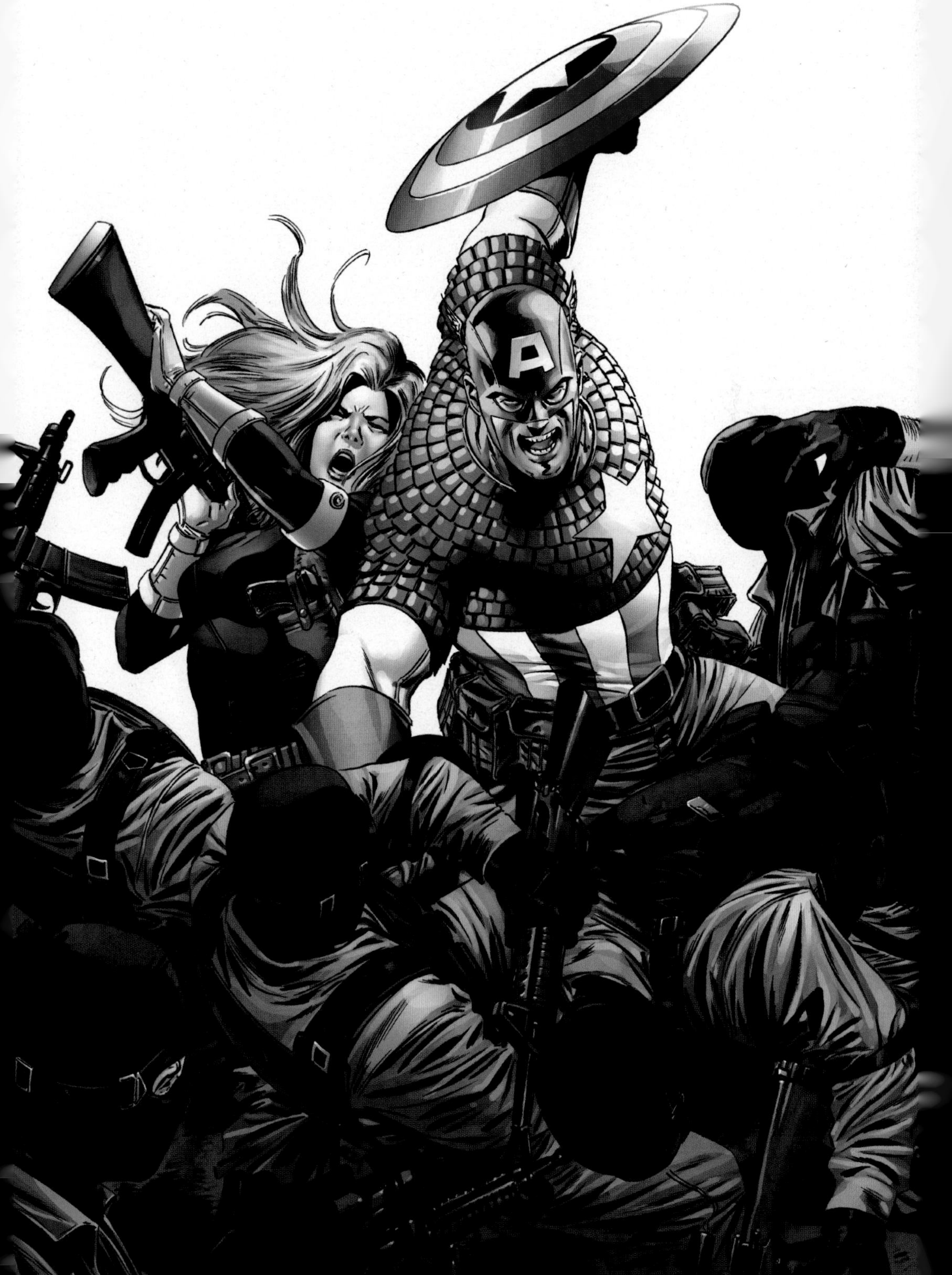

--ESTIMATED TIME OF ARRIVAL IS ONE HOUR TWENTY MINUTES, SO I WANT TO KNOW *EXACTLY* WHAT WE'RE LOOKING AT HERE.

CONTAINMENT LEVELS, CIVILIAN TRAFFIC, EVERYTHING.

AND SOMEONE GET ME A *LINK-UP* WITH WHOEVER'S HANDLING THE *LONDON* TEAM. THEY SHOULD BE INSIDE BY NOW.

YES, MA'AM. I'LL GET ON IT. AGENT HEINBERG HAS BEEN WORKING ON THE DATA FOR OUR STRIKE.

RIGHT, THE TRACE FROM THE SKULL'S RECEIVER APPEARS TO BE TRACKING TO *THIS* LOCATION, AND IF THE *MANHATTAN* DEVICE IS ANY INDICATION, IT'LL BE *UNDERGROUND*...

AND UNFORTUNATELY, THIS IS *AVENUE FOCH*, ALONG THE CHAMPS-ELYSEES...

...SO WE'RE LOOKING AT A SERIOUS *TARGET-RICH ENVIRONMENT* IF THIS GOES BADLY.

HOLD THAT THOUGHT, HEINBERG. I NEED TO GET SOME TACTICAL INSIGHT.

WALK WITH ME.

TACTICAL INSIGHT? WHAT'S UP?

YOU. LOOK LIKE YOU'RE IN ANOTHER *TIME ZONE,* STEVE.

I KNOW THIS HAS BEEN A HELL OF A NIGHT, AND IT JUST KEEPS GETTING *WORSE,* BUT I NEED YOU TO BE *FOCUSED* WHEN WE HIT PARIS.

SHARON... I'M JUST TIRED-- A LOT ON MY MIND.

LOOK, I'VE *GOT* THIS. WHY DON'T YOU TAKE A BREAK? CATCH A FEW MINUTES SHUT-EYE OR GRAB A CUP OF COFFEE?

YOU'LL CALL ME?

THE *SECOND* FURY GETS IN TOUCH. SCOUT'S HONOR. GO.

C'MON, ROGERS, WAKE UP...WHAT'S YOUR *PROBLEM?*

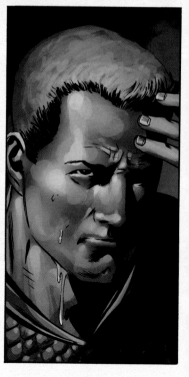

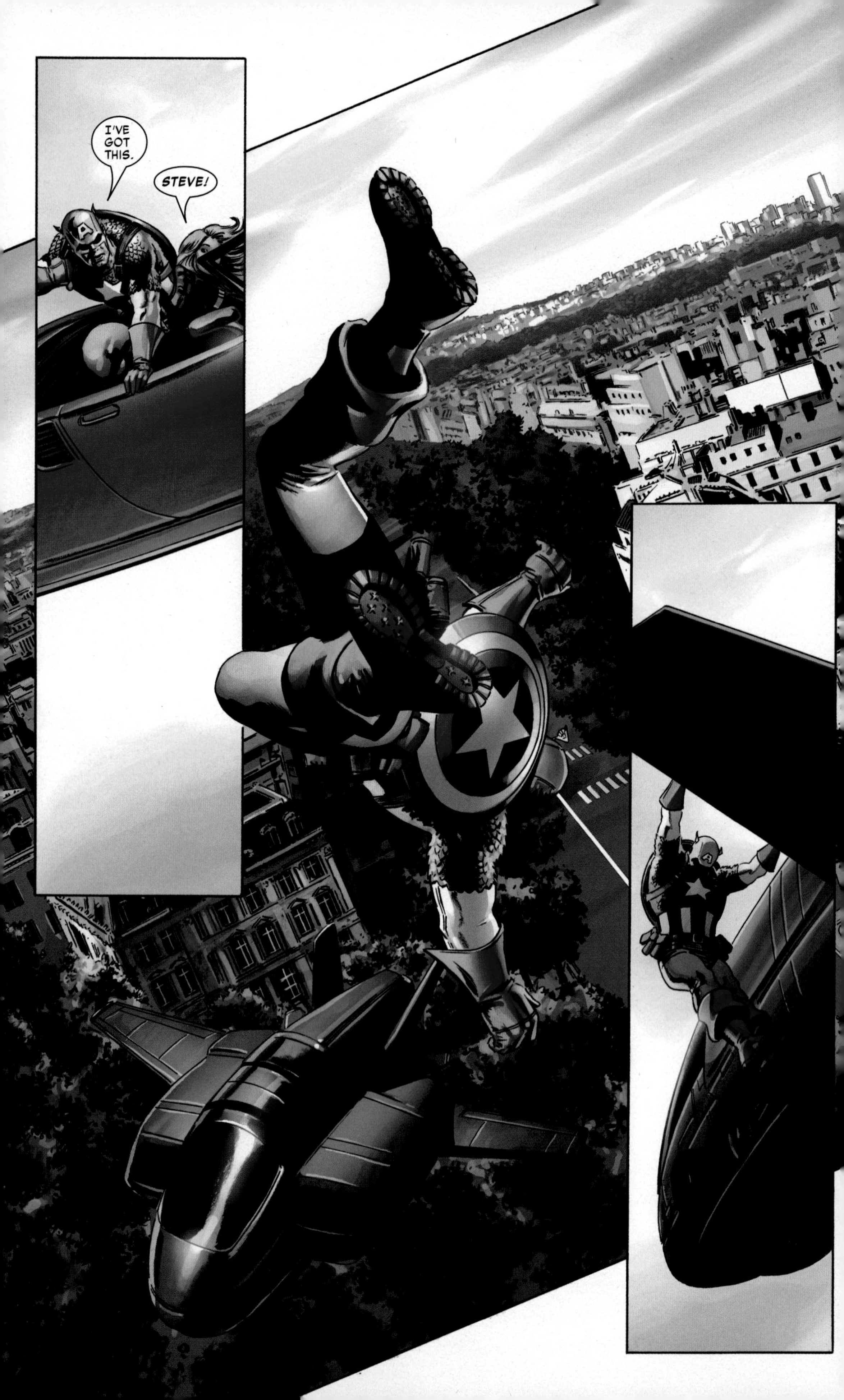
I'VE GOT THIS.
STEVE!

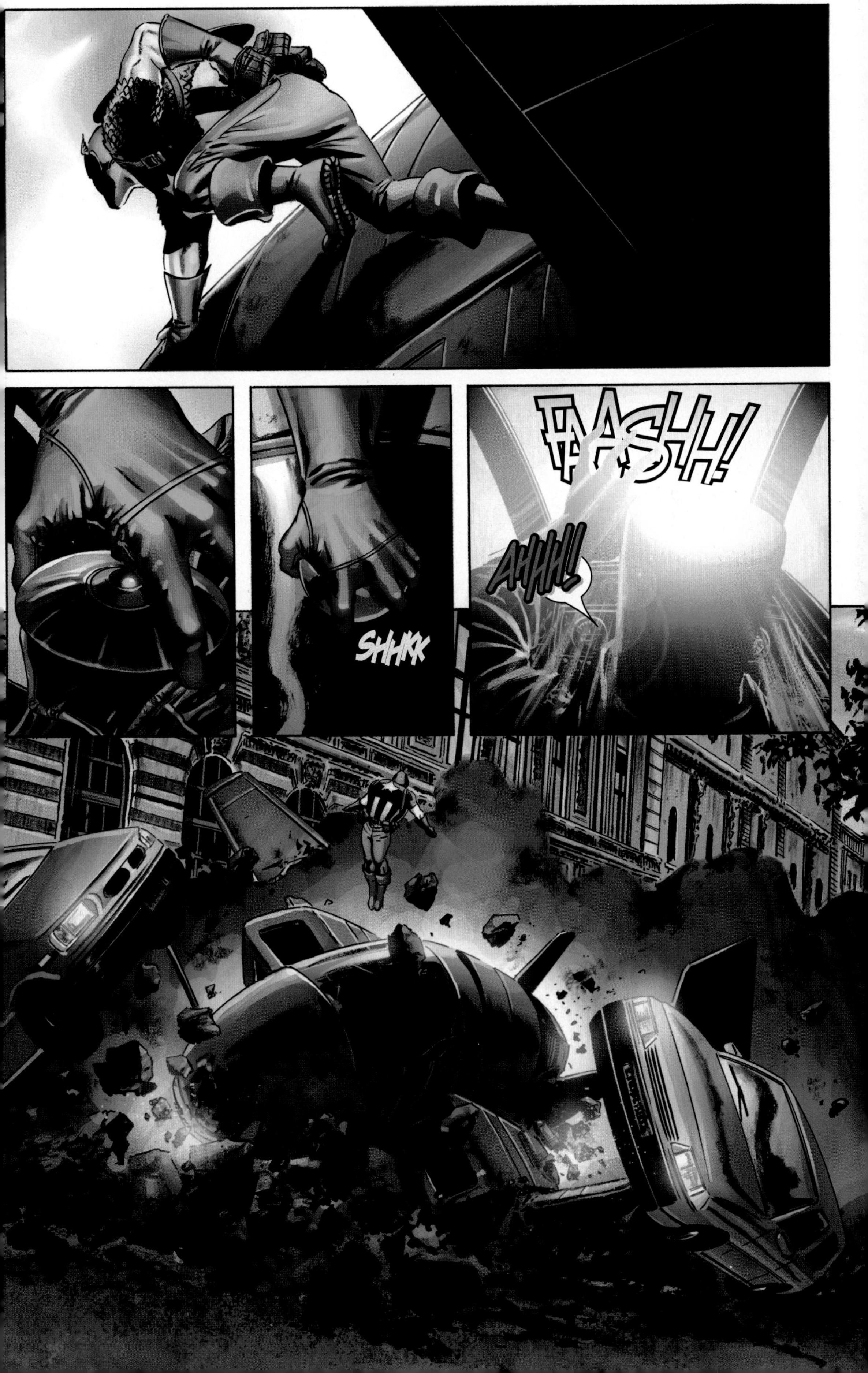
SHHKK
FAASHH!
AHHH!!

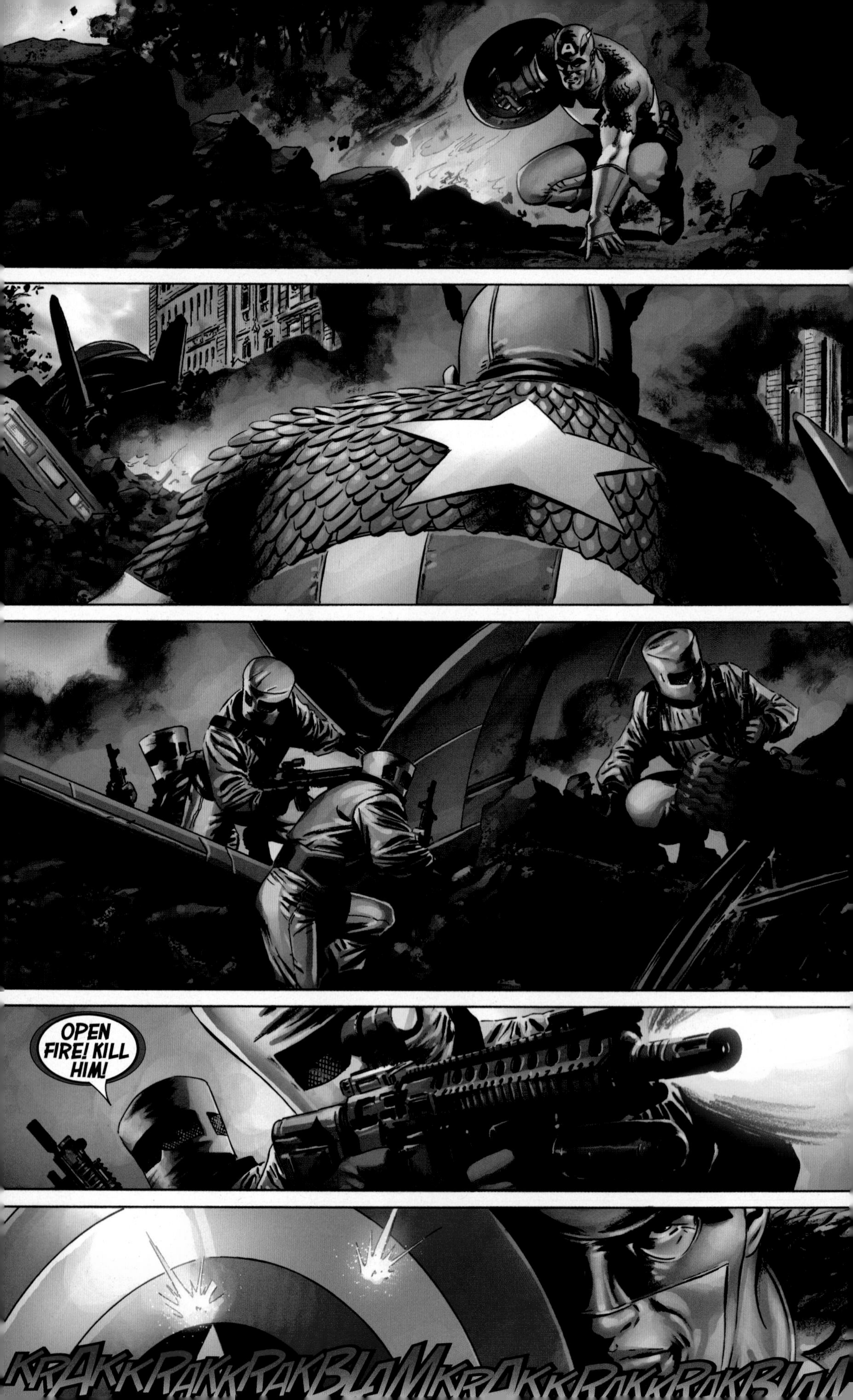
OPEN FIRE! KILL HIM!
KRAKKRAKKRAKBLAMKRAKKRAKKRAKBLAM

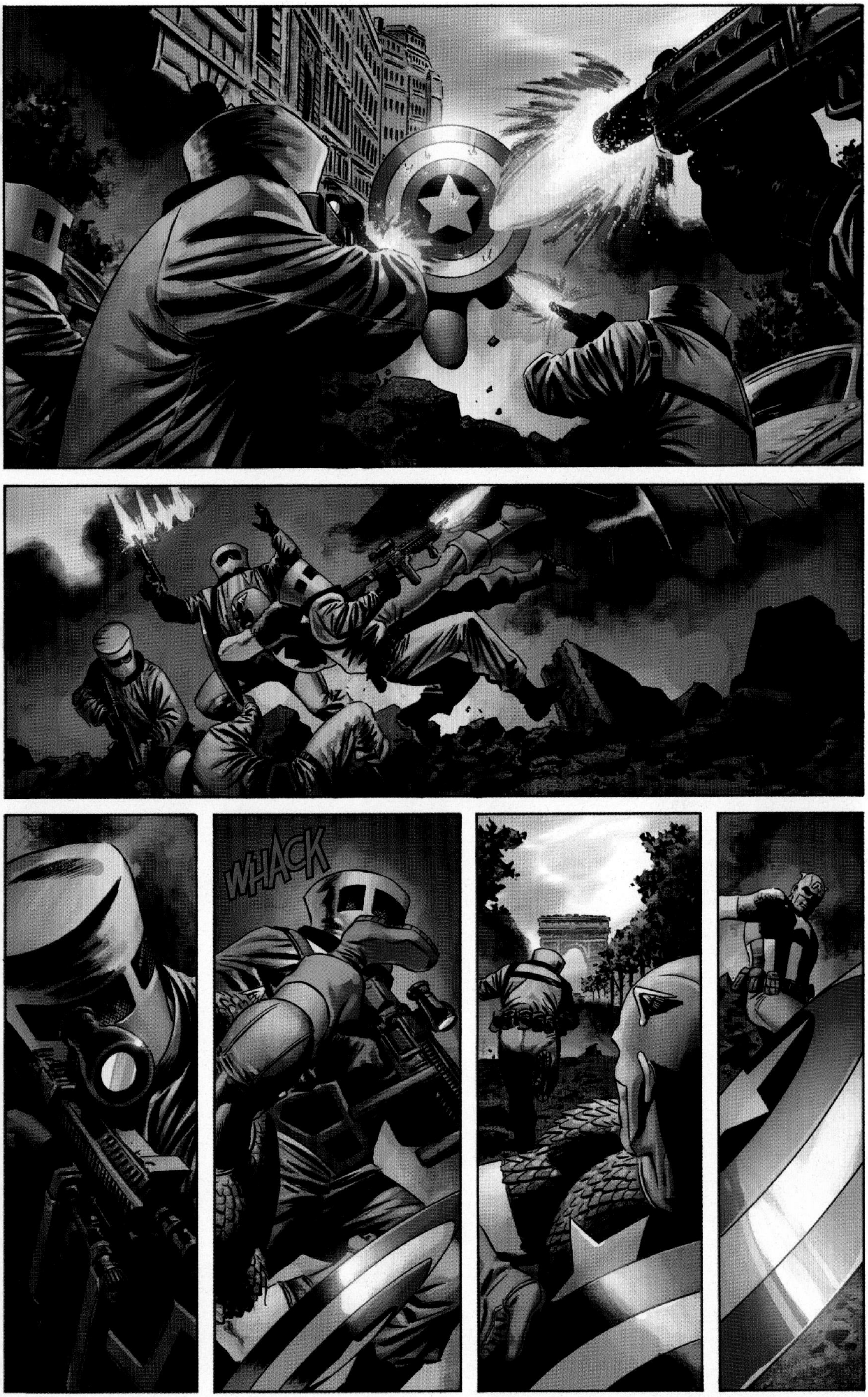
WHACK

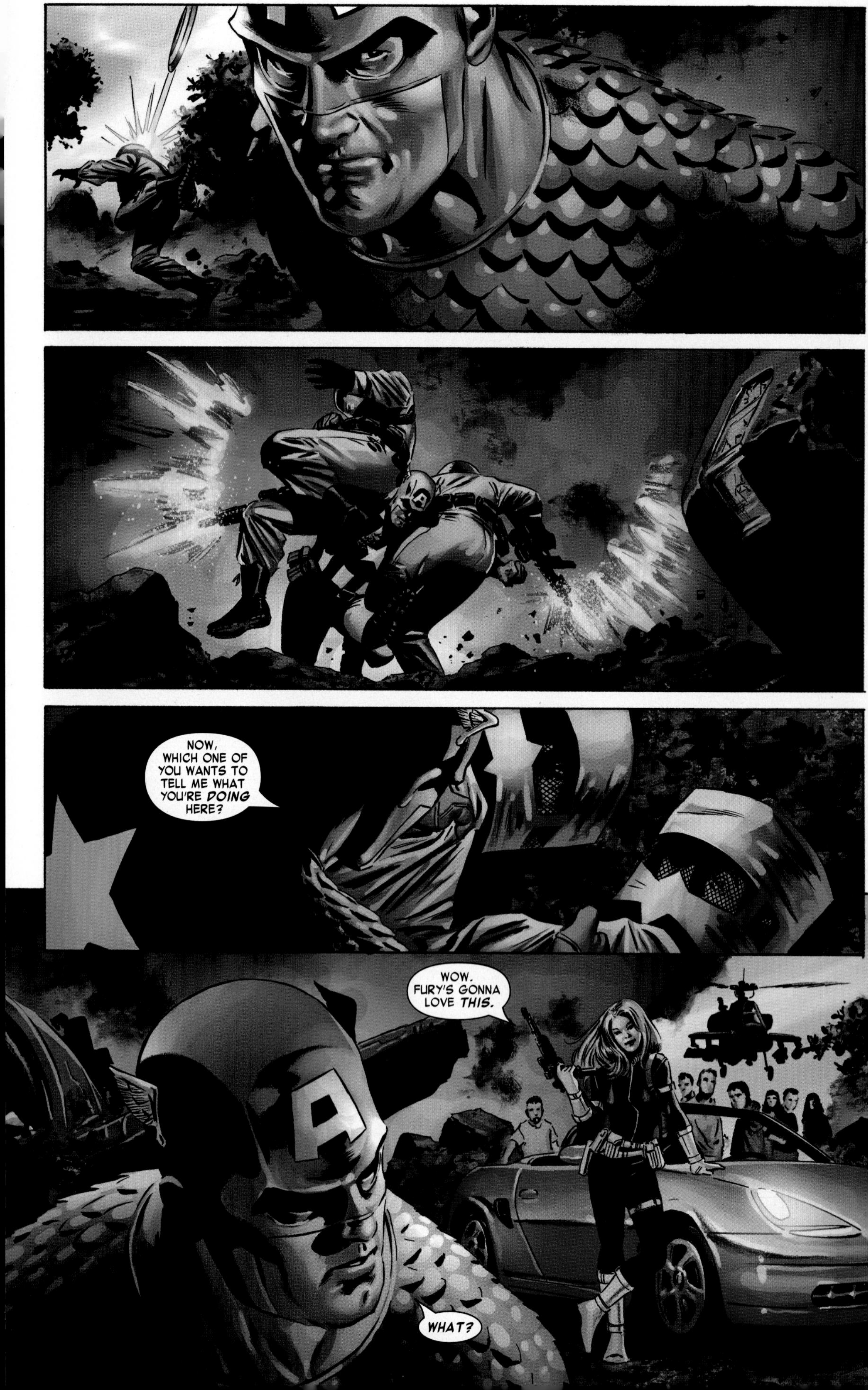
NOW, WHICH ONE OF YOU WANTS TO TELL ME WHAT YOU'RE *DOING* HERE?
WOW. FURY'S GONNA LOVE *THIS.*
WHAT?

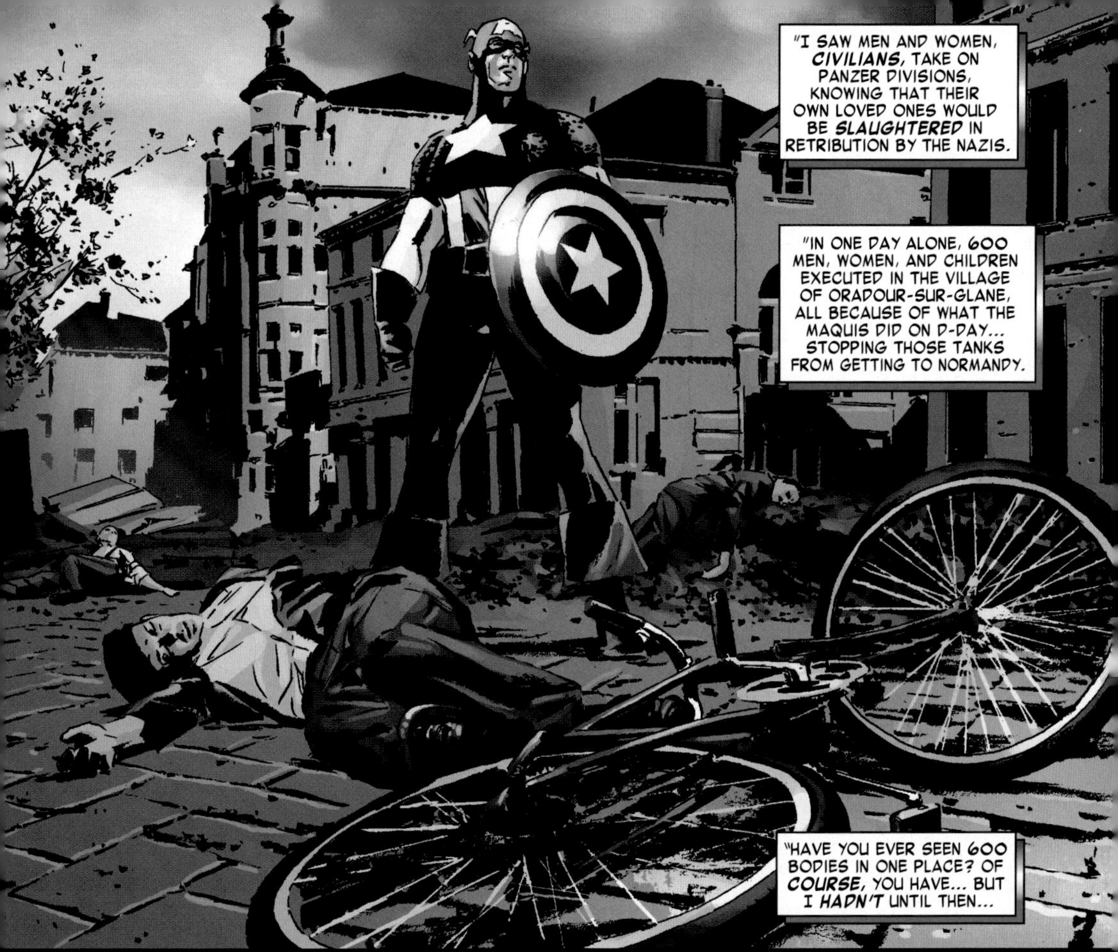
"I SAW MEN AND WOMEN, CIVILIANS, TAKE ON PANZER DIVISIONS, KNOWING THAT THEIR OWN LOVED ONES WOULD BE SLAUGHTERED IN RETRIBUTION BY THE NAZIS.
"IN ONE DAY ALONE, 600 MEN, WOMEN, AND CHILDREN EXECUTED IN THE VILLAGE OF ORADOUR-SUR-GLANE, ALL BECAUSE OF WHAT THE MAQUIS DID ON D-DAY... STOPPING THOSE TANKS FROM GETTING TO NORMANDY.
"HAVE YOU EVER SEEN 600 BODIES IN ONE PLACE? OF COURSE, YOU HAVE... BUT I HADN'T UNTIL THEN...

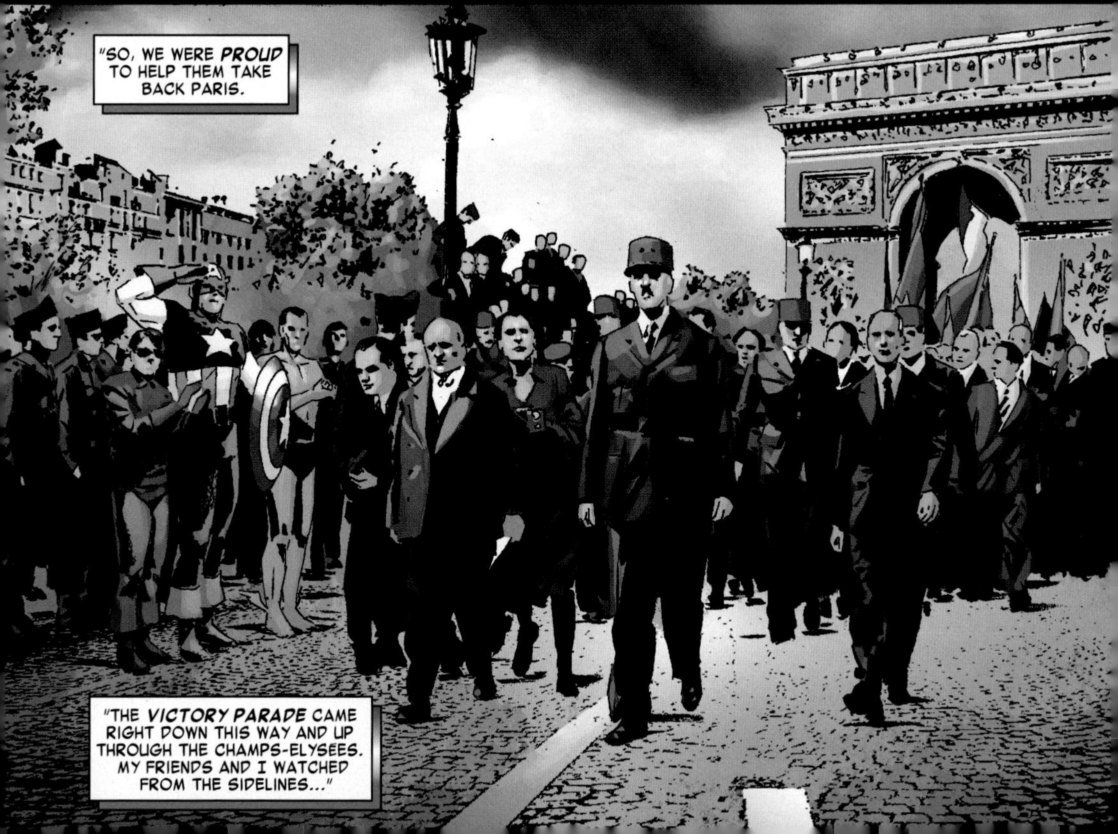
"SO, WE WERE PROUD TO HELP THEM TAKE BACK PARIS.
"THE VICTORY PARADE CAME RIGHT DOWN THIS WAY AND UP THROUGH THE CHAMPS-ELYSEES. MY FRIENDS AND I WATCHED FROM THE SIDELINES..."

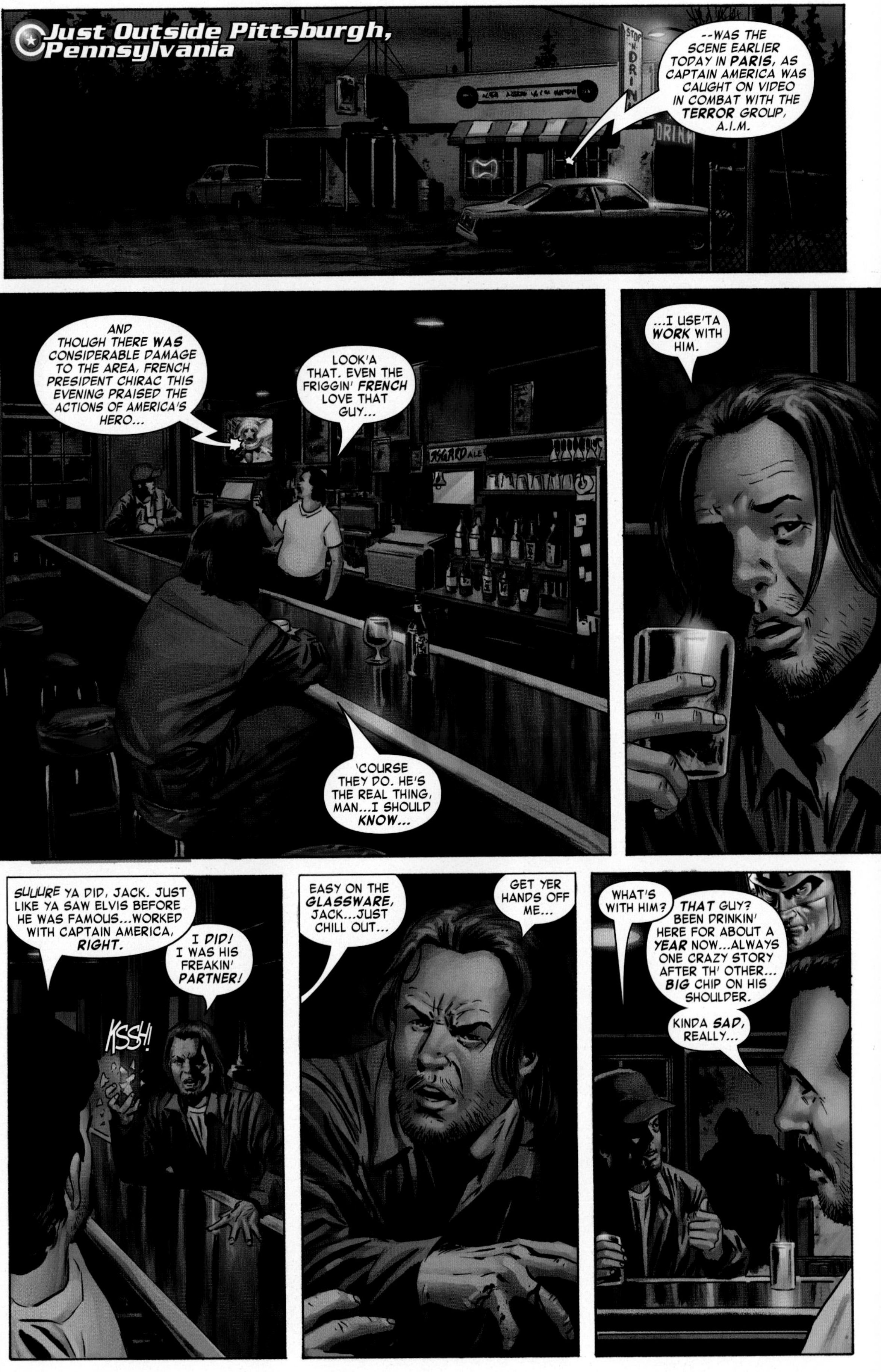
Just Outside Pittsburgh, Pennsylvania
--WAS THE SCENE EARLIER TODAY IN PARIS, AS CAPTAIN AMERICA WAS CAUGHT ON VIDEO IN COMBAT WITH THE TERROR GROUP, A.I.M.
AND THOUGH THERE WAS CONSIDERABLE DAMAGE TO THE AREA, FRENCH PRESIDENT CHIRAC THIS EVENING PRAISED THE ACTIONS OF AMERICA'S HERO...
LOOK'A THAT. EVEN THE FRIGGIN' FRENCH LOVE THAT GUY...
'COURSE THEY DO. HE'S THE REAL THING, MAN...I SHOULD KNOW...
...I USE'TA WORK WITH HIM.
SUUURE YA DID, JACK. JUST LIKE YA SAW ELVIS BEFORE HE WAS FAMOUS...WORKED WITH CAPTAIN AMERICA, RIGHT.
I DID! I WAS HIS FREAKIN' PARTNER!
KSSH!
EASY ON THE GLASSWARE, JACK...JUST CHILL OUT...
GET YER HANDS OFF ME...
WHAT'S WITH HIM?
THAT GUY? BEEN DRINKIN' HERE FOR ABOUT A YEAR NOW...ALWAYS ONE CRAZY STORY AFTER TH' OTHER... BIG CHIP ON HIS SHOULDER.
KINDA SAD, REALLY...

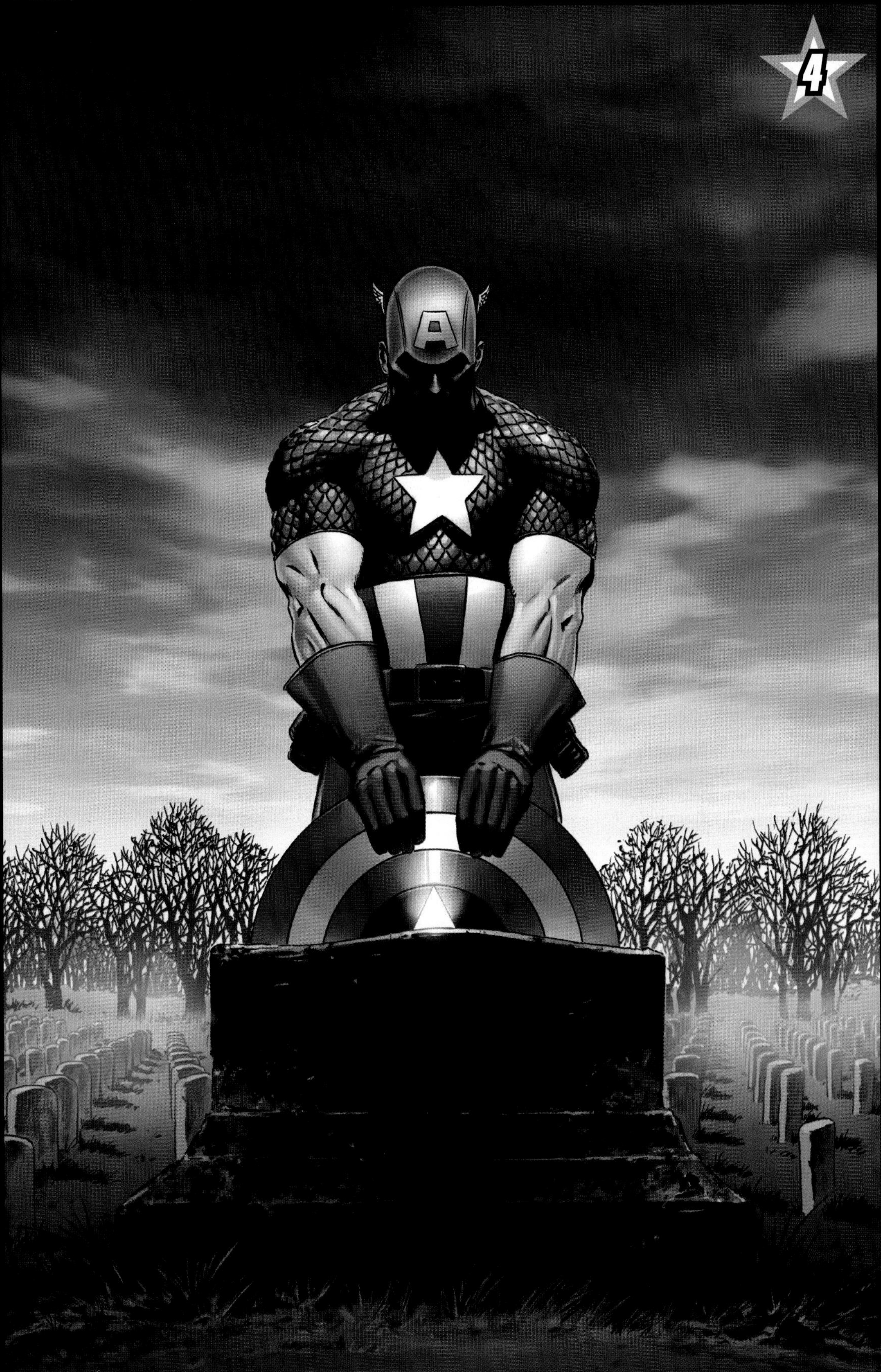
4

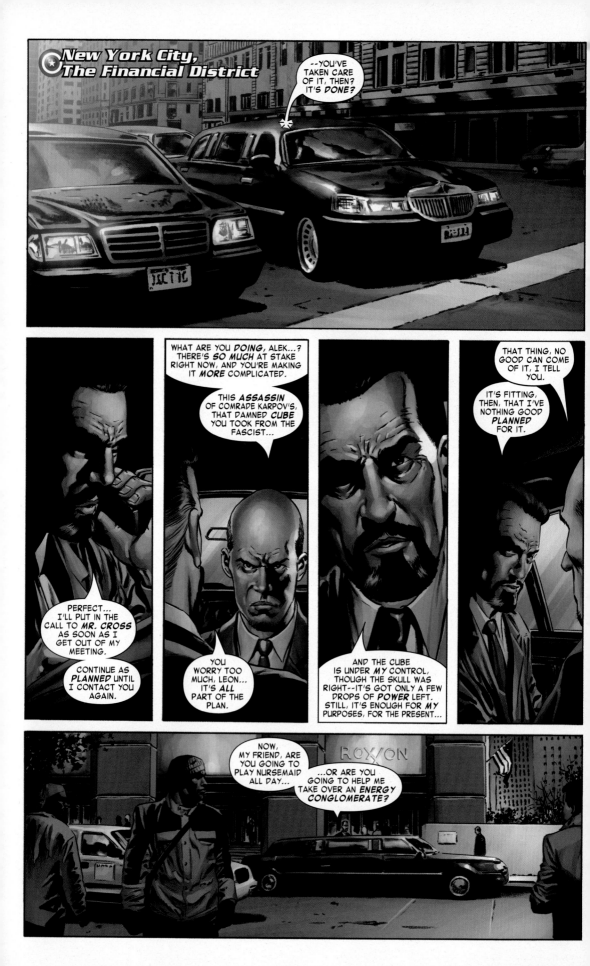

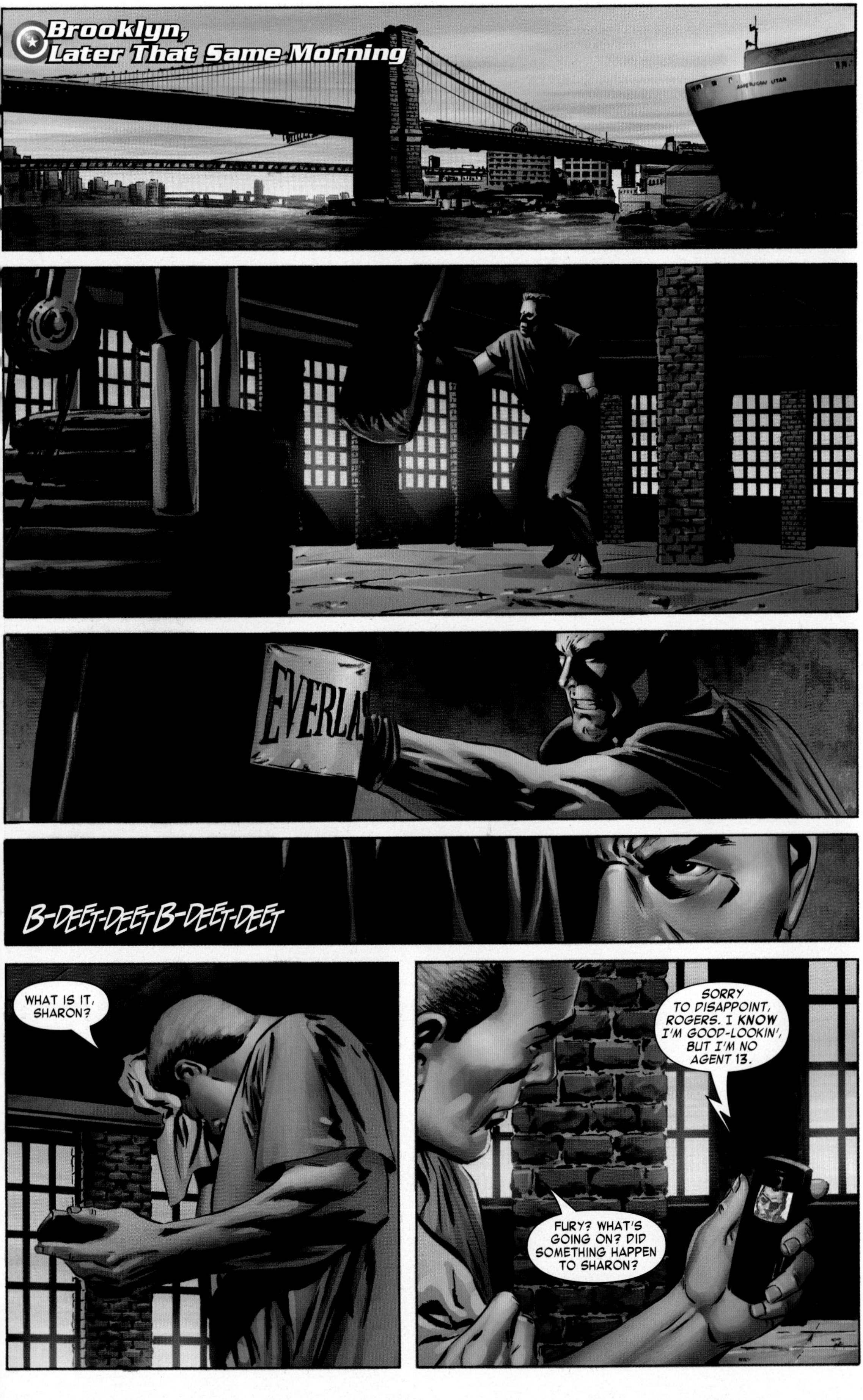

Brooklyn, Later That Same Morning
EVERLAS
B-DEET-DEET B-DEET-DEET
WHAT IS IT, SHARON?
SORRY TO DISAPPOINT, ROGERS. I KNOW I'M GOOD-LOOKIN', BUT I'M NO AGENT 13.
FURY? WHAT'S GOING ON? DID SOMETHING HAPPEN TO SHARON?

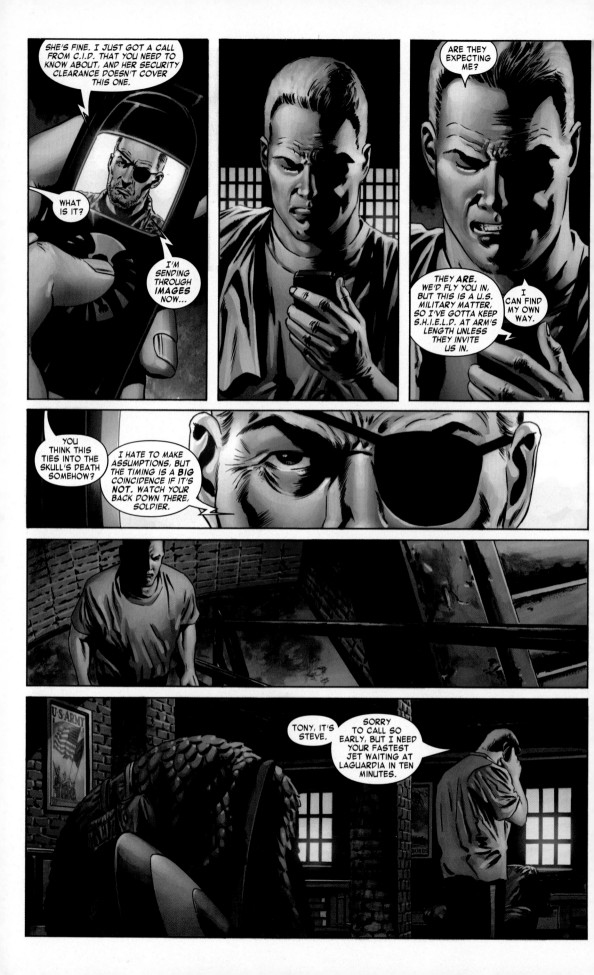

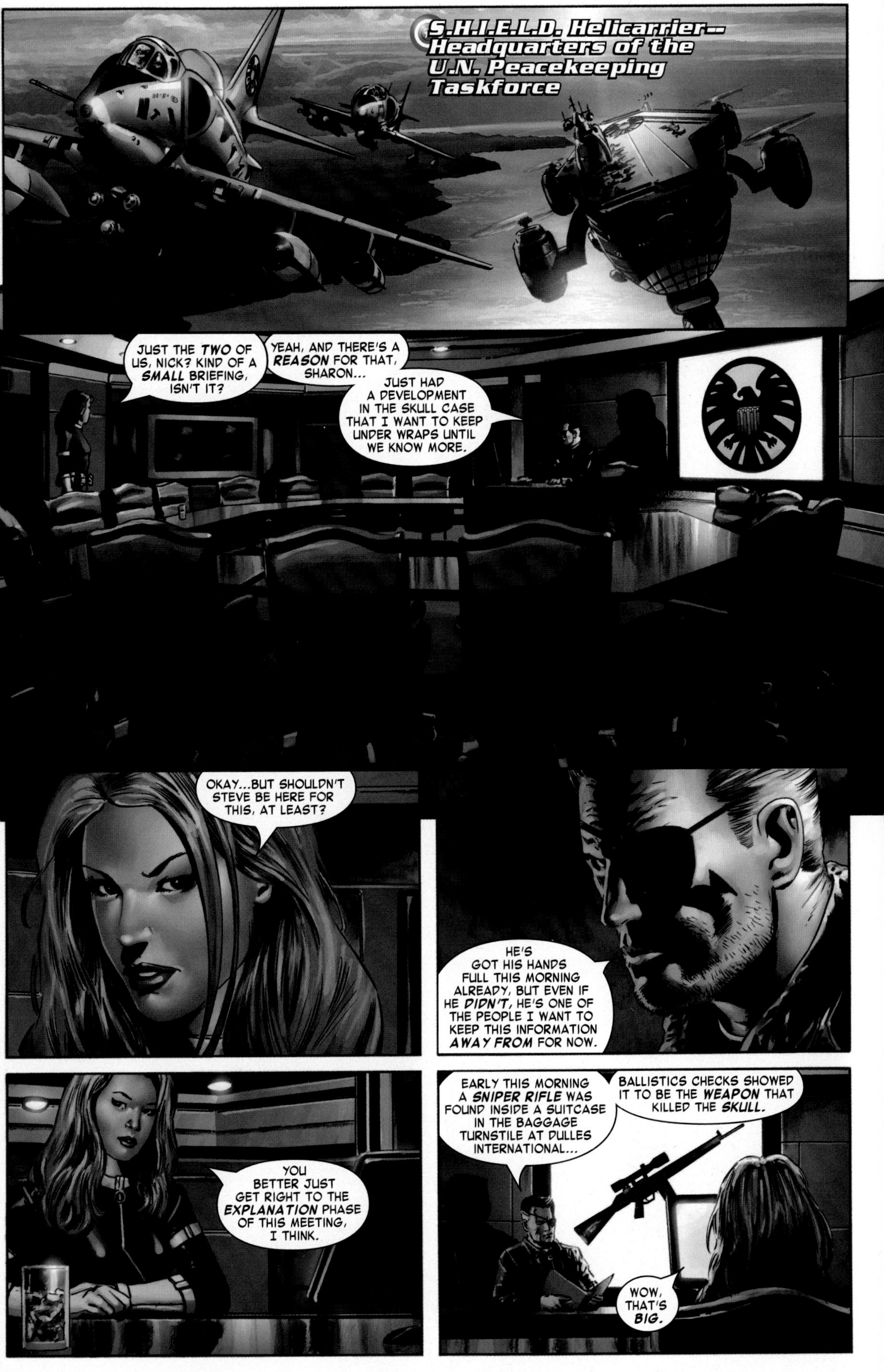
S.H.I.E.L.D. Helicarrier--Headquarters of the U.N. Peacekeeping Taskforce
JUST THE TWO OF US, NICK? KIND OF A SMALL BRIEFING, ISN'T IT?
YEAH, AND THERE'S A REASON FOR THAT, SHARON...
JUST HAD A DEVELOPMENT IN THE SKULL CASE THAT I WANT TO KEEP UNDER WRAPS UNTIL WE KNOW MORE.
OKAY...BUT SHOULDN'T STEVE BE HERE FOR THIS, AT LEAST?
HE'S GOT HIS HANDS FULL THIS MORNING ALREADY, BUT EVEN IF HE DIDN'T, HE'S ONE OF THE PEOPLE I WANT TO KEEP THIS INFORMATION AWAY FROM FOR NOW.
YOU BETTER JUST GET RIGHT TO THE EXPLANATION PHASE OF THIS MEETING, I THINK.
EARLY THIS MORNING A SNIPER RIFLE WAS FOUND INSIDE A SUITCASE IN THE BAGGAGE TURNSTILE AT DULLES INTERNATIONAL...
BALLISTICS CHECKS SHOWED IT TO BE THE WEAPON THAT KILLED THE SKULL.
WOW, THAT'S BIG.

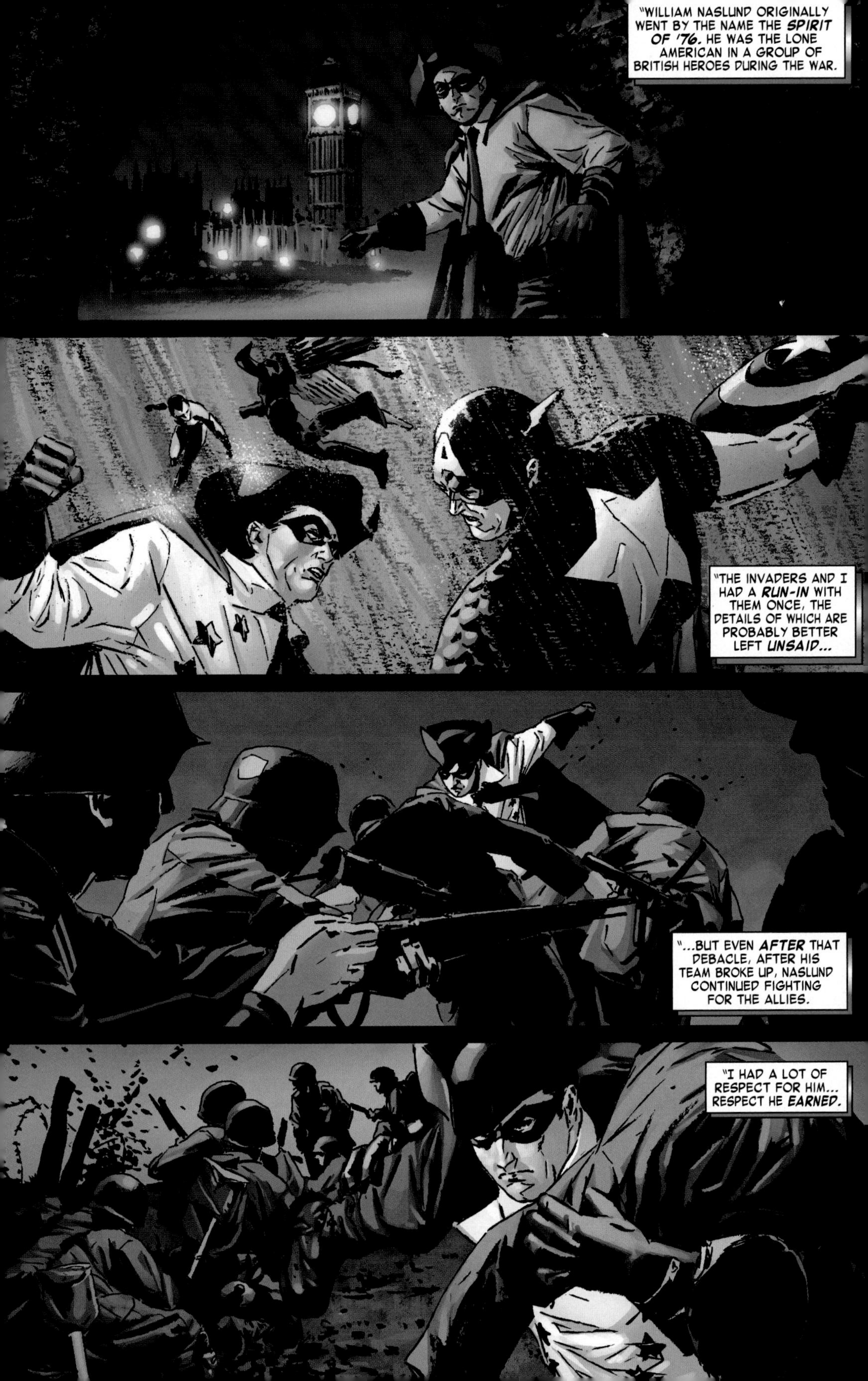
"WILLIAM NASLUND ORIGINALLY WENT BY THE NAME THE SPIRIT OF '76. HE WAS THE LONE AMERICAN IN A GROUP OF BRITISH HEROES DURING THE WAR.
"THE INVADERS AND I HAD A RUN-IN WITH THEM ONCE, THE DETAILS OF WHICH ARE PROBABLY BETTER LEFT UNSAID...
"...BUT EVEN AFTER THAT DEBACLE, AFTER HIS TEAM BROKE UP, NASLUND CONTINUED FIGHTING FOR THE ALLIES.
"I HAD A LOT OF RESPECT FOR HIM... RESPECT HE EARNED.

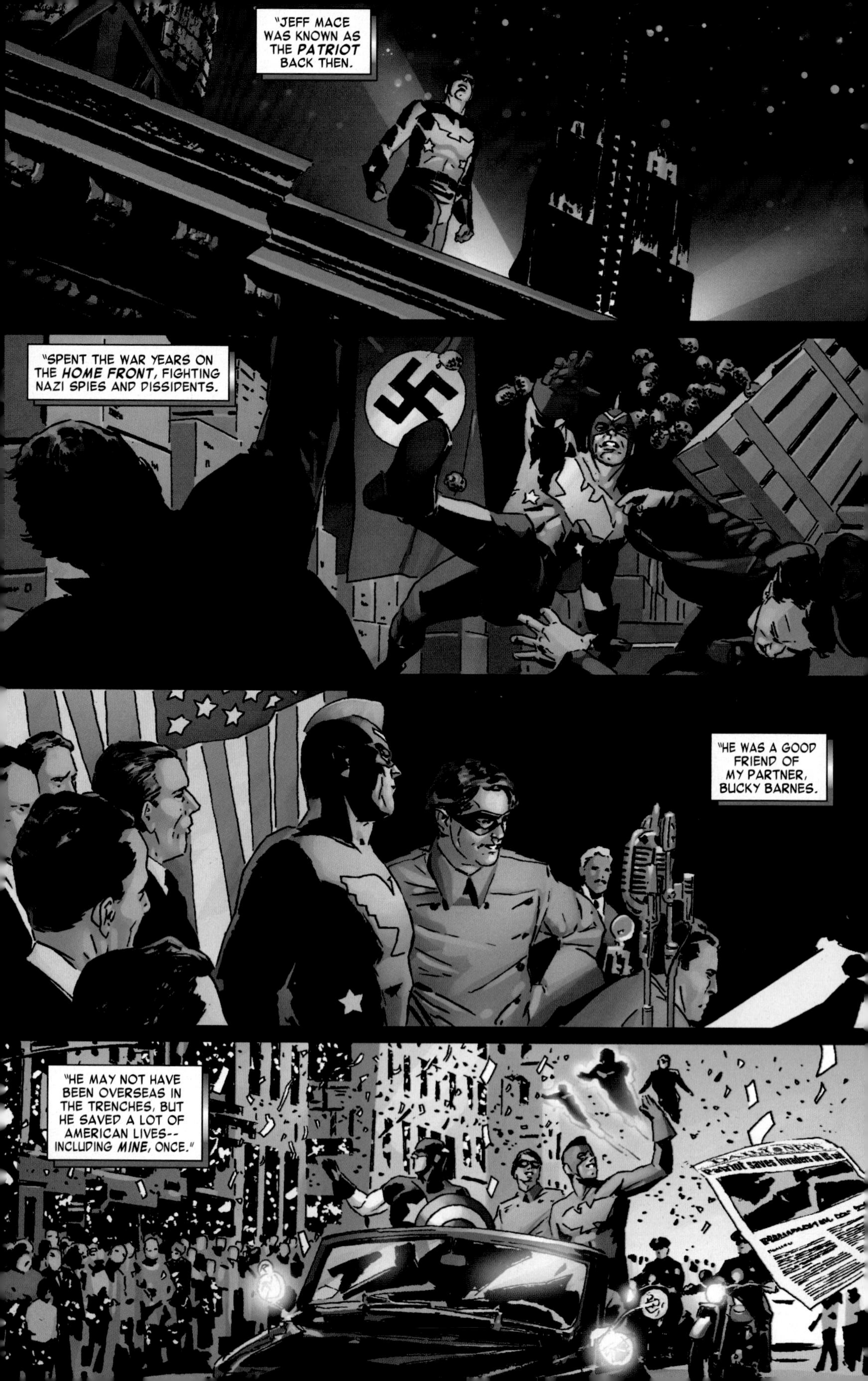
"JEFF MACE WAS KNOWN AS THE *PATRIOT* BACK THEN.
"SPENT THE WAR YEARS ON THE *HOME FRONT*, FIGHTING NAZI SPIES AND DISSIDENTS.
"HE WAS A GOOD FRIEND OF MY PARTNER, BUCKY BARNES.
"HE MAY NOT HAVE BEEN OVERSEAS IN THE TRENCHES, BUT HE SAVED A LOT OF AMERICAN LIVES-- INCLUDING *MINE*, ONCE."

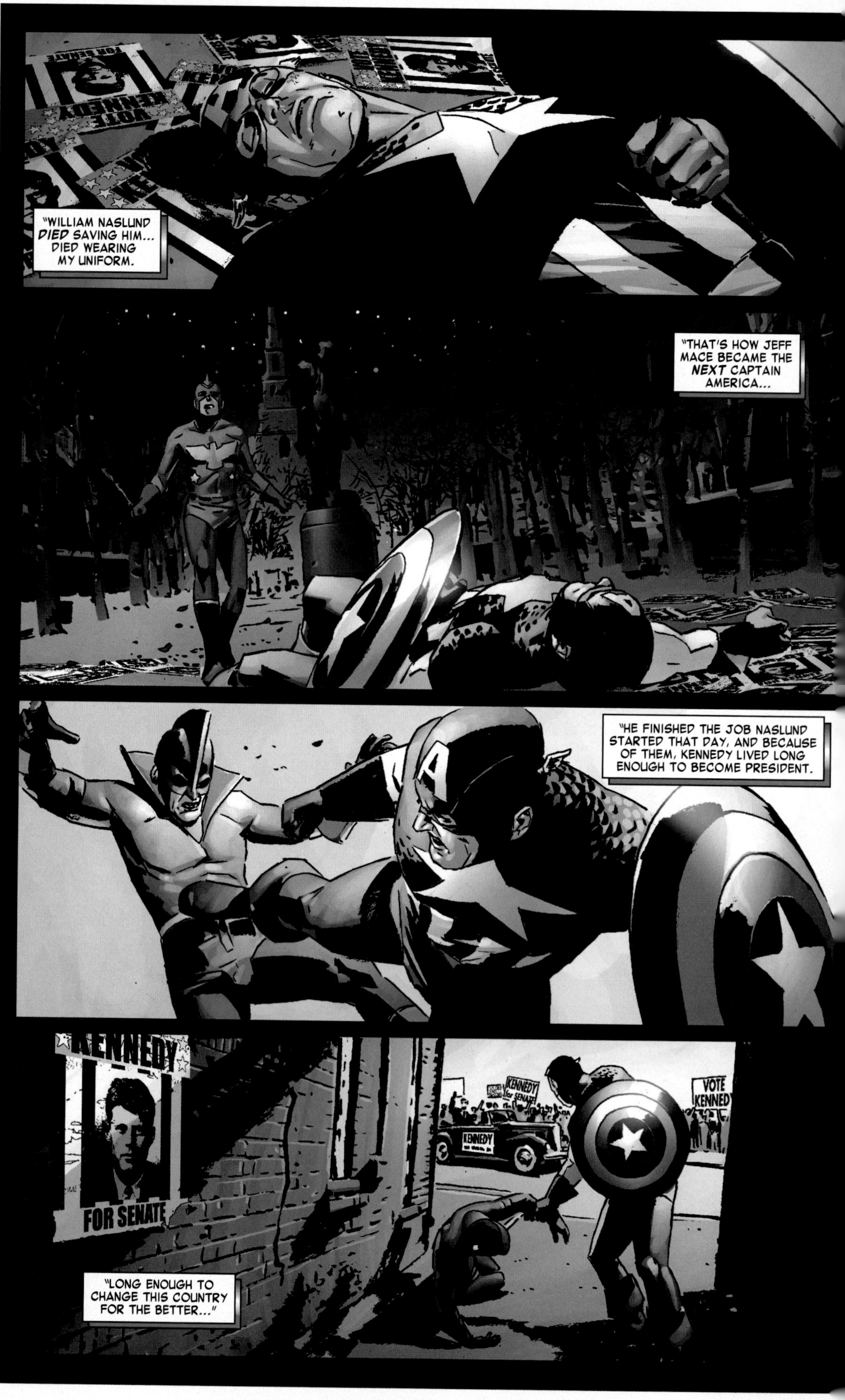
"WILLIAM NASLUND DIED SAVING HIM... DIED WEARING MY UNIFORM.
"THAT'S HOW JEFF MACE BECAME THE NEXT CAPTAIN AMERICA...
"HE FINISHED THE JOB NASLUND STARTED THAT DAY, AND BECAUSE OF THEM, KENNEDY LIVED LONG ENOUGH TO BECOME PRESIDENT.
KENNEDY
FOR SENATE
KENNEDY for SENATE
KENNEDY
"LONG ENOUGH TO CHANGE THIS COUNTRY FOR THE BETTER..."

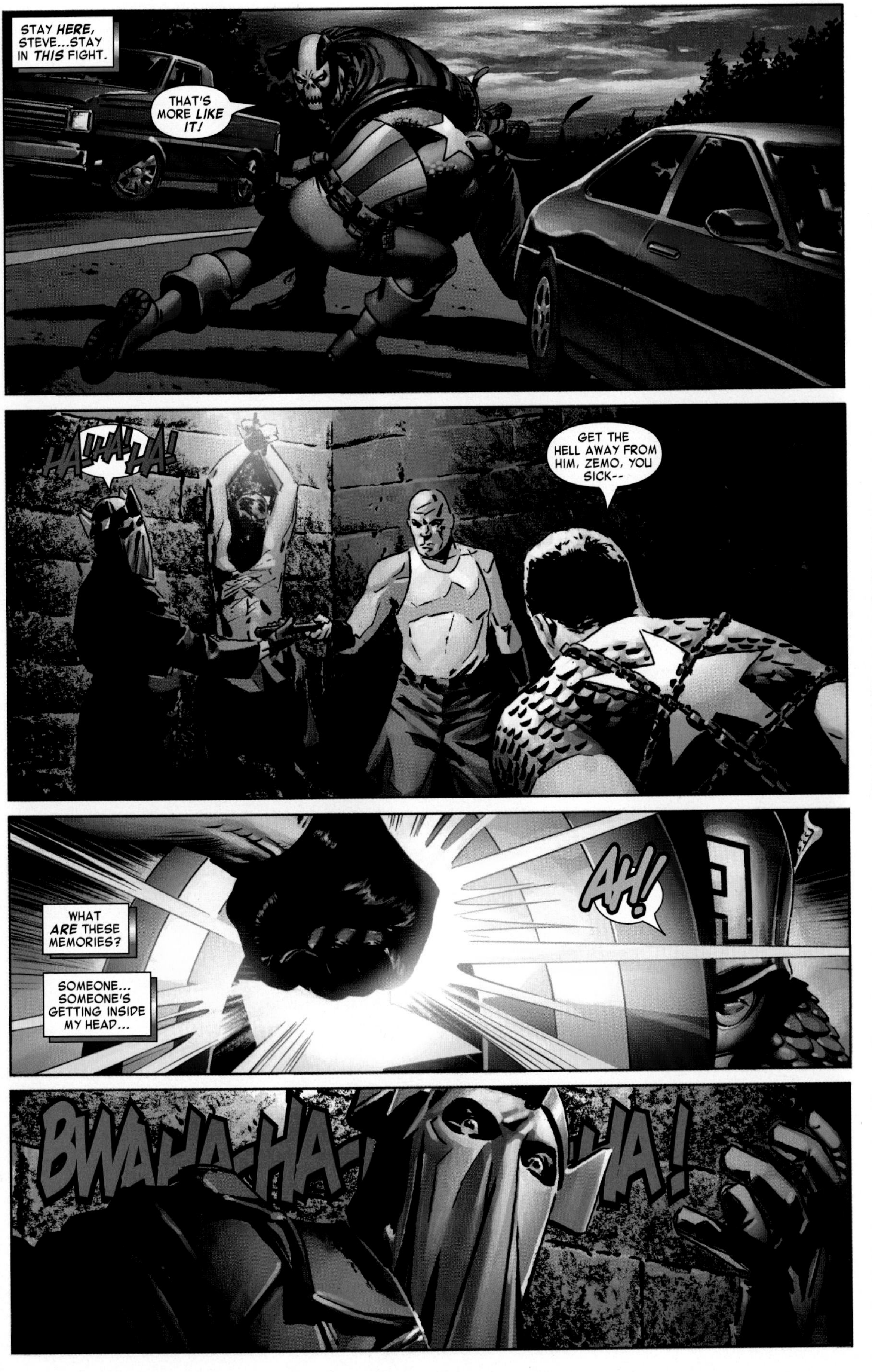
STAY HERE, STEVE...STAY IN THIS FIGHT.
THAT'S MORE LIKE IT!
HA!HA!HA!
GET THE HELL AWAY FROM HIM, ZEMO, YOU SICK--
AH!
WHAT ARE THESE MEMORIES?
SOMEONE... SOMEONE'S GETTING INSIDE MY HEAD...
BWAHA-HA-HA!

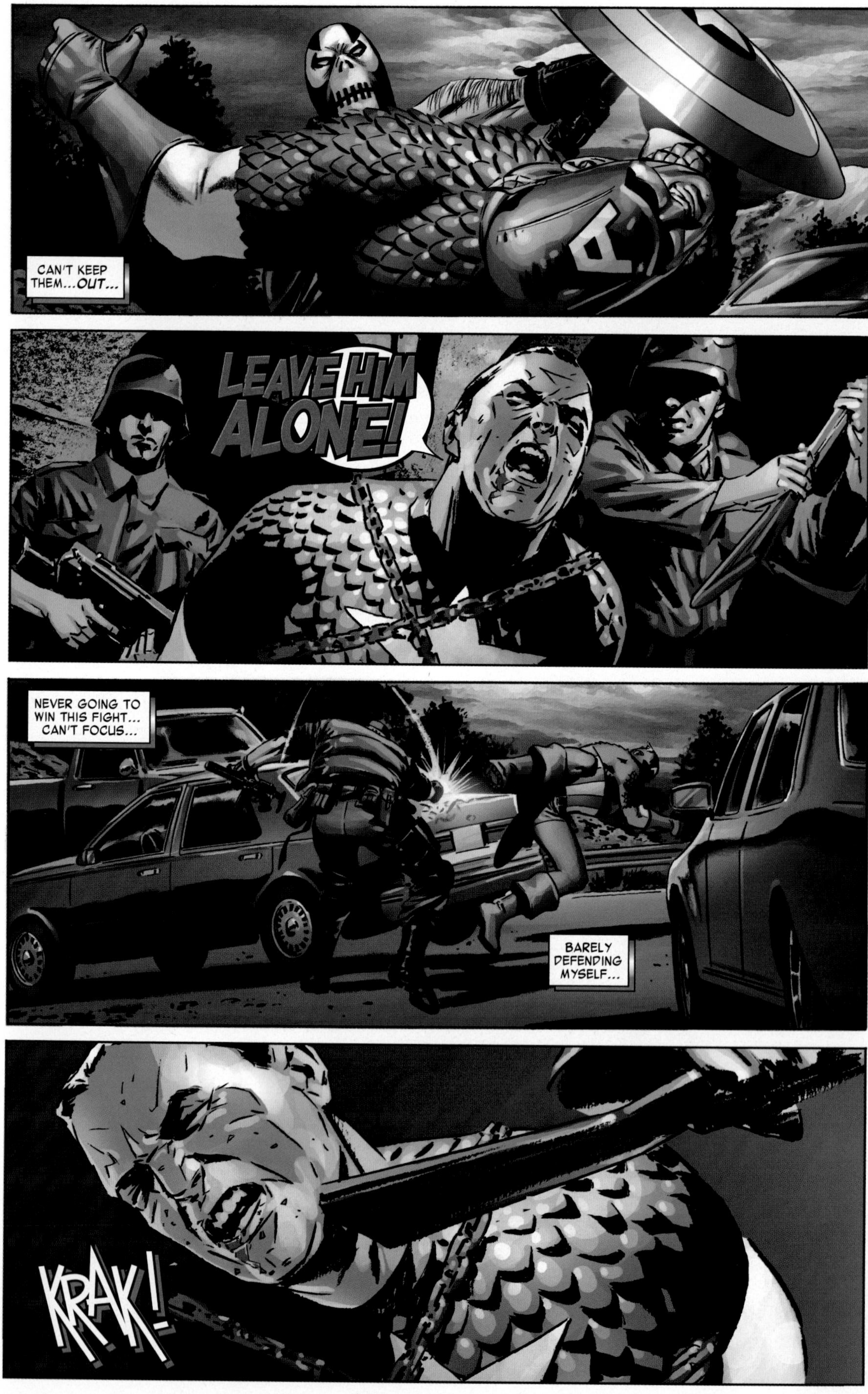
CAN'T KEEP THEM...OUT...
LEAVE HIM ALONE!
NEVER GOING TO WIN THIS FIGHT... CAN'T FOCUS...
BARELY DEFENDING MYSELF...
KRAK!

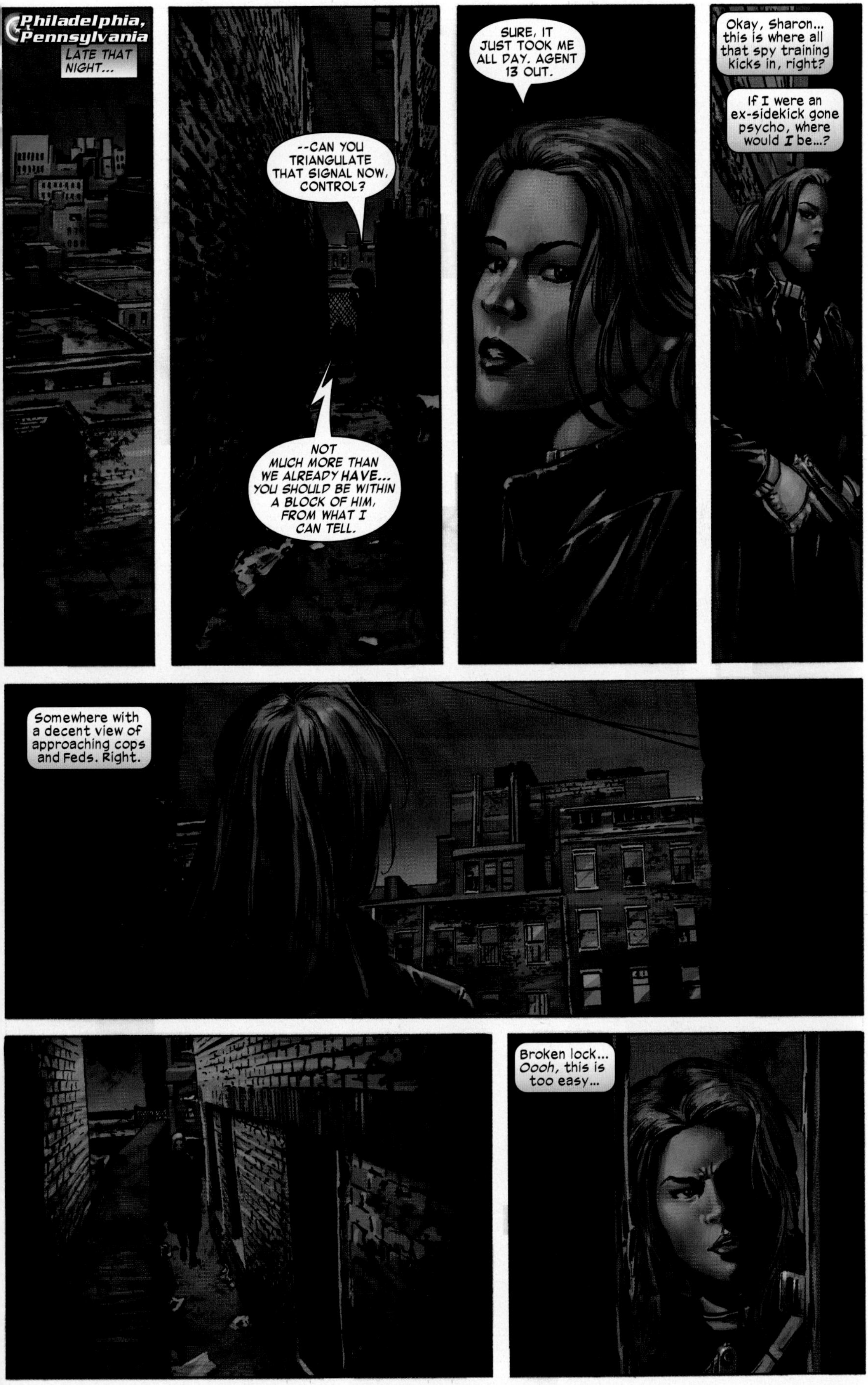
Philadelphia, Pennsylvania
LATE THAT NIGHT...
--CAN YOU TRIANGULATE THAT SIGNAL NOW, CONTROL?
NOT MUCH MORE THAN WE ALREADY HAVE... YOU SHOULD BE WITHIN A BLOCK OF HIM, FROM WHAT I CAN TELL.
SURE, IT JUST TOOK ME ALL DAY. AGENT 13 OUT.
Okay, Sharon... this is where all that spy training kicks in, right?
If I were an ex-sidekick gone psycho, where would I be...?
Somewhere with a decent view of approaching cops and Feds. Right.
Broken lock... Oooh, this is too easy...

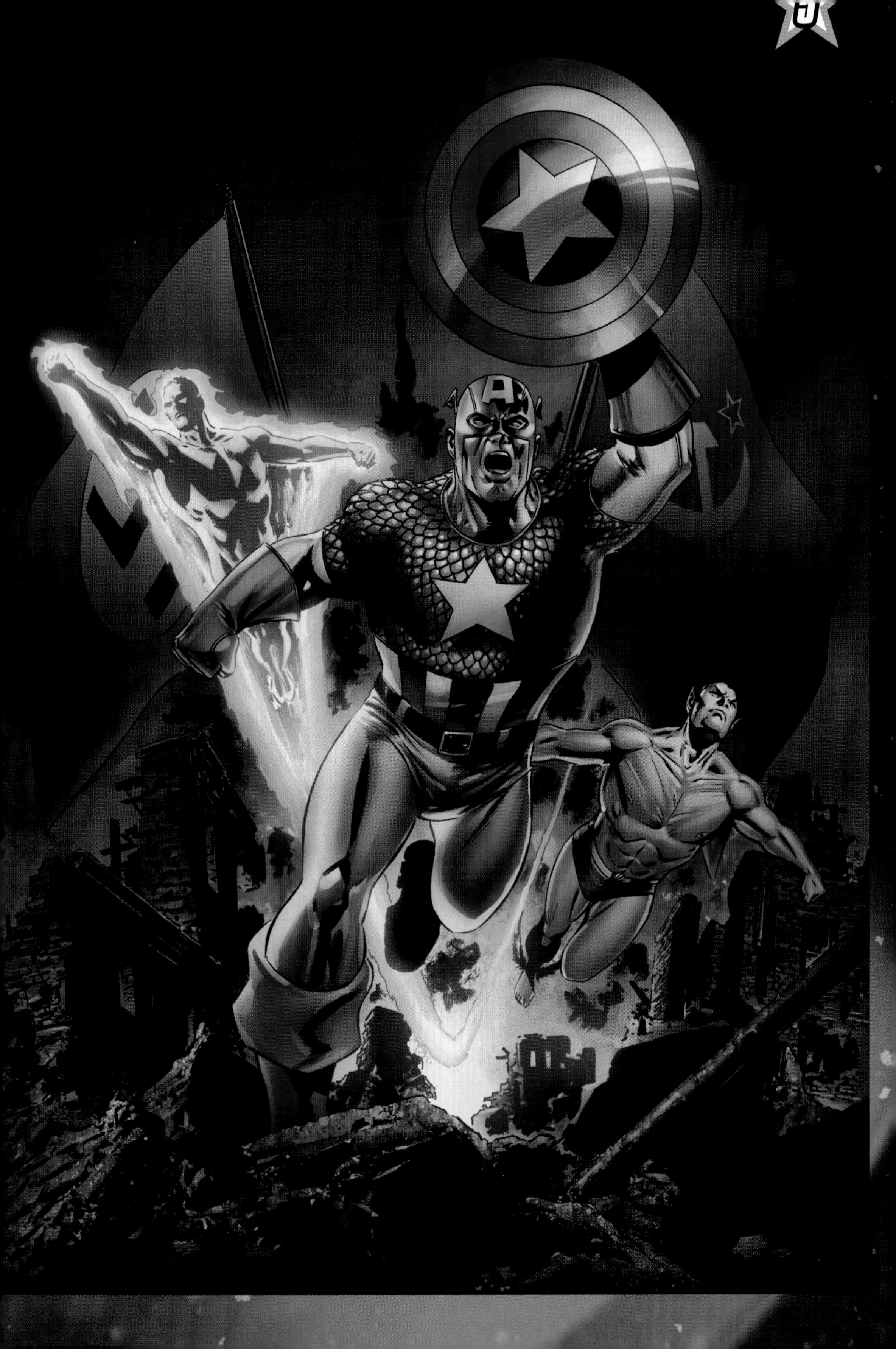

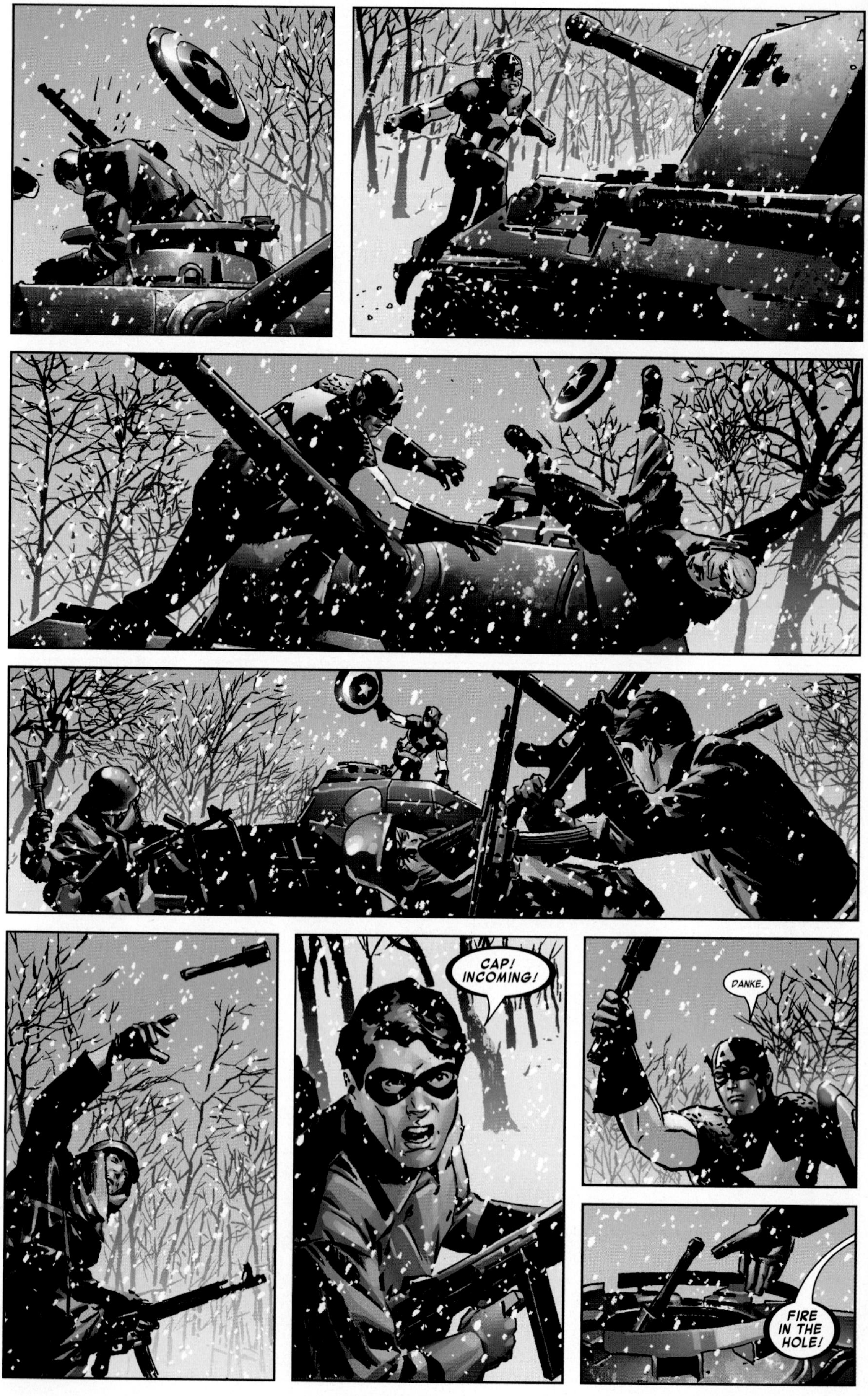
CAP! INCOMING!
DANKE.
FIRE IN THE HOLE!

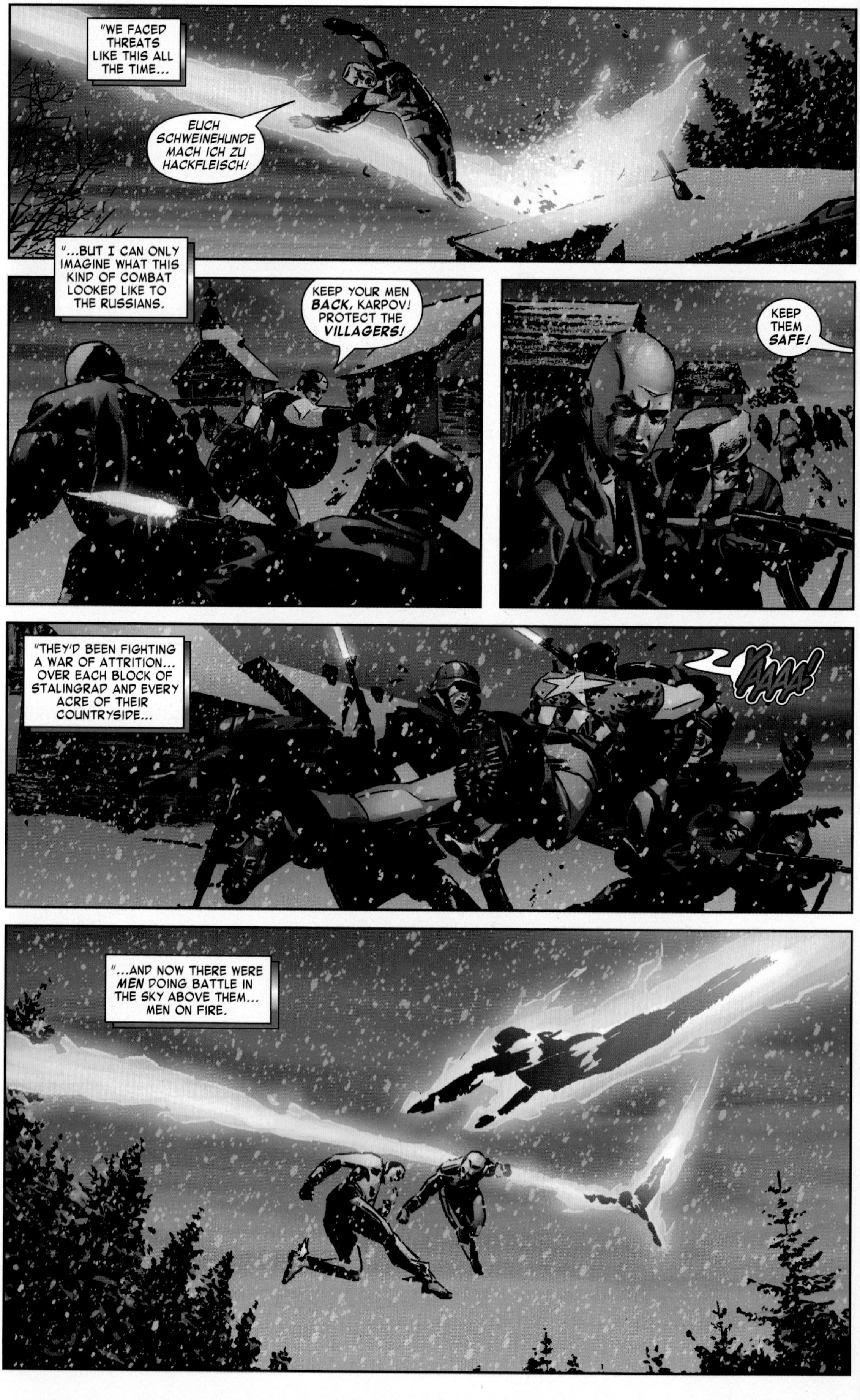
"WE FACED THREATS LIKE THIS ALL THE TIME...
EUCH SCHWEINEHUNDE MACH ICH ZU HACKFLEISCH!
"...BUT I CAN ONLY IMAGINE WHAT THIS KIND OF COMBAT LOOKED LIKE TO THE RUSSIANS.
KEEP YOUR MEN BACK, KARPOV! PROTECT THE VILLAGERS!
KEEP THEM SAFE!
"THEY'D BEEN FIGHTING A WAR OF ATTRITION... OVER EACH BLOCK OF STALINGRAD AND EVERY ACRE OF THEIR COUNTRYSIDE...
YAAAA!
"...AND NOW THERE WERE MEN DOING BATTLE IN THE SKY ABOVE THEM... MEN ON FIRE.

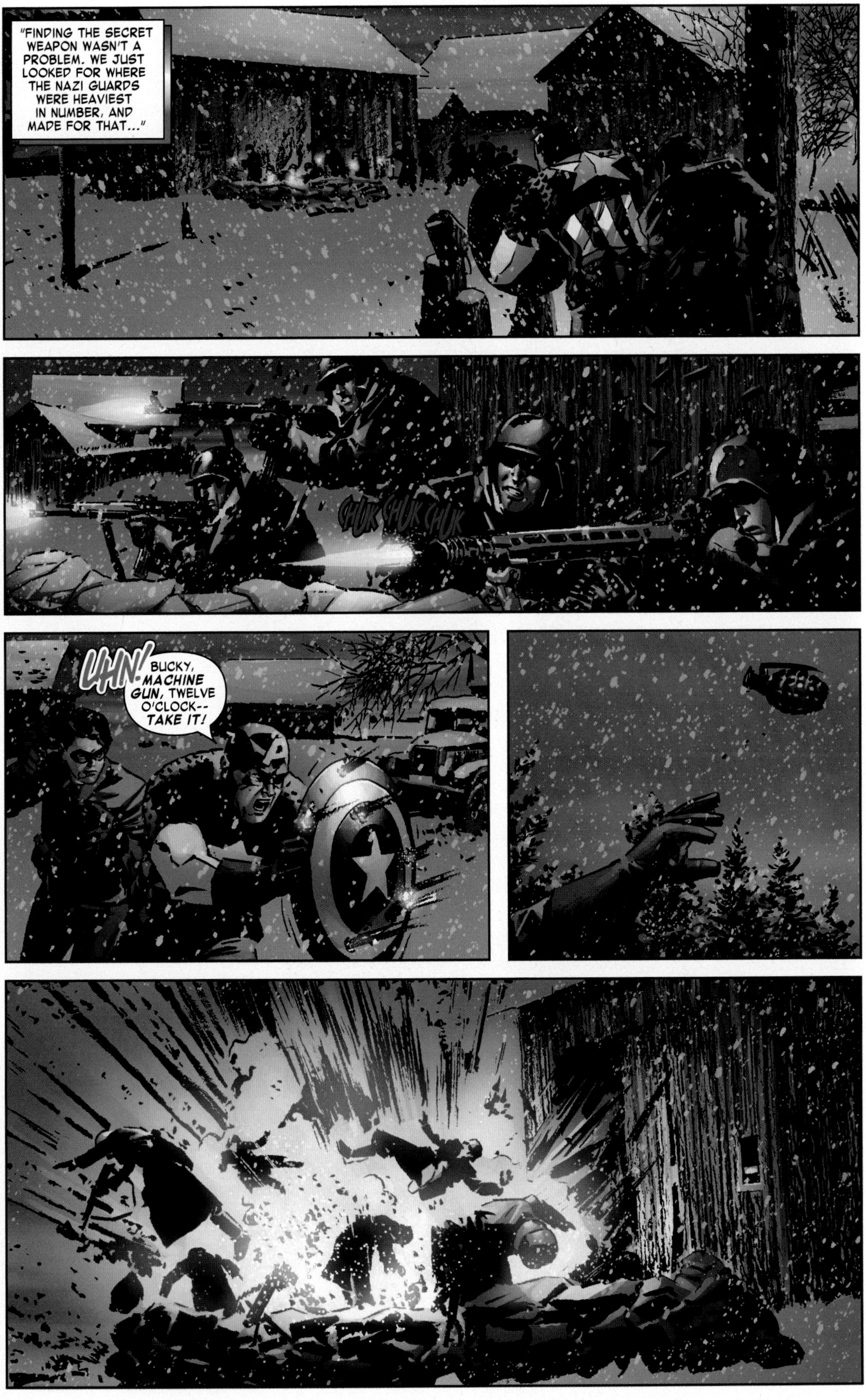
"FINDING THE SECRET WEAPON WASN'T A PROBLEM. WE JUST LOOKED FOR WHERE THE NAZI GUARDS WERE HEAVIEST IN NUMBER, AND MADE FOR THAT..."
CHUK CHUK CHUK
UHN!
BUCKY, MACHINE GUN, TWELVE O'CLOCK-- TAKE IT!

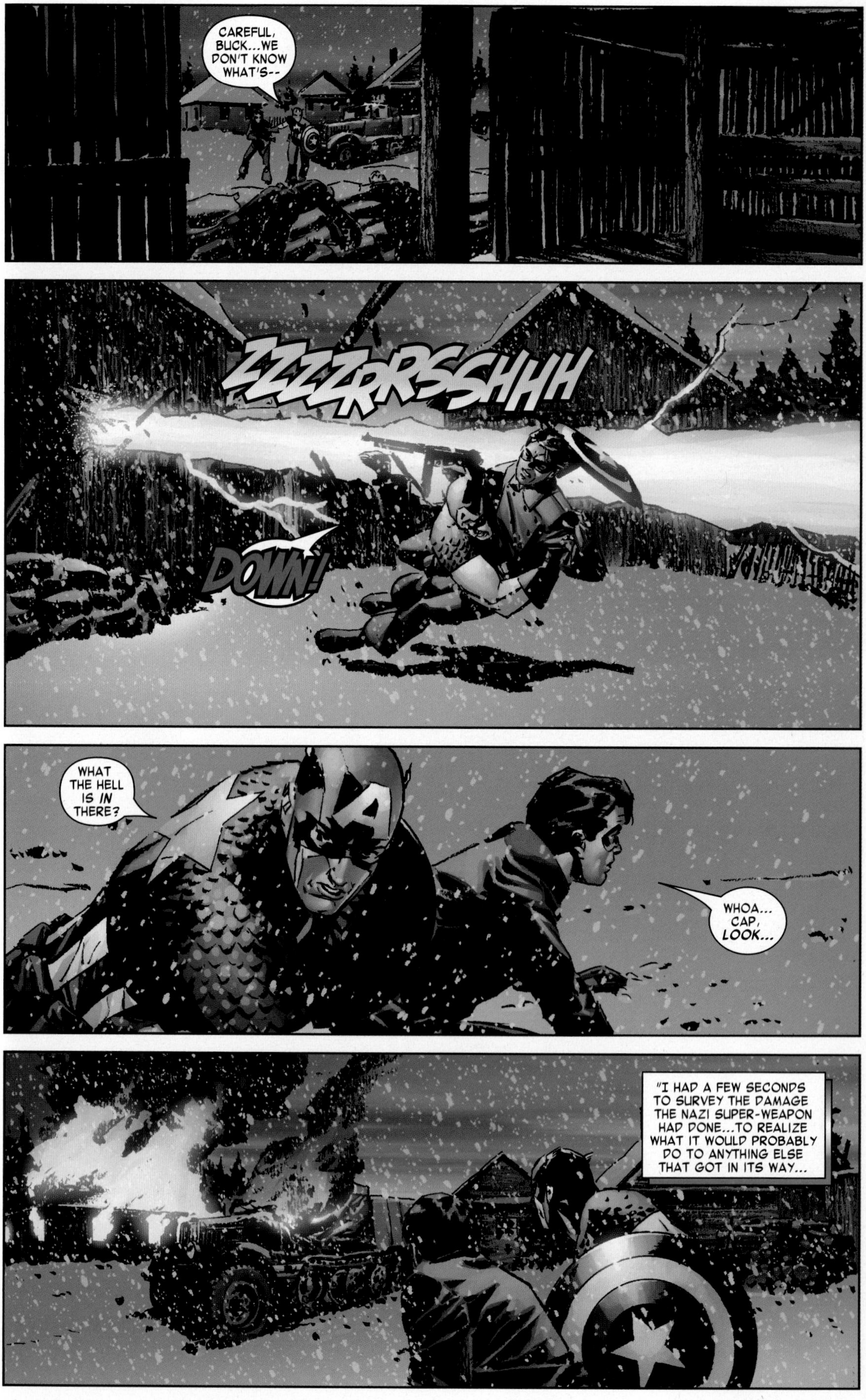
CAREFUL, BUCK...WE DON'T KNOW WHAT'S--
ZZZZZRRSSHHH
DOWN!
WHAT THE HELL IS IN THERE?
WHOA... CAP, LOOK...
"I HAD A FEW SECONDS TO SURVEY THE DAMAGE THE NAZI SUPER-WEAPON HAD DONE...TO REALIZE WHAT IT WOULD PROBABLY DO TO ANYTHING ELSE THAT GOT IN ITS WAY...

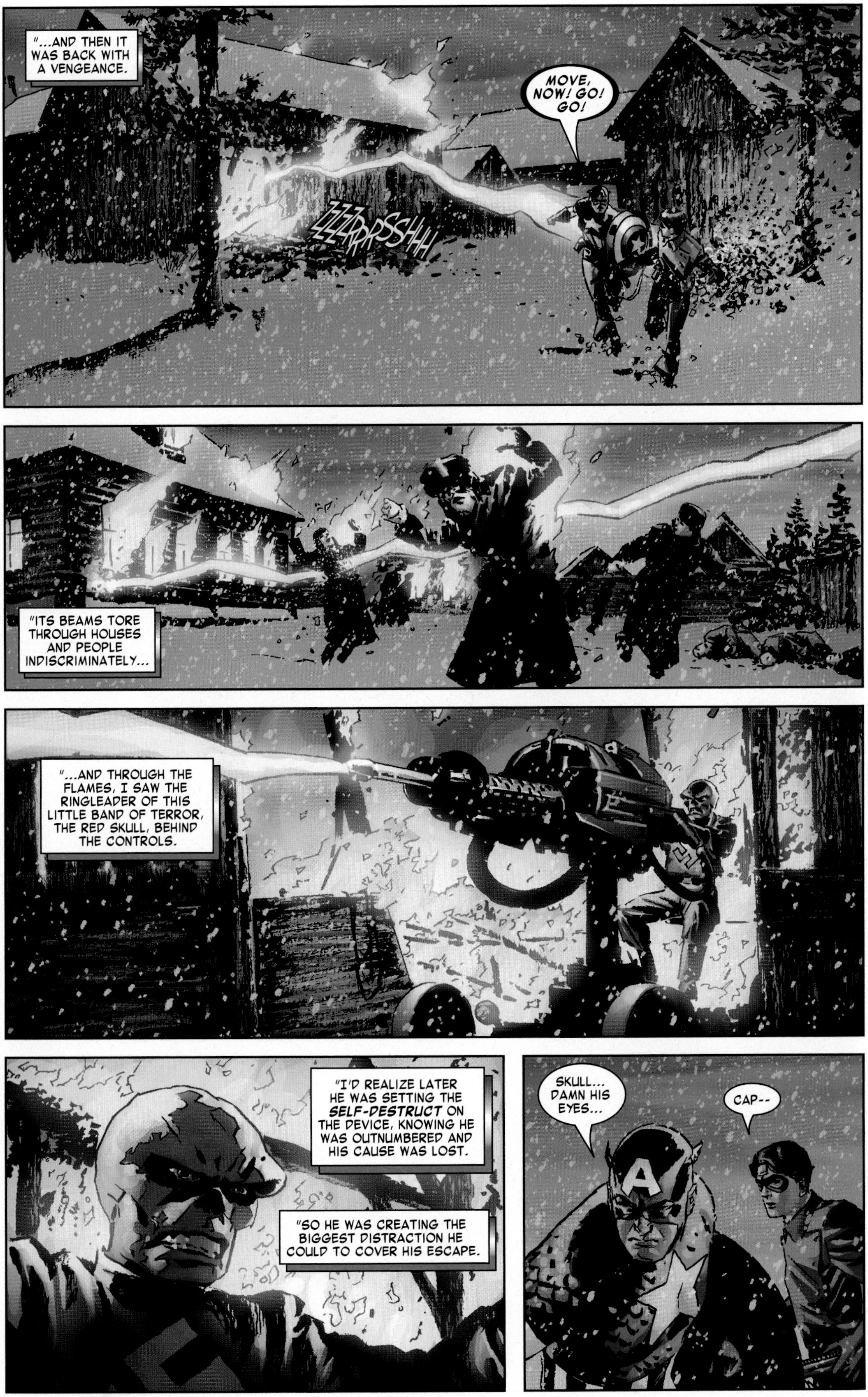
"...AND THEN IT WAS BACK WITH A VENGEANCE.
MOVE, NOW! GO! GO!
ZZZRRRSSHHH
"ITS BEAMS TORE THROUGH HOUSES AND PEOPLE INDISCRIMINATELY...
"...AND THROUGH THE FLAMES, I SAW THE RINGLEADER OF THIS LITTLE BAND OF TERROR, THE RED SKULL, BEHIND THE CONTROLS.
"I'D REALIZE LATER HE WAS SETTING THE SELF-DESTRUCT ON THE DEVICE, KNOWING HE WAS OUTNUMBERED AND HIS CAUSE WAS LOST.
"SO HE WAS CREATING THE BIGGEST DISTRACTION HE COULD TO COVER HIS ESCAPE.
SKULL... DAMN HIS EYES...
CAP--

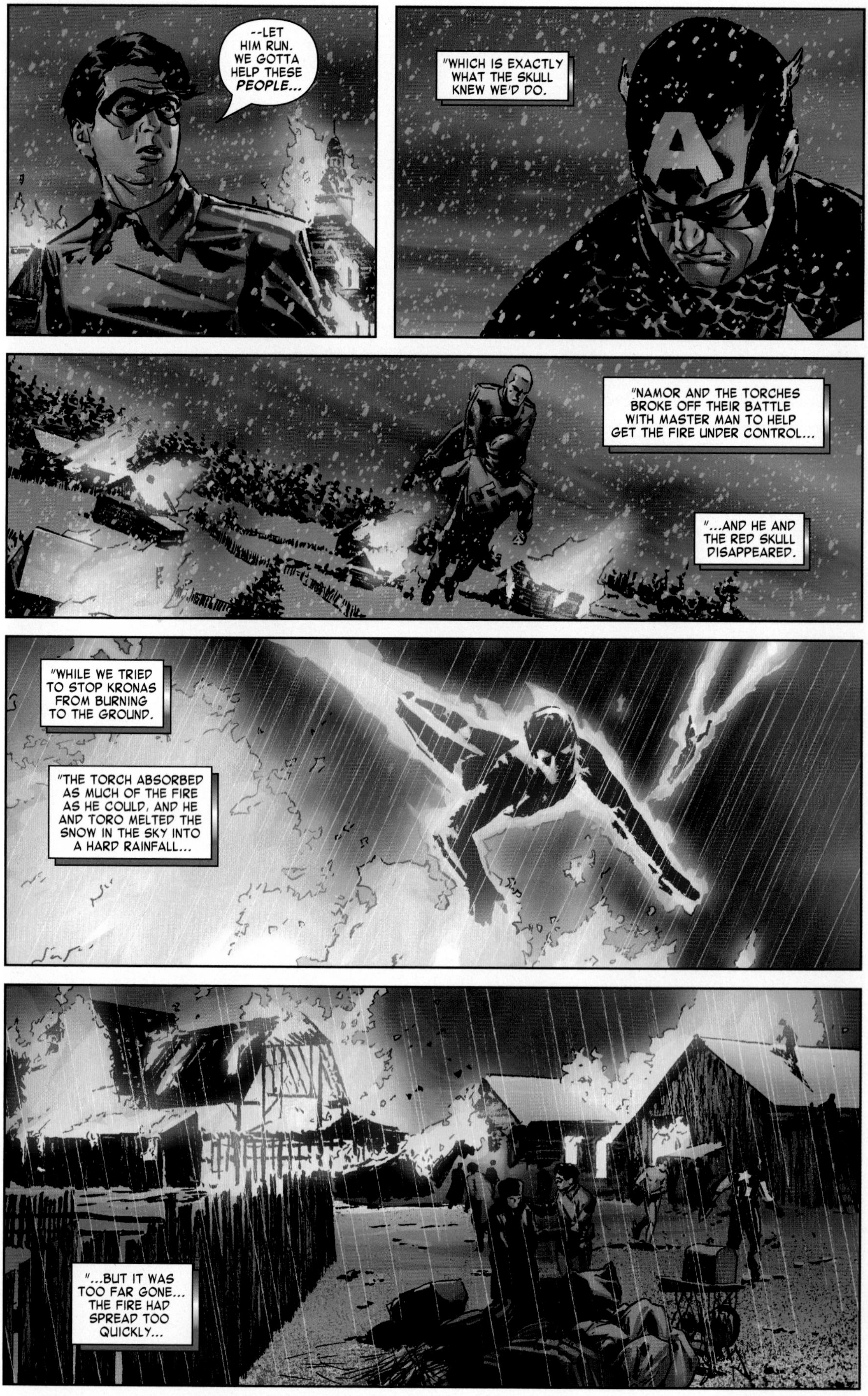
--LET HIM RUN. WE GOTTA HELP THESE PEOPLE...
"WHICH IS EXACTLY WHAT THE SKULL KNEW WE'D DO.
"NAMOR AND THE TORCHES BROKE OFF THEIR BATTLE WITH MASTER MAN TO HELP GET THE FIRE UNDER CONTROL...
"...AND HE AND THE RED SKULL DISAPPEARED.
"WHILE WE TRIED TO STOP KRONAS FROM BURNING TO THE GROUND.
"THE TORCH ABSORBED AS MUCH OF THE FIRE AS HE COULD, AND HE AND TORO MELTED THE SNOW IN THE SKY INTO A HARD RAINFALL...
"...BUT IT WAS TOO FAR GONE... THE FIRE HAD SPREAD TOO QUICKLY...

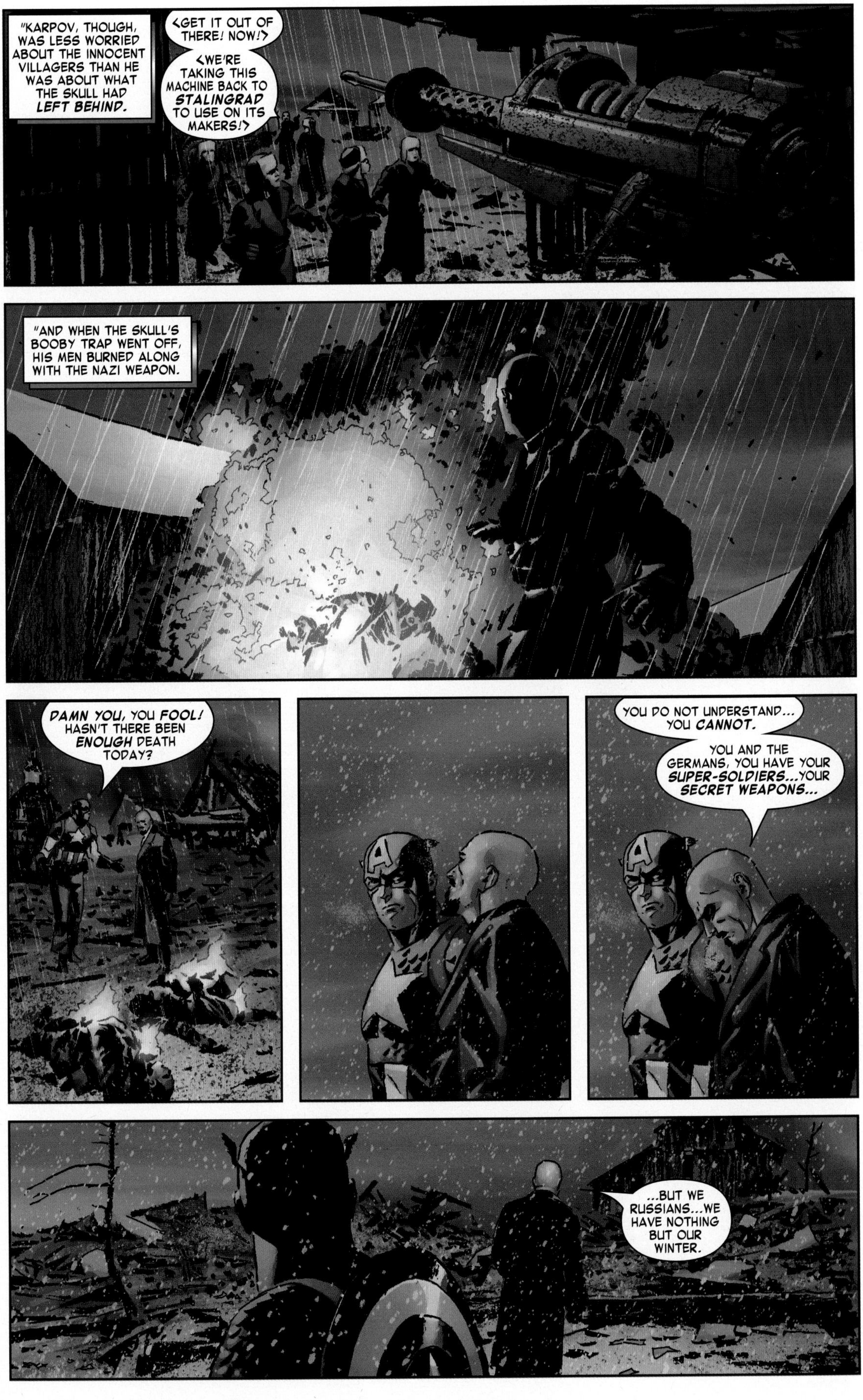
"KARPOV, THOUGH, WAS LESS WORRIED ABOUT THE INNOCENT VILLAGERS THAN HE WAS ABOUT WHAT THE SKULL HAD LEFT BEHIND.
<GET IT OUT OF THERE! NOW!>
<WE'RE TAKING THIS MACHINE BACK TO STALINGRAD TO USE ON ITS MAKERS!>
"AND WHEN THE SKULL'S BOOBY TRAP WENT OFF, HIS MEN BURNED ALONG WITH THE NAZI WEAPON.
DAMN YOU, YOU FOOL! HASN'T THERE BEEN ENOUGH DEATH TODAY?
YOU DO NOT UNDERSTAND... YOU CANNOT.
YOU AND THE GERMANS, YOU HAVE YOUR SUPER-SOLDIERS...YOUR SECRET WEAPONS...
...BUT WE RUSSIANS...WE HAVE NOTHING BUT OUR WINTER.

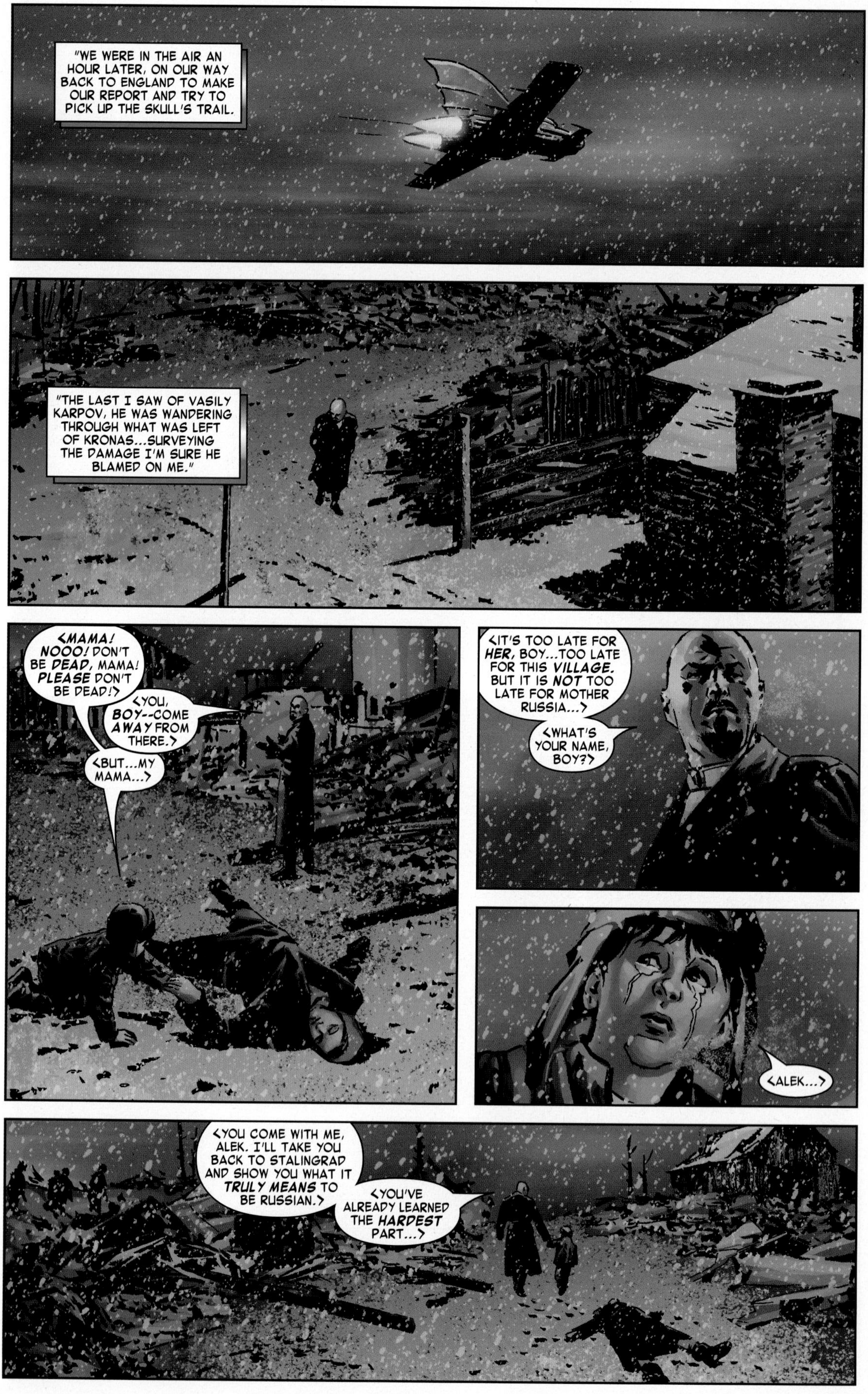
"WE WERE IN THE AIR AN HOUR LATER, ON OUR WAY BACK TO ENGLAND TO MAKE OUR REPORT AND TRY TO PICK UP THE SKULL'S TRAIL.
"THE LAST I SAW OF VASILY KARPOV, HE WAS WANDERING THROUGH WHAT WAS LEFT OF KRONAS...SURVEYING THE DAMAGE I'M SURE HE BLAMED ON ME."
<MAMA! NOOO! DON'T BE DEAD, MAMA! PLEASE DON'T BE DEAD!>
<YOU, BOY--COME AWAY FROM THERE.>
<BUT...MY MAMA...>
<IT'S TOO LATE FOR HER, BOY...TOO LATE FOR THIS VILLAGE. BUT IT IS NOT TOO LATE FOR MOTHER RUSSIA...>
<WHAT'S YOUR NAME, BOY?>
<ALEK...>
<YOU COME WITH ME, ALEK. I'LL TAKE YOU BACK TO STALINGRAD AND SHOW YOU WHAT IT TRULY MEANS TO BE RUSSIAN.>
<YOU'VE ALREADY LEARNED THE HARDEST PART...>

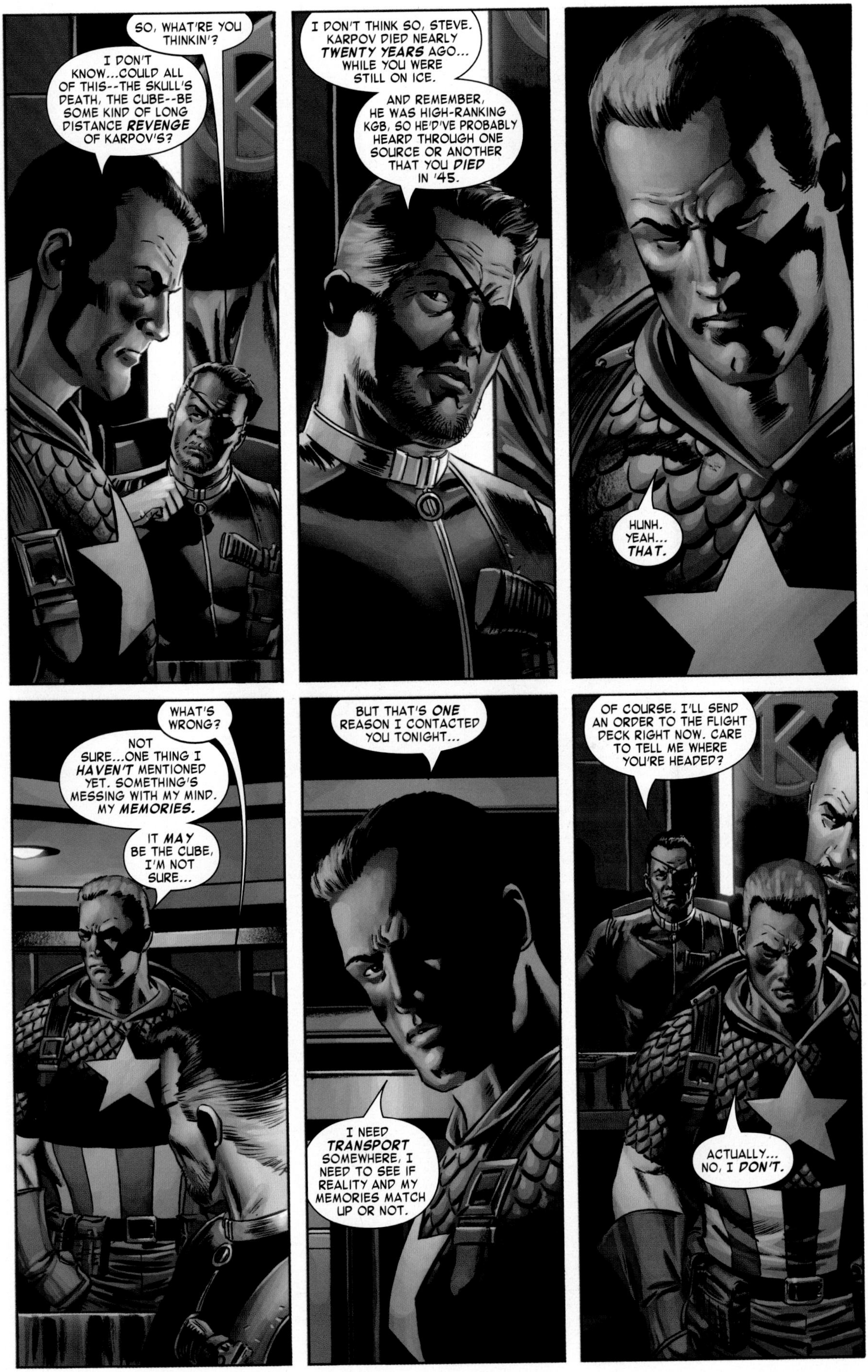
SO, WHAT'RE YOU THINKIN'?
I DON'T KNOW...COULD ALL OF THIS--THE SKULL'S DEATH, THE CUBE--BE SOME KIND OF LONG DISTANCE REVENGE OF KARPOV'S?
I DON'T THINK SO, STEVE. KARPOV DIED NEARLY TWENTY YEARS AGO... WHILE YOU WERE STILL ON ICE.
AND REMEMBER, HE WAS HIGH-RANKING KGB, SO HE'D'VE PROBABLY HEARD THROUGH ONE SOURCE OR ANOTHER THAT YOU DIED IN '45.
HUNH. YEAH... THAT.
WHAT'S WRONG?
NOT SURE...ONE THING I HAVEN'T MENTIONED YET. SOMETHING'S MESSING WITH MY MIND. MY MEMORIES.
IT MAY BE THE CUBE, I'M NOT SURE...
BUT THAT'S ONE REASON I CONTACTED YOU TONIGHT...
I NEED TRANSPORT SOMEWHERE. I NEED TO SEE IF REALITY AND MY MEMORIES MATCH UP OR NOT.
OF COURSE. I'LL SEND AN ORDER TO THE FLIGHT DECK RIGHT NOW. CARE TO TELL ME WHERE YOU'RE HEADED?
ACTUALLY... NO, I DON'T.

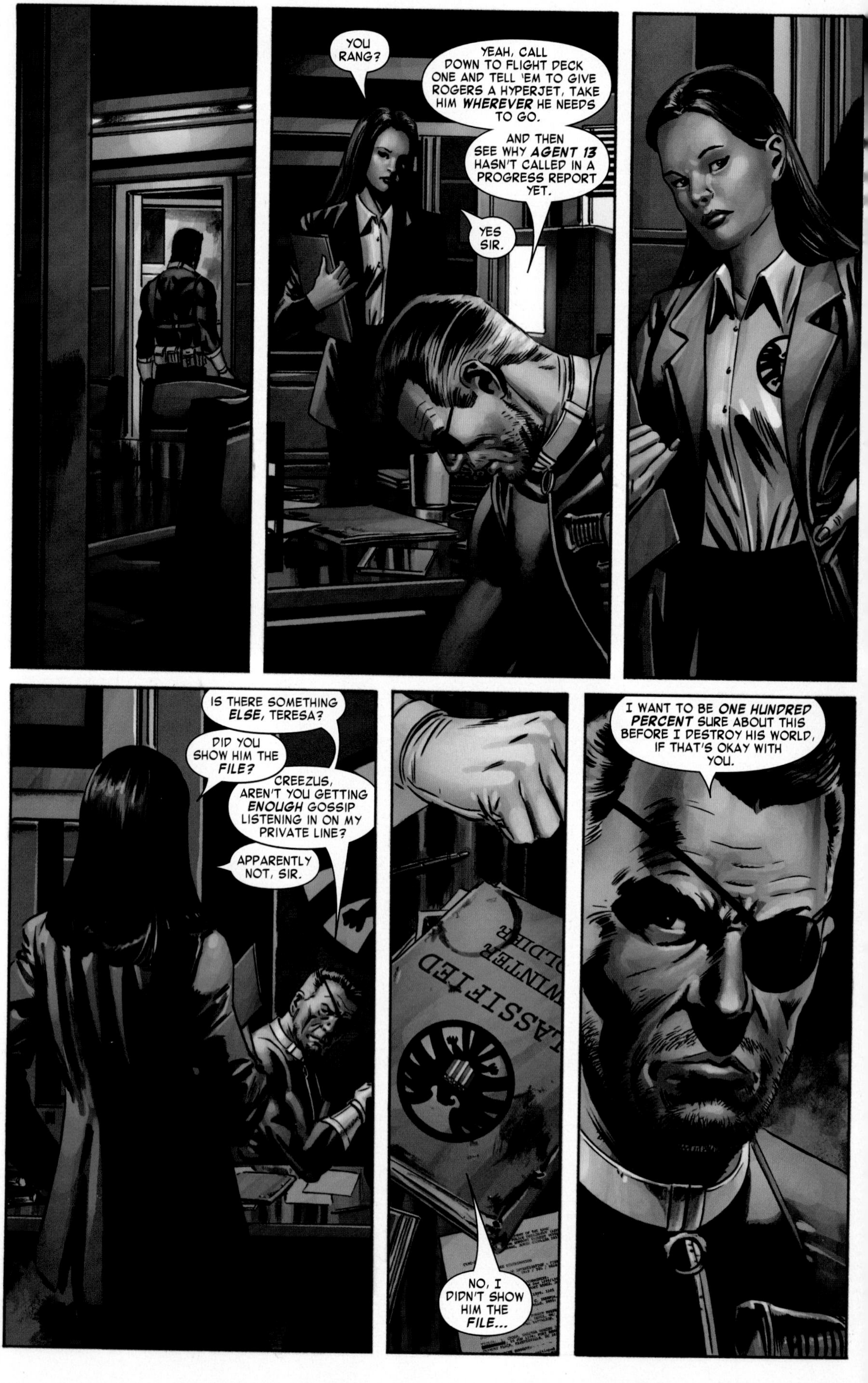
YOU RANG?
YEAH, CALL DOWN TO FLIGHT DECK ONE AND TELL 'EM TO GIVE ROGERS A HYPERJET, TAKE HIM *WHEREVER* HE NEEDS TO GO.
AND THEN SEE WHY *AGENT 13* HASN'T CALLED IN A PROGRESS REPORT YET.
YES SIR.
IS THERE SOMETHING *ELSE*, TERESA?
DID YOU SHOW HIM THE *FILE?*
CREEZUS, AREN'T YOU GETTING *ENOUGH* GOSSIP LISTENING IN ON MY PRIVATE LINE?
APPARENTLY NOT, SIR.
NO, I DIDN'T SHOW HIM THE *FILE...*
I WANT TO BE *ONE HUNDRED PERCENT* SURE ABOUT THIS BEFORE I DESTROY HIS WORLD, IF THAT'S OKAY WITH YOU.

6

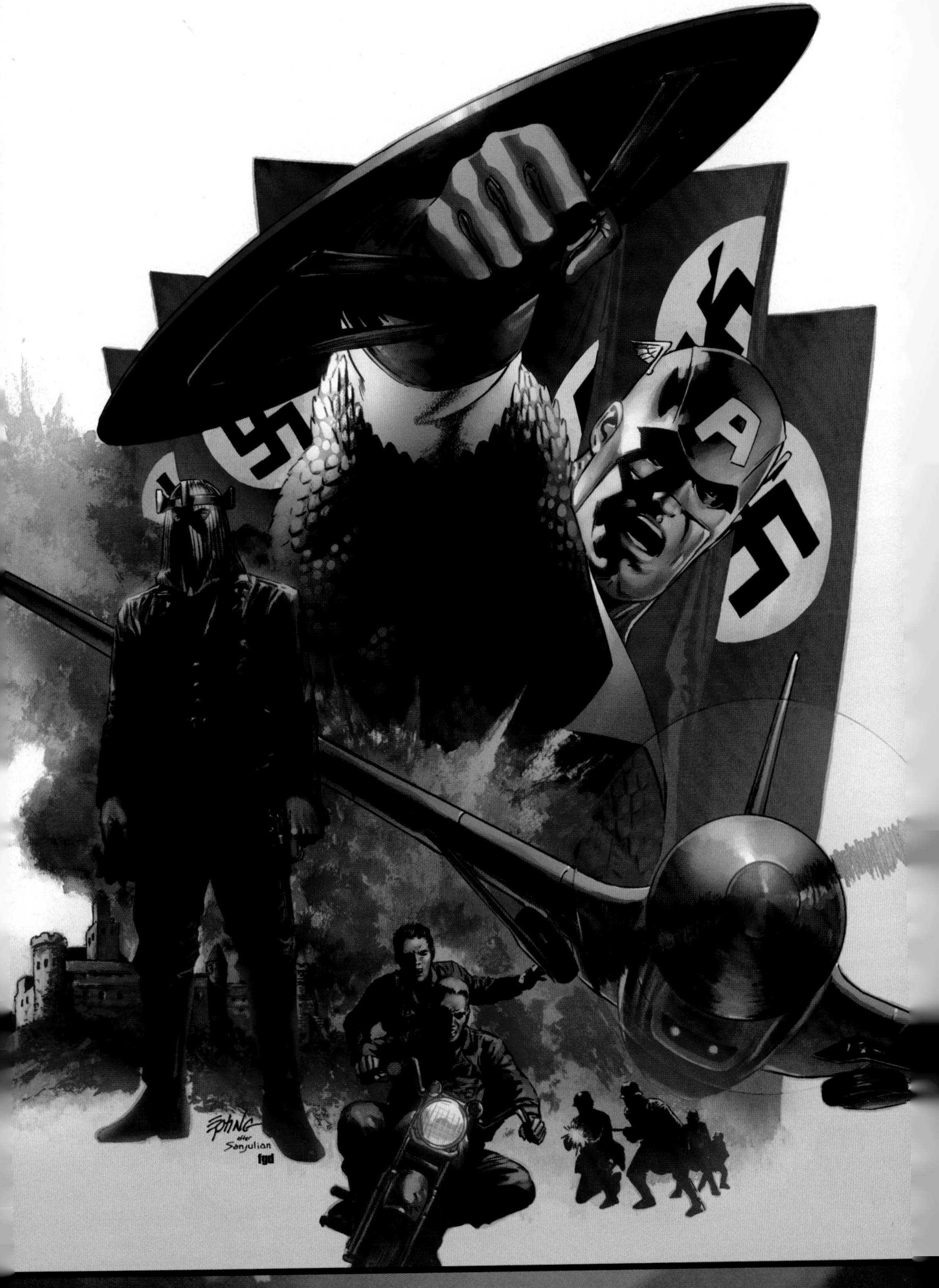
Epting
after
Sanjulian
fgd

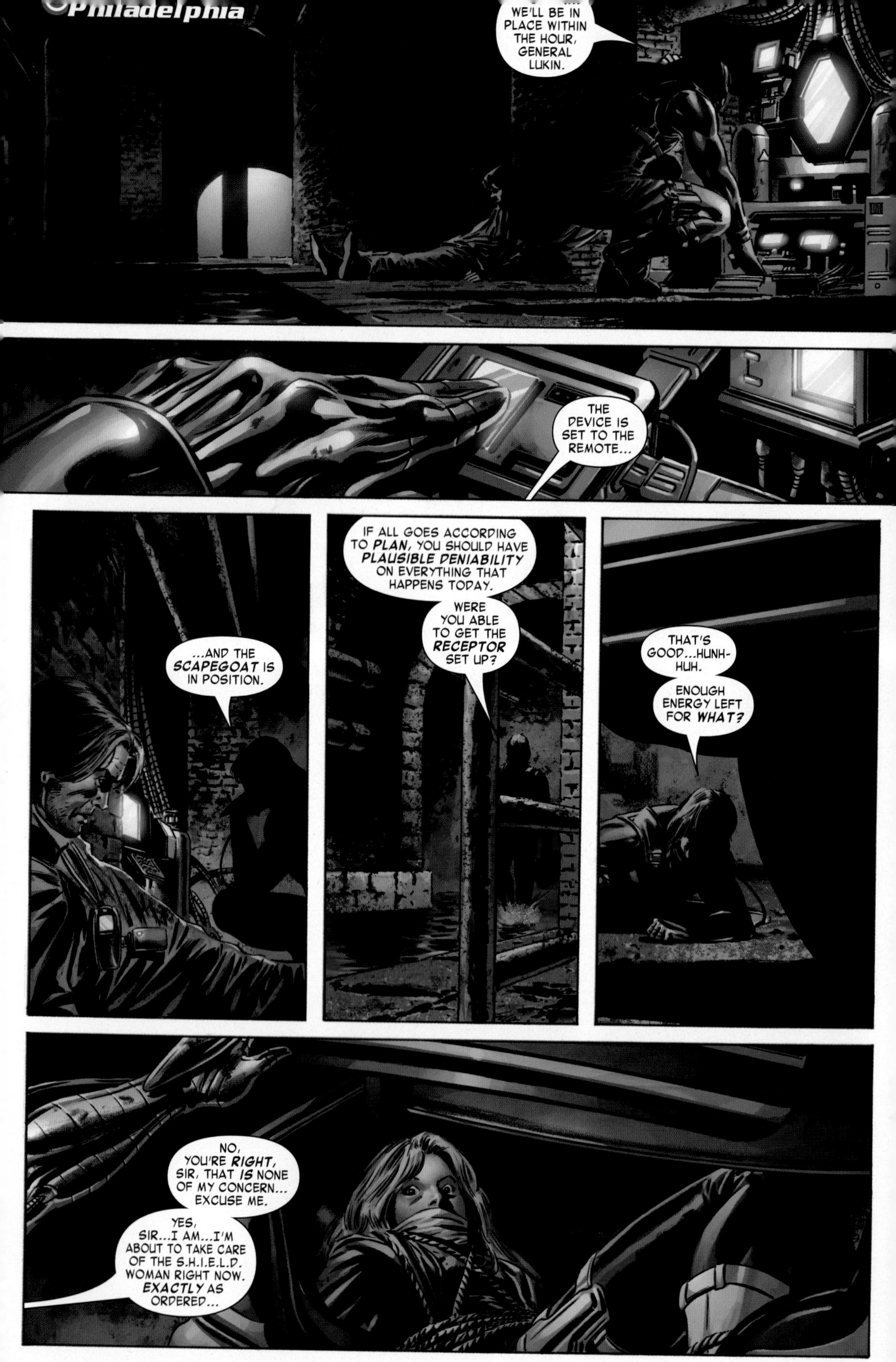
Philadelphia
WE'LL BE IN PLACE WITHIN THE HOUR, GENERAL LUKIN.
THE DEVICE IS SET TO THE REMOTE...
...AND THE SCAPEGOAT IS IN POSITION.
IF ALL GOES ACCORDING TO PLAN, YOU SHOULD HAVE PLAUSIBLE DENIABILITY ON EVERYTHING THAT HAPPENS TODAY.
WERE YOU ABLE TO GET THE RECEPTOR SET UP?
THAT'S GOOD...HUNH-HUH.
ENOUGH ENERGY LEFT FOR WHAT?
NO, YOU'RE RIGHT, SIR, THAT IS NONE OF MY CONCERN... EXCUSE ME.
YES, SIR...I AM...I'M ABOUT TO TAKE CARE OF THE S.H.I.E.L.D. WOMAN RIGHT NOW. EXACTLY AS ORDERED...

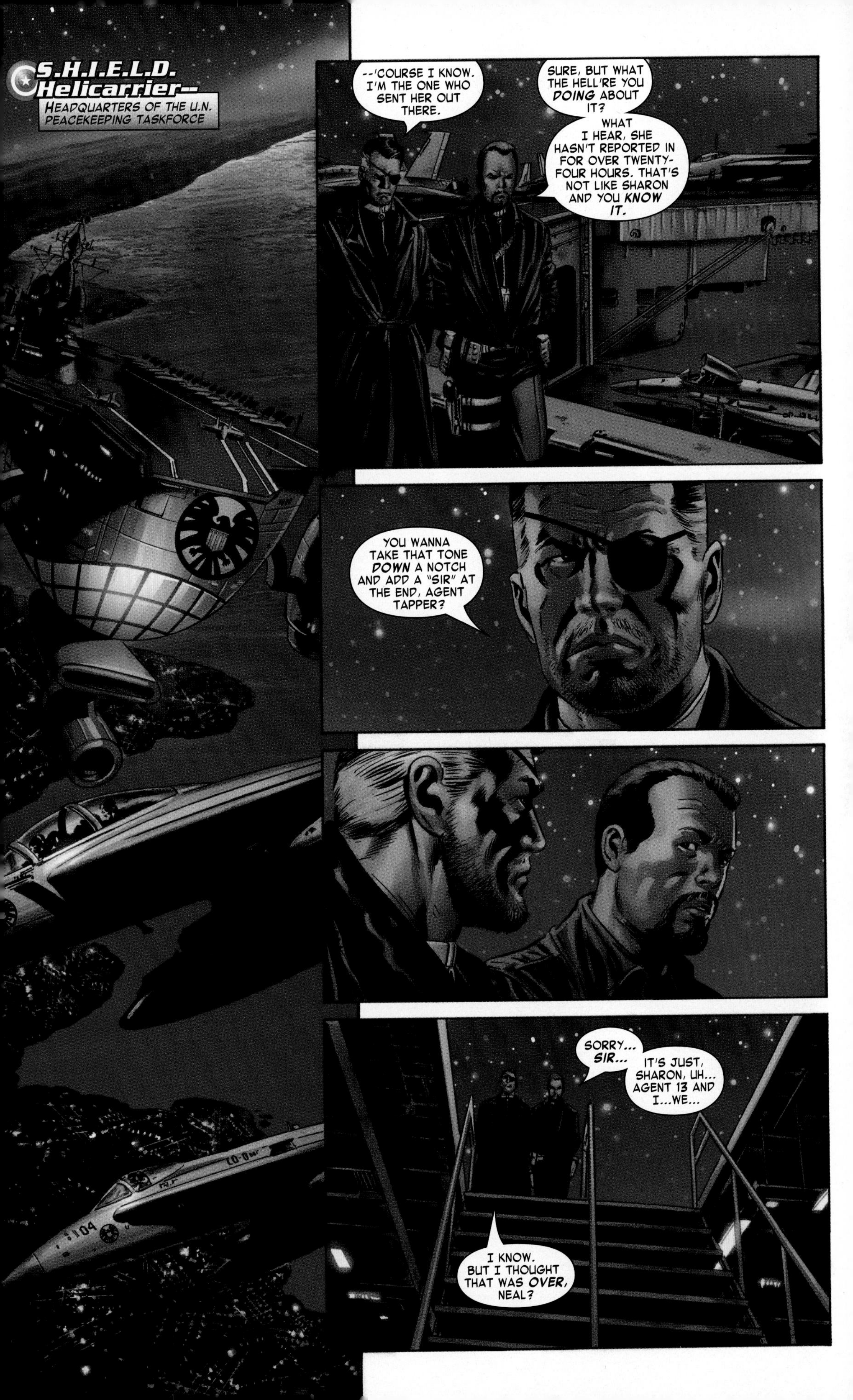

S.H.I.E.L.D. Helicarrier--
HEADQUARTERS OF THE U.N. PEACEKEEPING TASKFORCE
--'COURSE I KNOW. I'M THE ONE WHO SENT HER OUT THERE.
SURE, BUT WHAT THE HELL'RE YOU DOING ABOUT IT?
WHAT I HEAR, SHE HASN'T REPORTED IN FOR OVER TWENTY-FOUR HOURS. THAT'S NOT LIKE SHARON AND YOU KNOW IT.
YOU WANNA TAKE THAT TONE DOWN A NOTCH AND ADD A "SIR" AT THE END, AGENT TAPPER?
SORRY... SIR...
IT'S JUST, SHARON, UH... AGENT 13 AND I...WE...
I KNOW. BUT I THOUGHT THAT WAS OVER, NEAL?

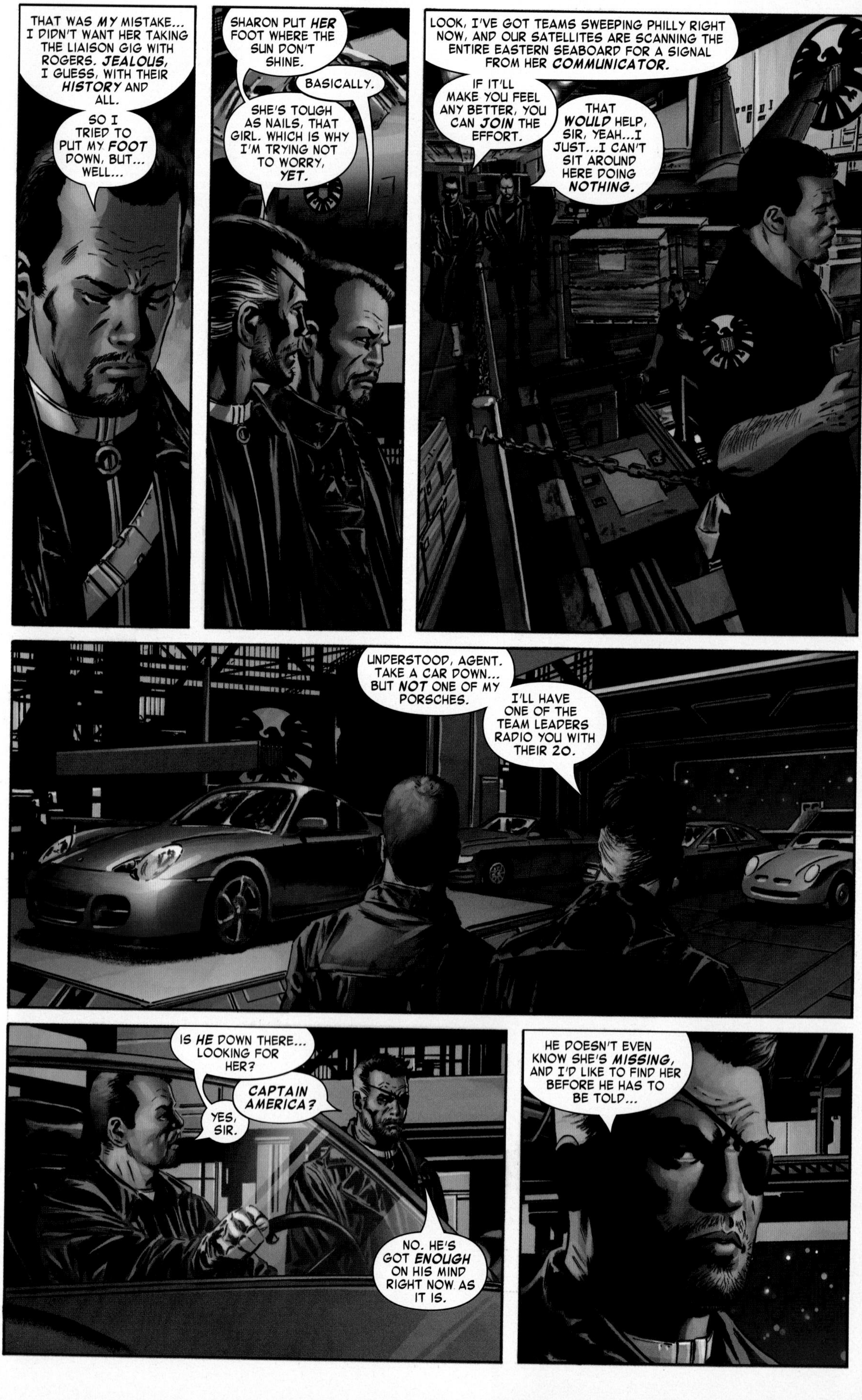
THAT WAS MY MISTAKE... I DIDN'T WANT HER TAKING THE LIAISON GIG WITH ROGERS. JEALOUS, I GUESS, WITH THEIR HISTORY AND ALL.
SO I TRIED TO PUT MY FOOT DOWN, BUT... WELL...
SHARON PUT HER FOOT WHERE THE SUN DON'T SHINE.
BASICALLY.
SHE'S TOUGH AS NAILS, THAT GIRL. WHICH IS WHY I'M TRYING NOT TO WORRY, YET.
LOOK, I'VE GOT TEAMS SWEEPING PHILLY RIGHT NOW, AND OUR SATELLITES ARE SCANNING THE ENTIRE EASTERN SEABOARD FOR A SIGNAL FROM HER COMMUNICATOR.
IF IT'LL MAKE YOU FEEL ANY BETTER, YOU CAN JOIN THE EFFORT.
THAT WOULD HELP, SIR, YEAH...I JUST...I CAN'T SIT AROUND HERE DOING NOTHING.
UNDERSTOOD, AGENT. TAKE A CAR DOWN... BUT NOT ONE OF MY PORSCHES.
I'LL HAVE ONE OF THE TEAM LEADERS RADIO YOU WITH THEIR 20.
IS HE DOWN THERE... LOOKING FOR HER?
CAPTAIN AMERICA?
YES, SIR.
NO. HE'S GOT ENOUGH ON HIS MIND RIGHT NOW AS IT IS.
HE DOESN'T EVEN KNOW SHE'S MISSING, AND I'D LIKE TO FIND HER BEFORE HE HAS TO BE TOLD...

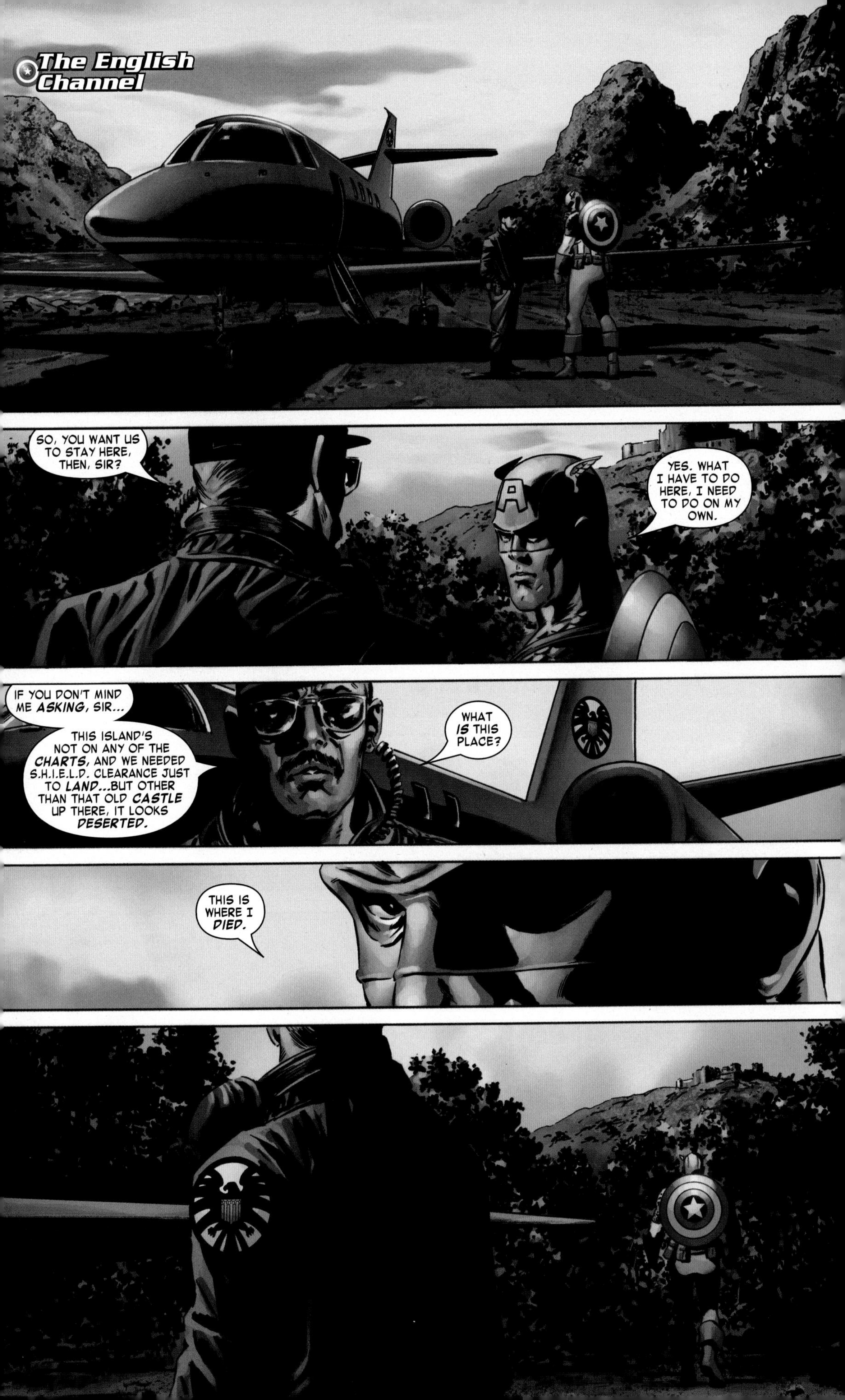
The English Channel
SO, YOU WANT US TO STAY HERE, THEN, SIR?
YES. WHAT I HAVE TO DO HERE, I NEED TO DO ON MY OWN.
IF YOU DON'T MIND ME ASKING, SIR...
THIS ISLAND'S NOT ON ANY OF THE CHARTS, AND WE NEEDED S.H.I.E.L.D. CLEARANCE JUST TO LAND...BUT OTHER THAN THAT OLD CASTLE UP THERE, IT LOOKS DESERTED.
WHAT IS THIS PLACE?
THIS IS WHERE I DIED.

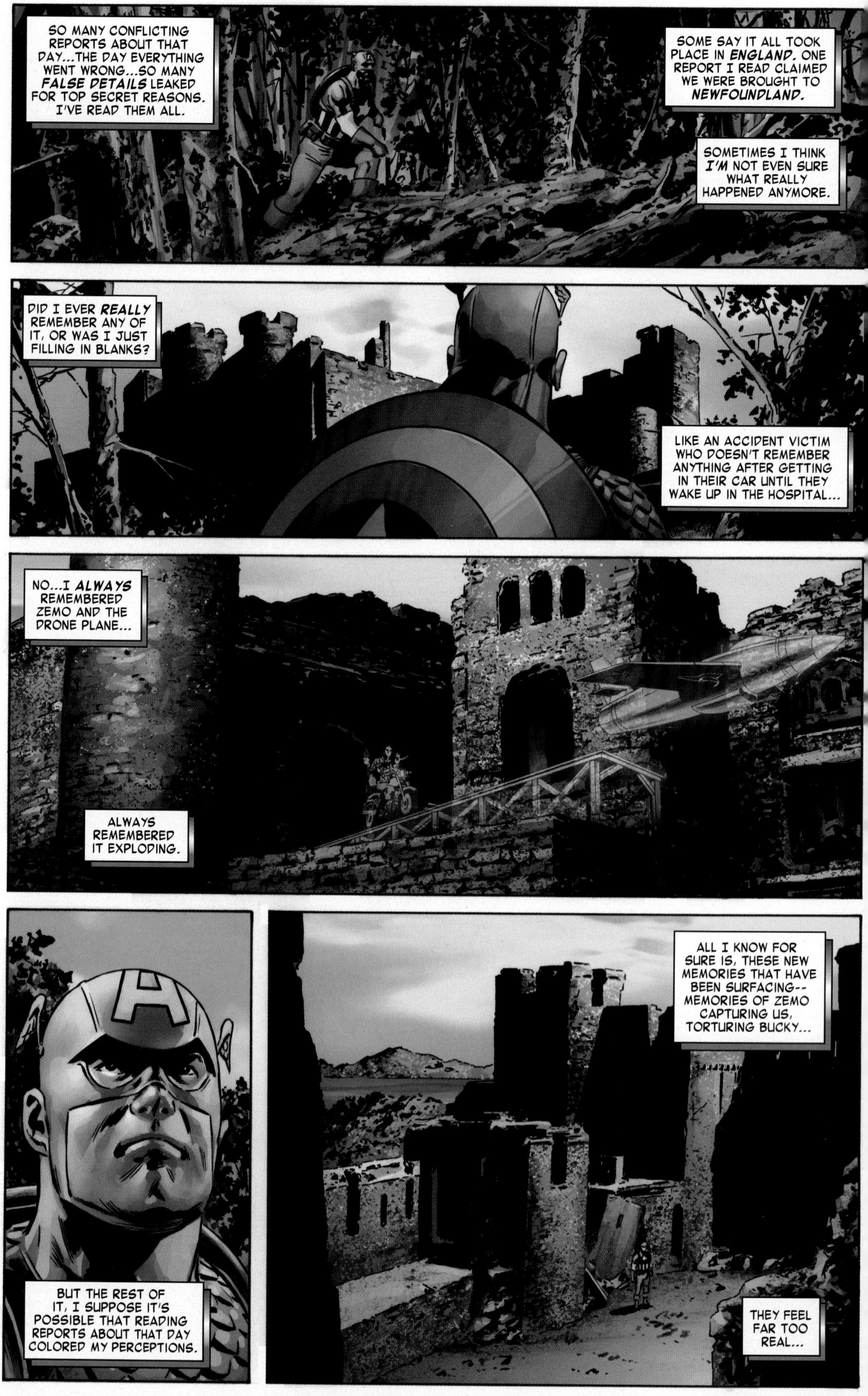
SO MANY CONFLICTING REPORTS ABOUT THAT DAY...THE DAY EVERYTHING WENT WRONG...SO MANY FALSE DETAILS LEAKED FOR TOP SECRET REASONS. I'VE READ THEM ALL.
SOME SAY IT ALL TOOK PLACE IN ENGLAND. ONE REPORT I READ CLAIMED WE WERE BROUGHT TO NEWFOUNDLAND.
SOMETIMES I THINK I'M NOT EVEN SURE WHAT REALLY HAPPENED ANYMORE.
DID I EVER REALLY REMEMBER ANY OF IT, OR WAS I JUST FILLING IN BLANKS?
LIKE AN ACCIDENT VICTIM WHO DOESN'T REMEMBER ANYTHING AFTER GETTING IN THEIR CAR UNTIL THEY WAKE UP IN THE HOSPITAL...
NO...I ALWAYS REMEMBERED ZEMO AND THE DRONE PLANE...
ALWAYS REMEMBERED IT EXPLODING.
BUT THE REST OF IT, I SUPPOSE IT'S POSSIBLE THAT READING REPORTS ABOUT THAT DAY COLORED MY PERCEPTIONS.
ALL I KNOW FOR SURE IS, THESE NEW MEMORIES THAT HAVE BEEN SURFACING-- MEMORIES OF ZEMO CAPTURING US, TORTURING BUCKY...
THEY FEEL FAR TOO REAL...

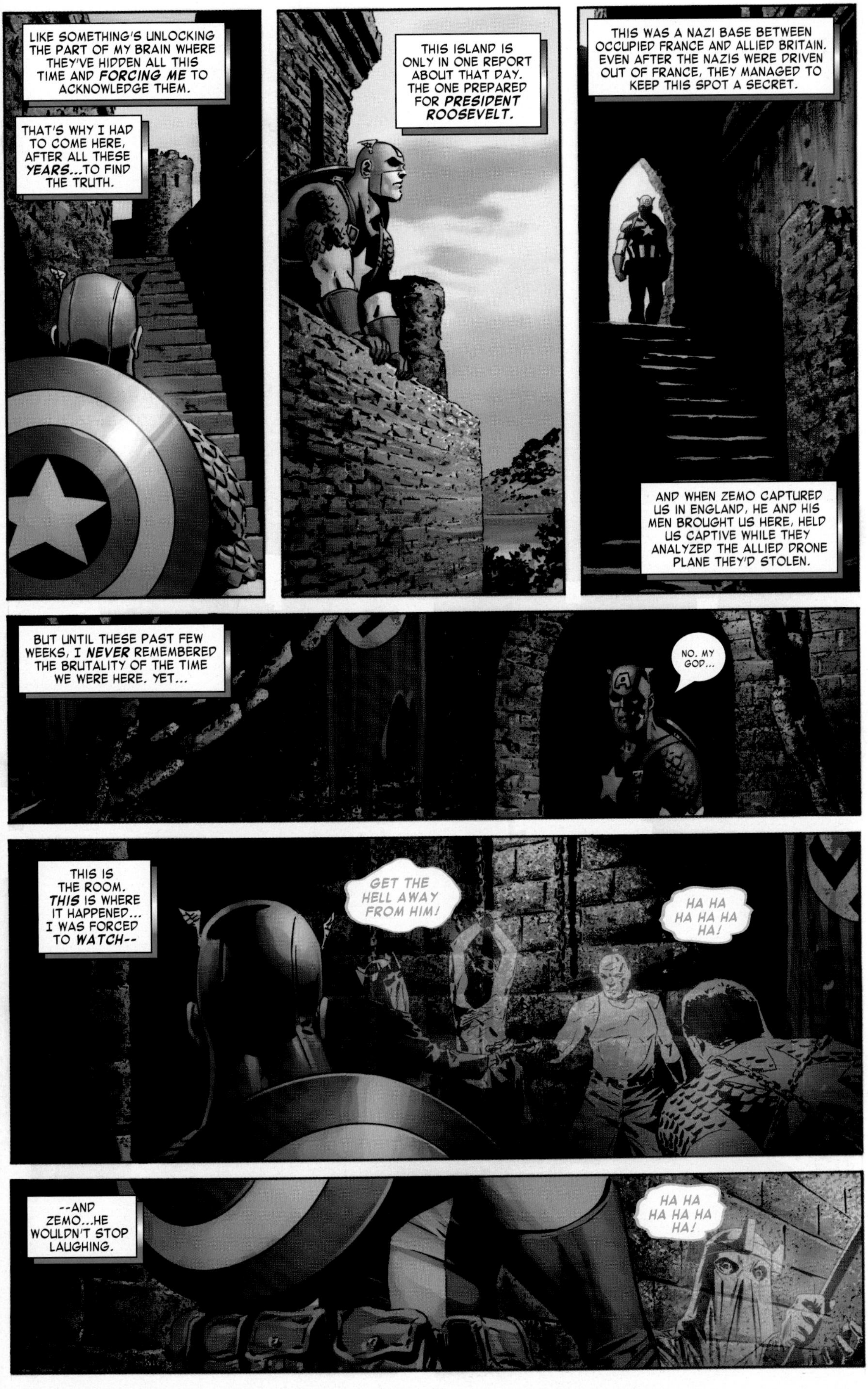
LIKE SOMETHING'S UNLOCKING THE PART OF MY BRAIN WHERE THEY'VE HIDDEN ALL THIS TIME AND FORCING ME TO ACKNOWLEDGE THEM.
THAT'S WHY I HAD TO COME HERE, AFTER ALL THESE YEARS...TO FIND THE TRUTH.
THIS ISLAND IS ONLY IN ONE REPORT ABOUT THAT DAY. THE ONE PREPARED FOR PRESIDENT ROOSEVELT.
THIS WAS A NAZI BASE BETWEEN OCCUPIED FRANCE AND ALLIED BRITAIN. EVEN AFTER THE NAZIS WERE DRIVEN OUT OF FRANCE, THEY MANAGED TO KEEP THIS SPOT A SECRET.
AND WHEN ZEMO CAPTURED US IN ENGLAND, HE AND HIS MEN BROUGHT US HERE, HELD US CAPTIVE WHILE THEY ANALYZED THE ALLIED DRONE PLANE THEY'D STOLEN.
BUT UNTIL THESE PAST FEW WEEKS, I NEVER REMEMBERED THE BRUTALITY OF THE TIME WE WERE HERE. YET...
NO. MY GOD...
THIS IS THE ROOM. THIS IS WHERE IT HAPPENED... I WAS FORCED TO WATCH--
GET THE HELL AWAY FROM HIM!
HA HA HA HA HA HA!
--AND ZEMO...HE WOULDN'T STOP LAUGHING.
HA HA HA HA HA HA!

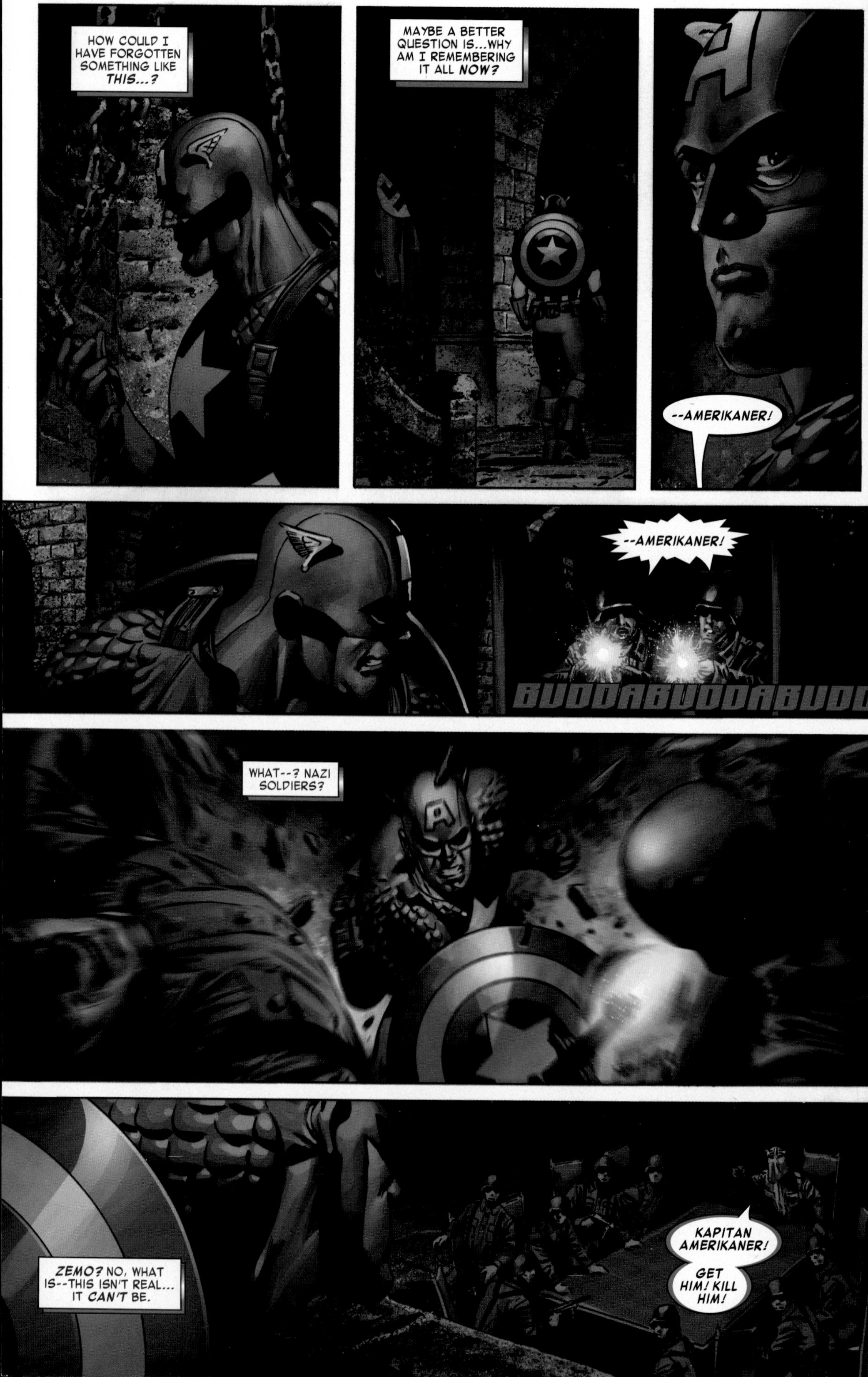
HOW COULD I HAVE FORGOTTEN SOMETHING LIKE THIS...?
MAYBE A BETTER QUESTION IS...WHY AM I REMEMBERING IT ALL NOW?
--AMERIKANER!
--AMERIKANER!
BUDDABUDDABUDD
WHAT--? NAZI SOLDIERS?
ZEMO? NO, WHAT IS--THIS ISN'T REAL... IT CAN'T BE.
KAPITAN AMERIKANER!
GET HIM! KILL HIM!

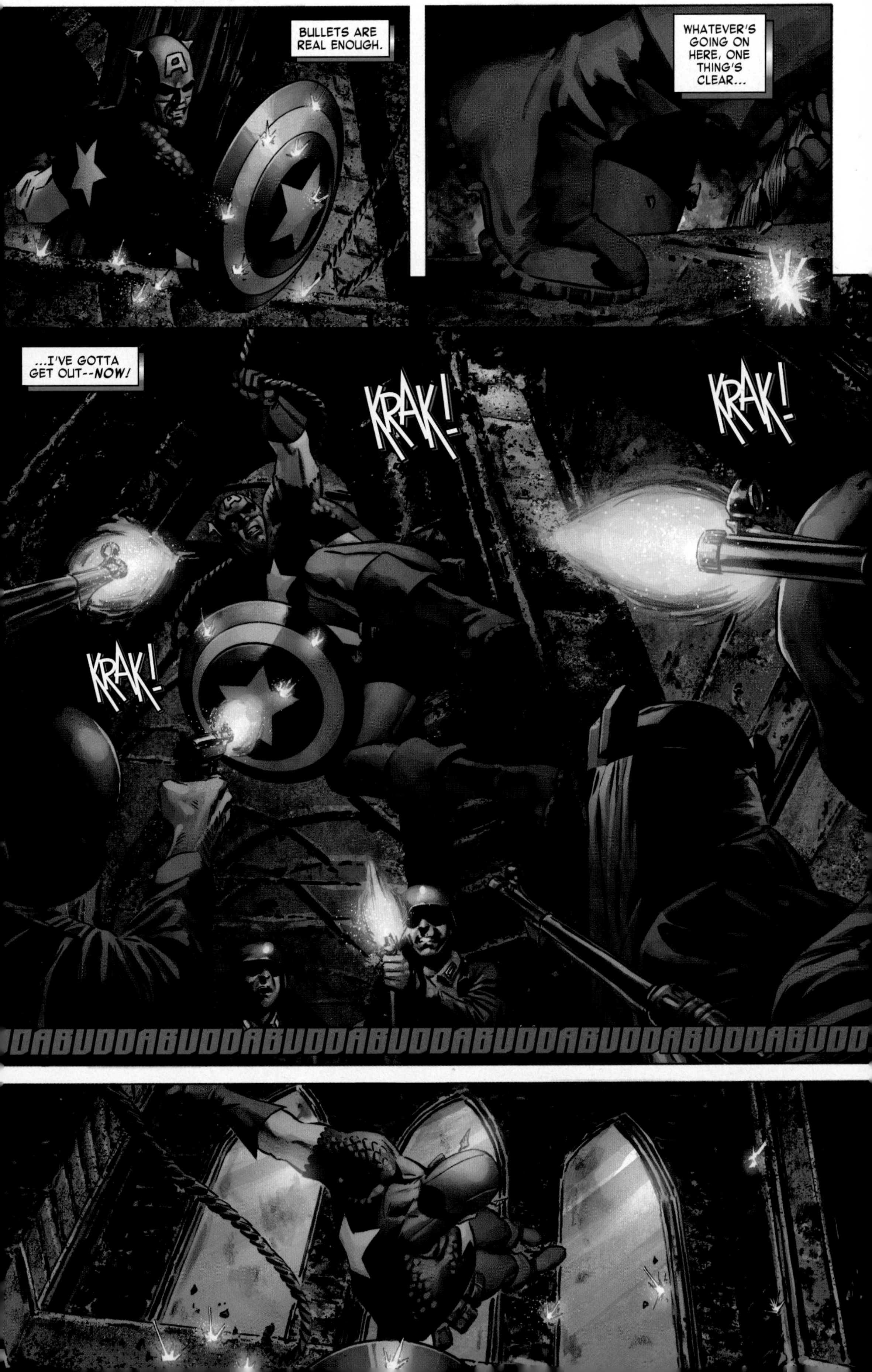
BULLETS ARE REAL ENOUGH.
WHATEVER'S GOING ON HERE, ONE THING'S CLEAR...
...I'VE GOTTA GET OUT--NOW!
KRAK!
KRAK!
KRAK!
DABUDDABUDDABUDDABUDDABUDDABUDDABUDDABUDD

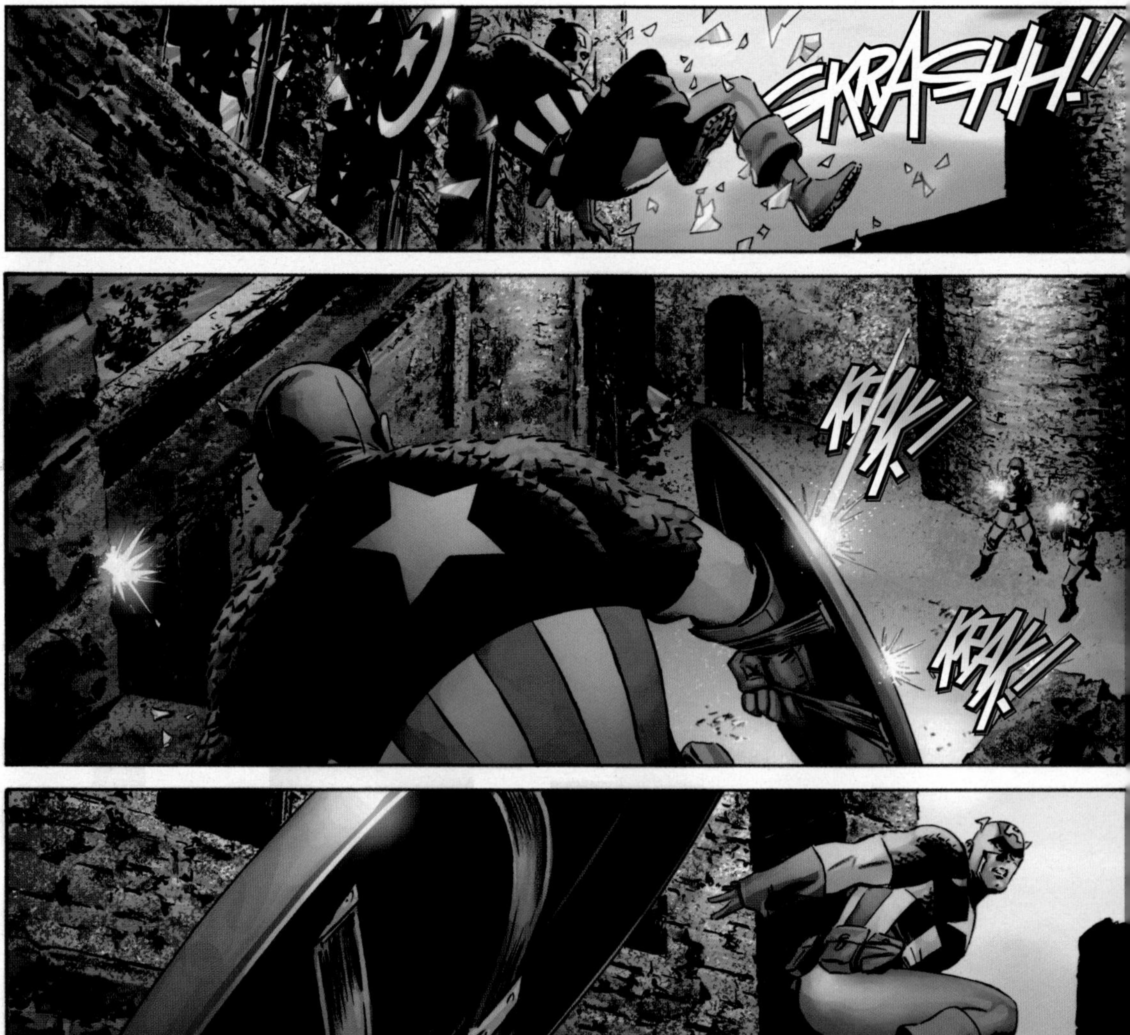
SKRASHH!
KRAK!
KRAK!
OF COURSE...
...THEY'RE ALL GONE.
NO EVIDENCE THEY WERE REALLY HERE AT ALL.

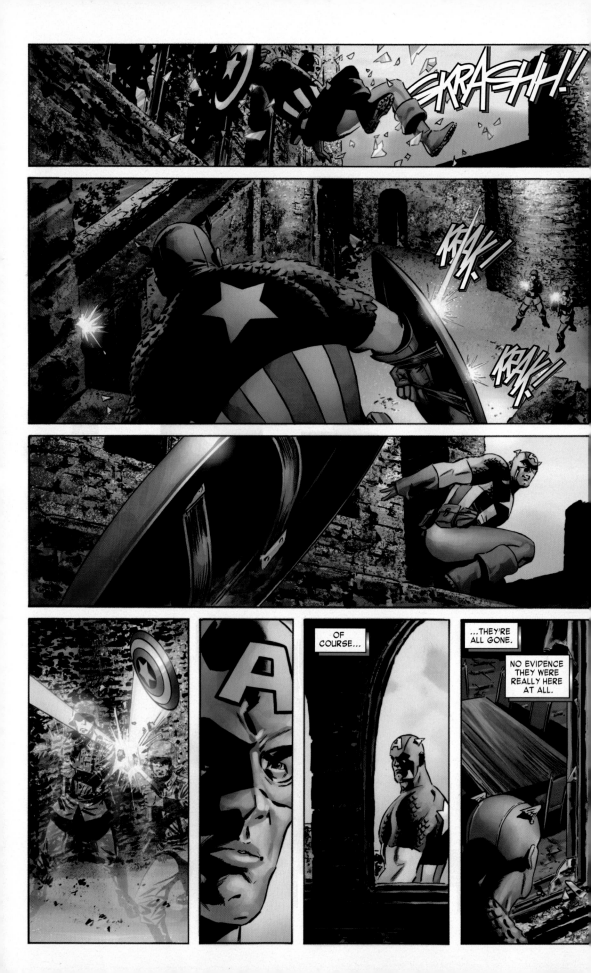

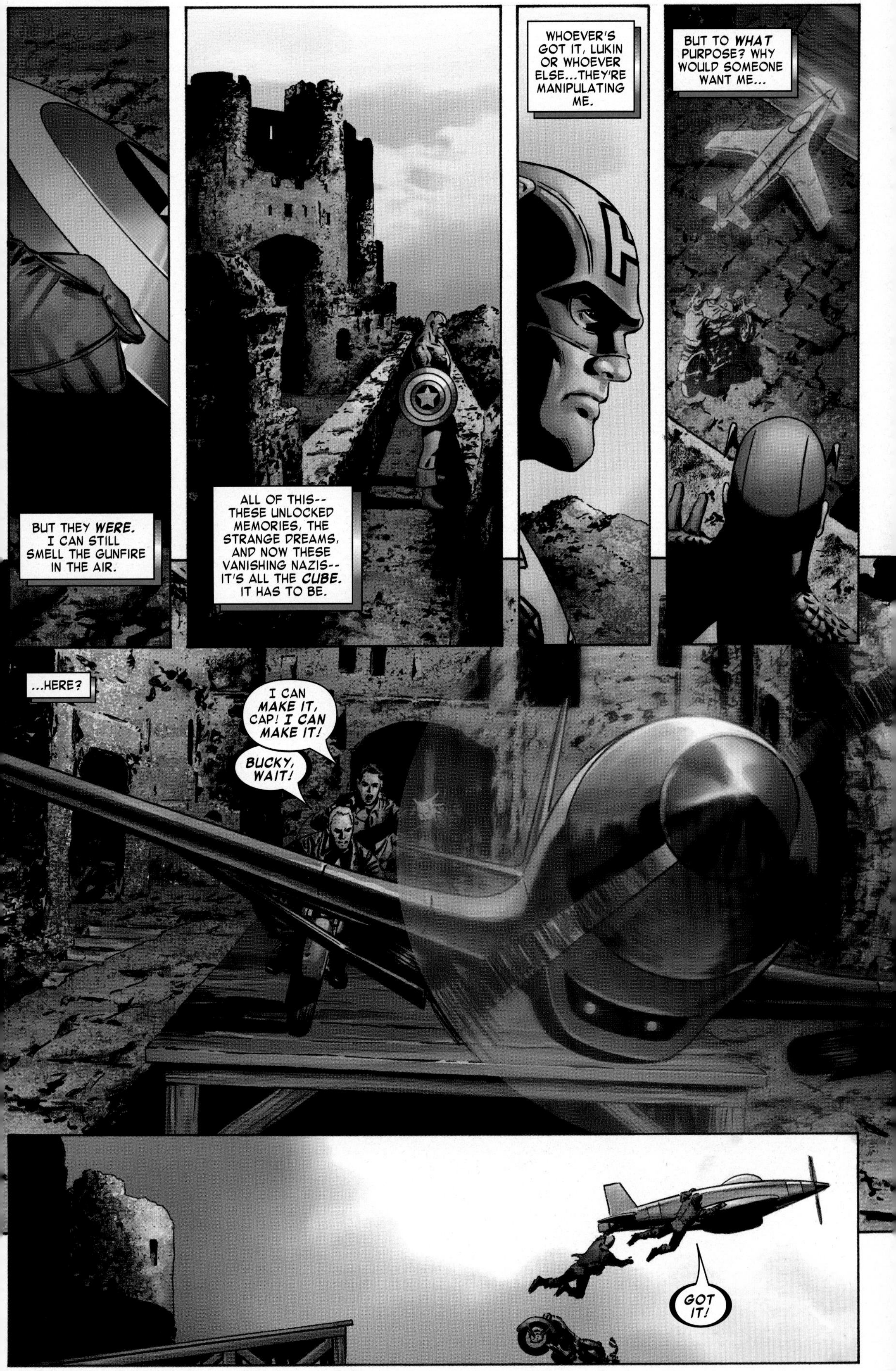
BUT THEY WERE. I CAN STILL SMELL THE GUNFIRE IN THE AIR.
ALL OF THIS-- THESE UNLOCKED MEMORIES, THE STRANGE DREAMS, AND NOW THESE VANISHING NAZIS-- IT'S ALL THE CUBE. IT HAS TO BE.
WHOEVER'S GOT IT, LUKIN OR WHOEVER ELSE...THEY'RE MANIPULATING ME.
BUT TO WHAT PURPOSE? WHY WOULD SOMEONE WANT ME...
...HERE?
I CAN MAKE IT, CAP! I CAN MAKE IT!
BUCKY, WAIT!
GOT IT!

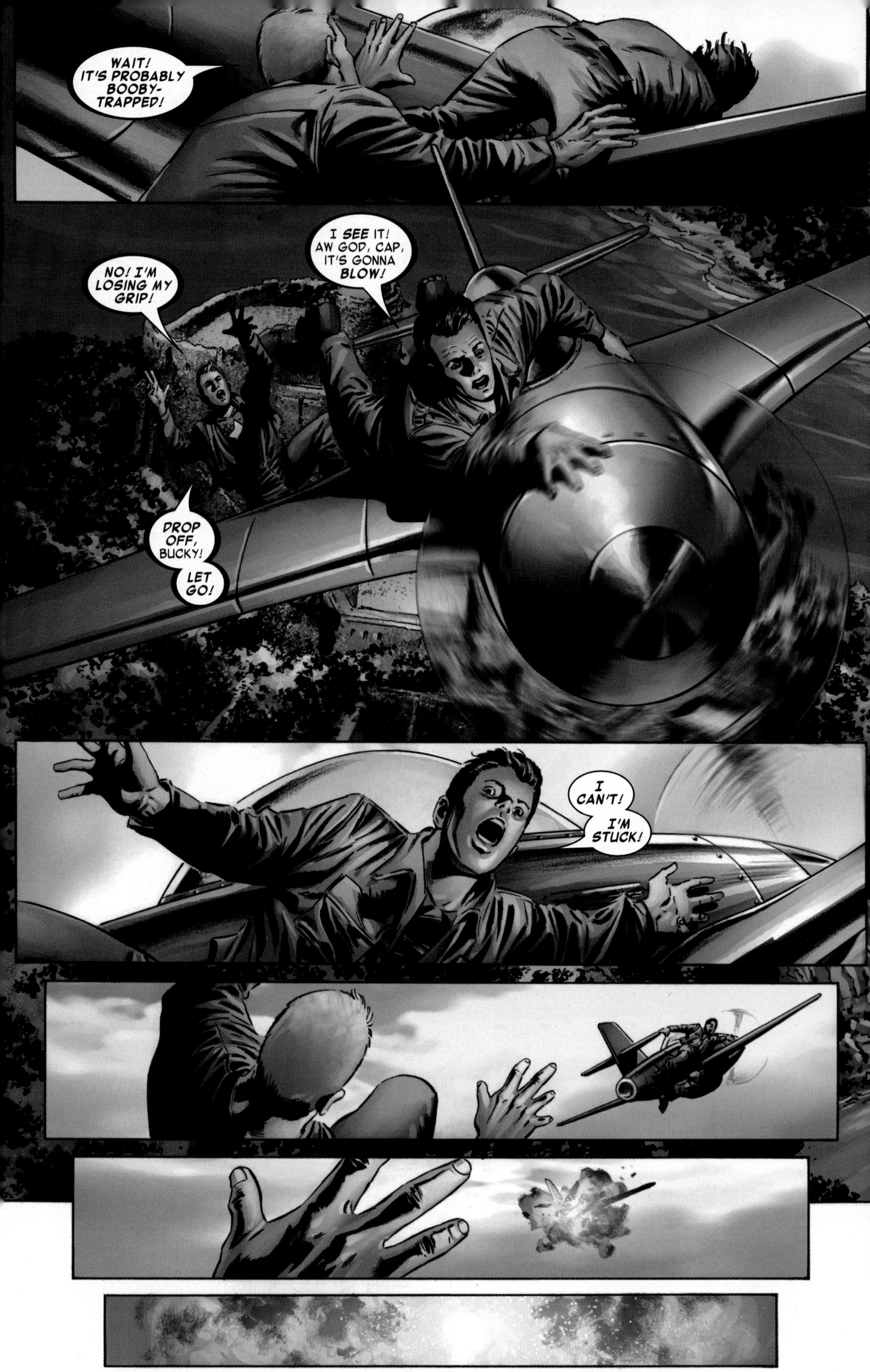
WAIT! IT'S PROBABLY BOOBY-TRAPPED!
NO! I'M LOSING MY GRIP!
I SEE IT! AW GOD, CAP, IT'S GONNA BLOW!
DROP OFF, BUCKY!
LET GO!
I CAN'T!
I'M STUCK!

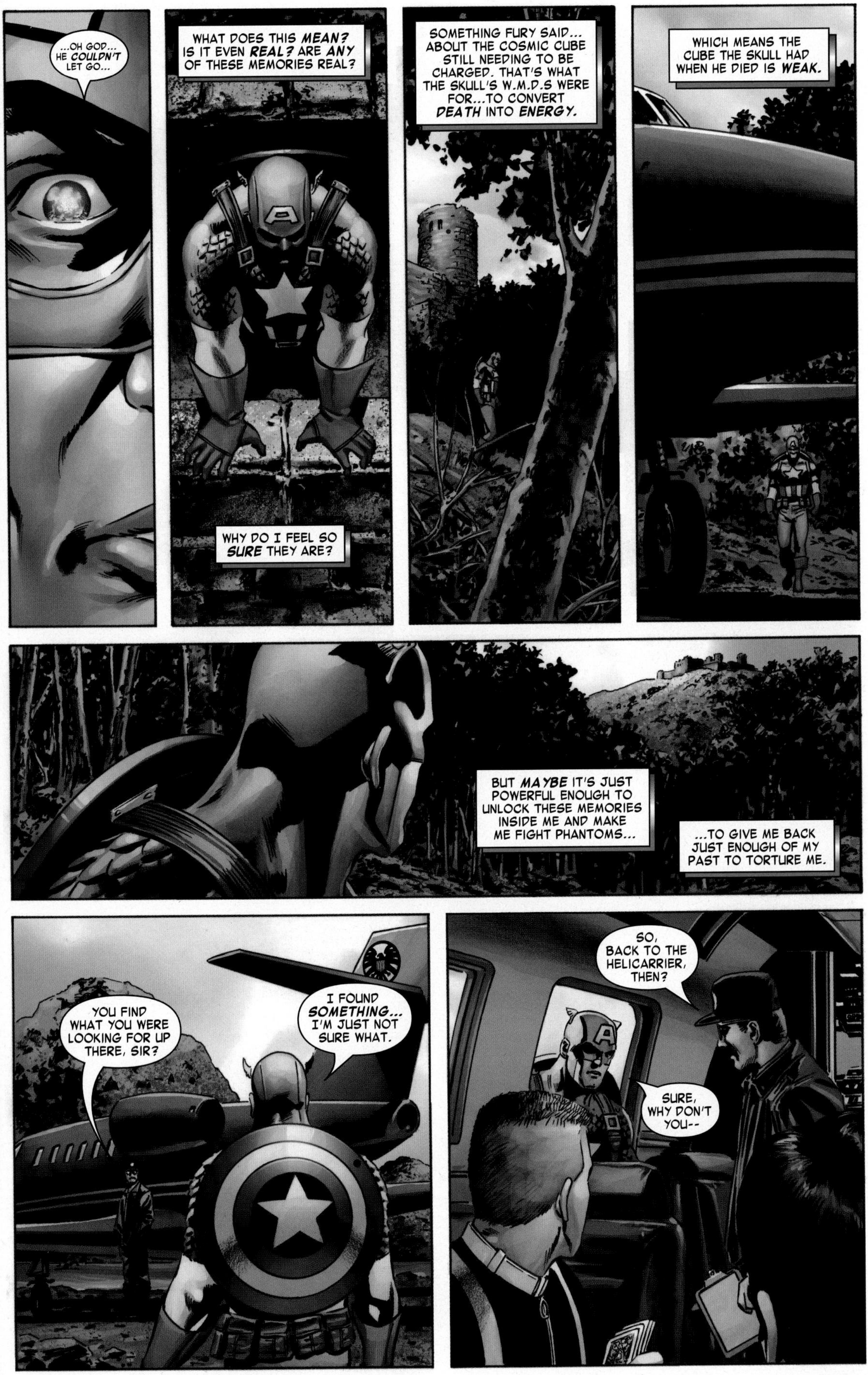

...OH GOD... HE COULDN'T LET GO...
WHAT DOES THIS MEAN? IS IT EVEN REAL? ARE ANY OF THESE MEMORIES REAL?
WHY DO I FEEL SO SURE THEY ARE?
SOMETHING FURY SAID... ABOUT THE COSMIC CUBE STILL NEEDING TO BE CHARGED. THAT'S WHAT THE SKULL'S W.M.D.S WERE FOR...TO CONVERT DEATH INTO ENERGY.
WHICH MEANS THE CUBE THE SKULL HAD WHEN HE DIED IS WEAK.
BUT MAYBE IT'S JUST POWERFUL ENOUGH TO UNLOCK THESE MEMORIES INSIDE ME AND MAKE ME FIGHT PHANTOMS...
...TO GIVE ME BACK JUST ENOUGH OF MY PAST TO TORTURE ME.
YOU FIND WHAT YOU WERE LOOKING FOR UP THERE, SIR?
I FOUND SOMETHING... I'M JUST NOT SURE WHAT.
SO, BACK TO THE HELICARRIER, THEN?
SURE, WHY DON'T YOU--

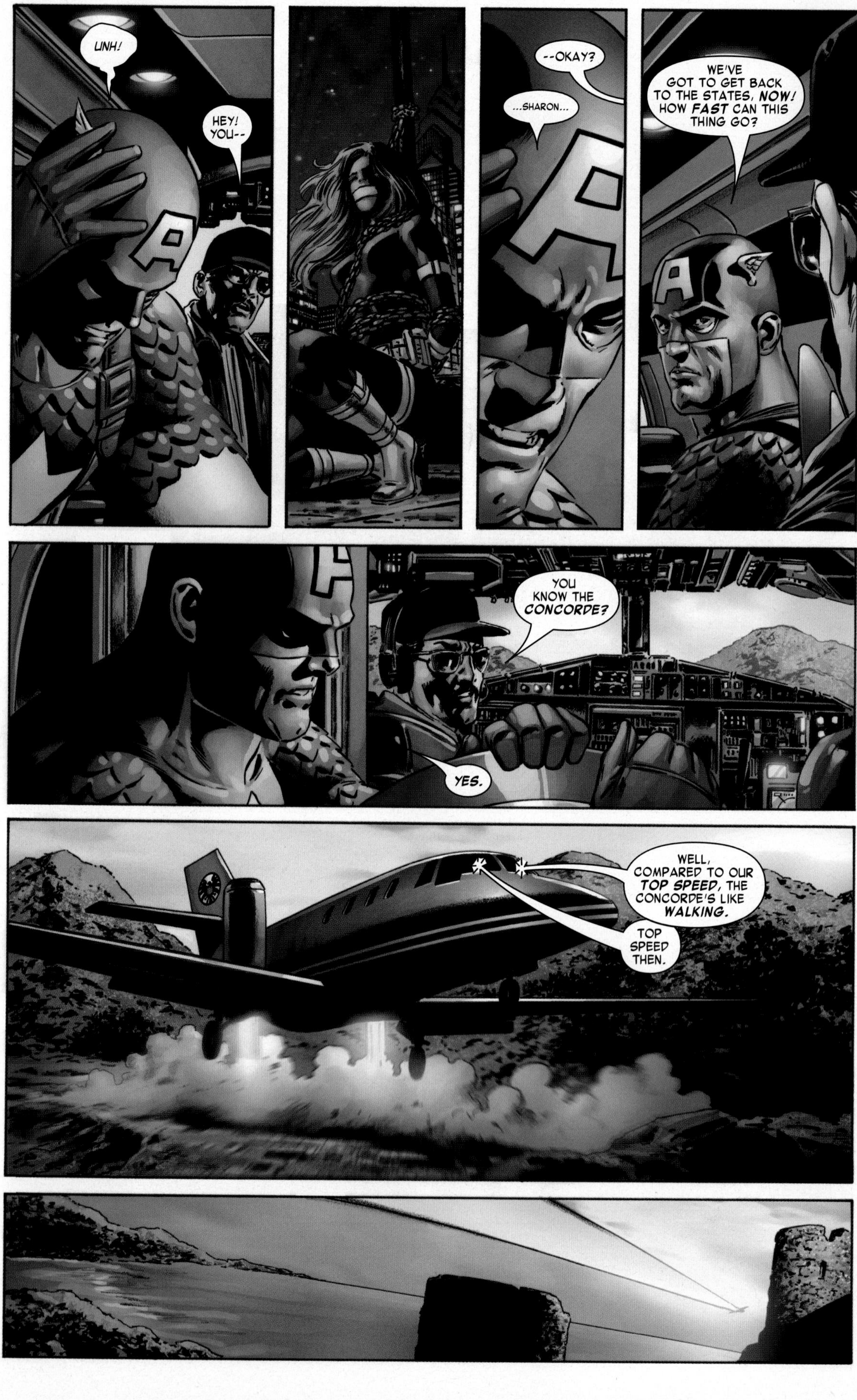
UNH!
HEY! YOU--
...SHARON...
--OKAY?
WE'VE GOT TO GET BACK TO THE STATES, NOW! HOW FAST CAN THIS THING GO?
YOU KNOW THE CONCORDE?
YES.
WELL, COMPARED TO OUR TOP SPEED, THE CONCORDE'S LIKE WALKING.
TOP SPEED THEN.

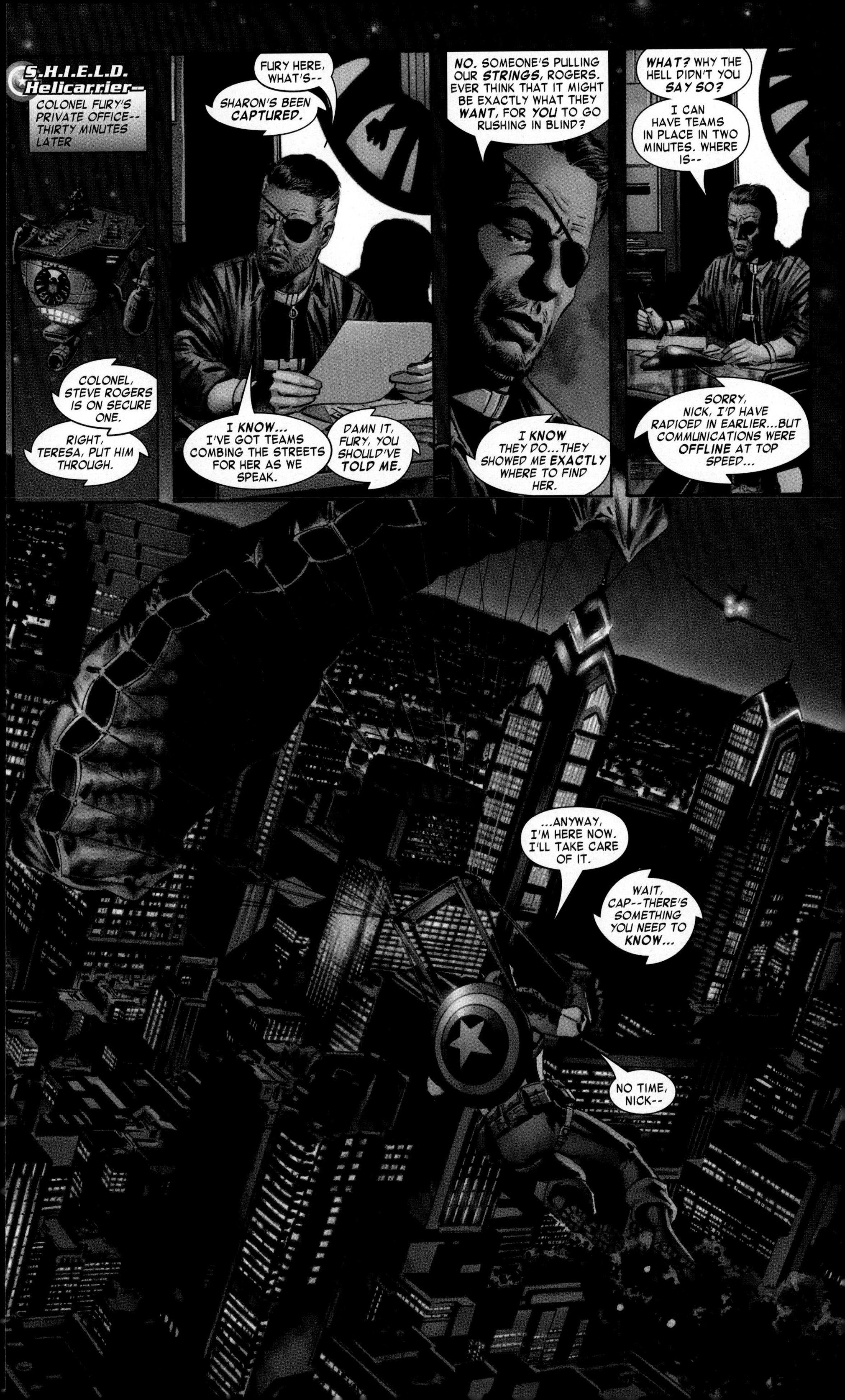
S.H.I.E.L.D. Helicarrier--
COLONEL FURY'S PRIVATE OFFICE--THIRTY MINUTES LATER
COLONEL, STEVE ROGERS IS ON SECURE ONE.
RIGHT, TERESA, PUT HIM THROUGH.
FURY HERE, WHAT'S--
SHARON'S BEEN CAPTURED.
I KNOW... I'VE GOT TEAMS COMBING THE STREETS FOR HER AS WE SPEAK.
DAMN IT, FURY, YOU SHOULD'VE TOLD ME.
NO. SOMEONE'S PULLING OUR STRINGS, ROGERS. EVER THINK THAT IT MIGHT BE EXACTLY WHAT THEY WANT, FOR YOU TO GO RUSHING IN BLIND?
I KNOW THEY DO... THEY SHOWED ME EXACTLY WHERE TO FIND HER.
WHAT? WHY THE HELL DIDN'T YOU SAY SO?
I CAN HAVE TEAMS IN PLACE IN TWO MINUTES. WHERE IS--
SORRY, NICK, I'D HAVE RADIOED IN EARLIER...BUT COMMUNICATIONS WERE OFFLINE AT TOP SPEED...
...ANYWAY, I'M HERE NOW. I'LL TAKE CARE OF IT.
WAIT, CAP--THERE'S SOMETHING YOU NEED TO KNOW...
NO TIME, NICK--

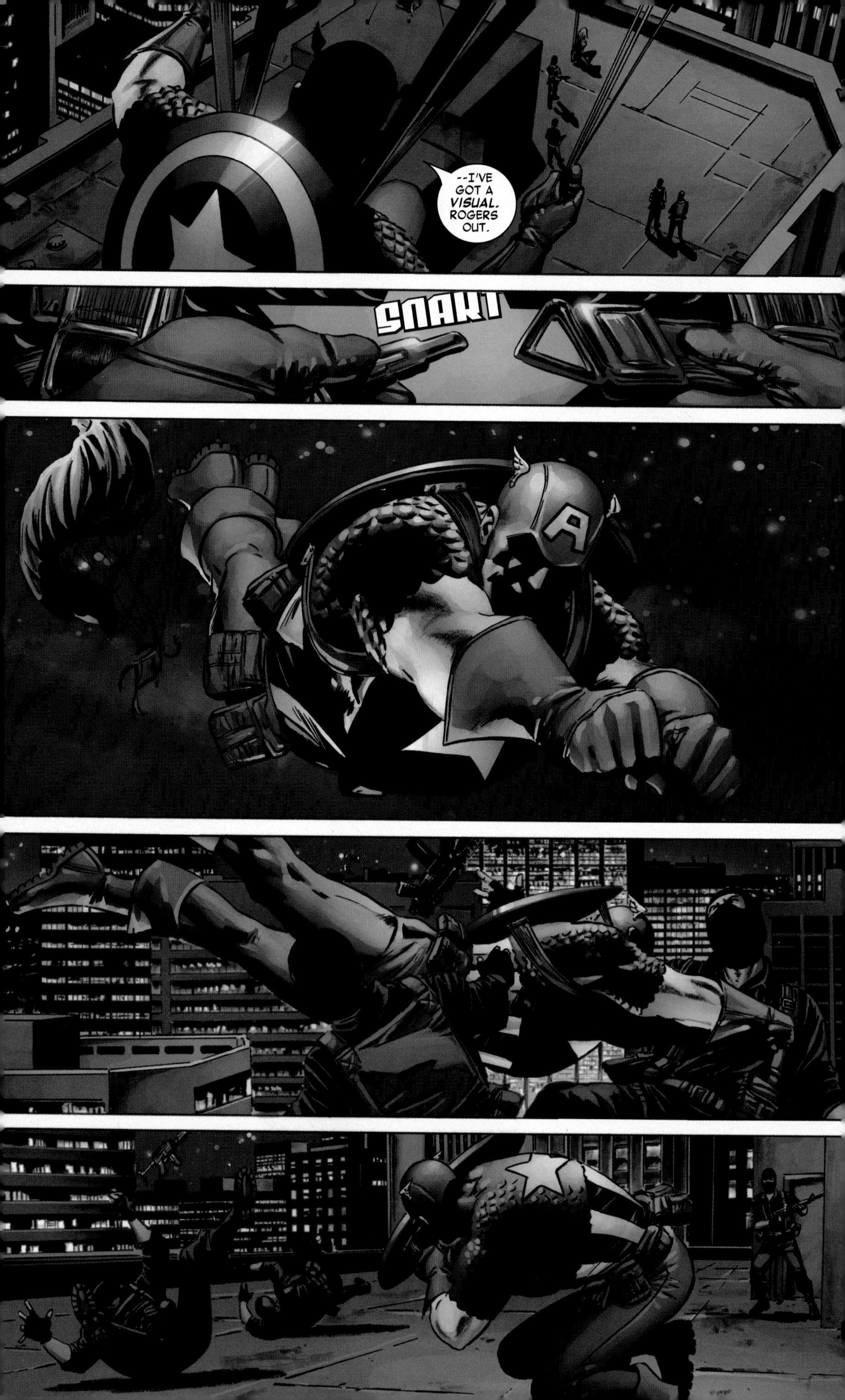
--I'VE GOT A VISUAL. ROGERS OUT.
SNAKT

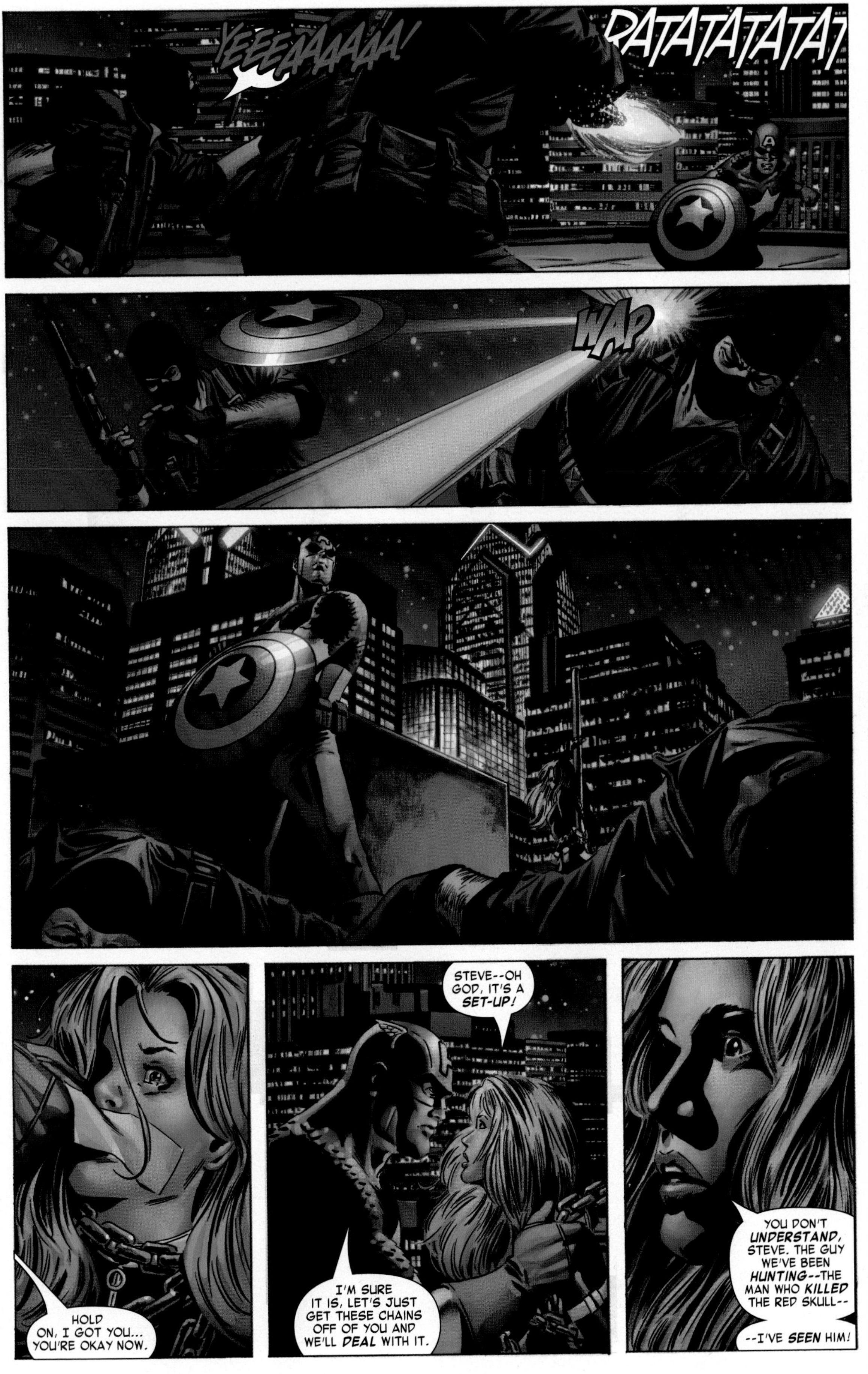
YEEEAAAAAA!
RATATATATAT
WAP
HOLD ON, I GOT YOU... YOU'RE OKAY NOW.
STEVE--OH GOD, IT'S A SET-UP!
I'M SURE IT IS, LET'S JUST GET THESE CHAINS OFF OF YOU AND WE'LL DEAL WITH IT.
YOU DON'T UNDERSTAND, STEVE. THE GUY WE'VE BEEN HUNTING--THE MAN WHO KILLED THE RED SKULL--
--I'VE SEEN HIM!

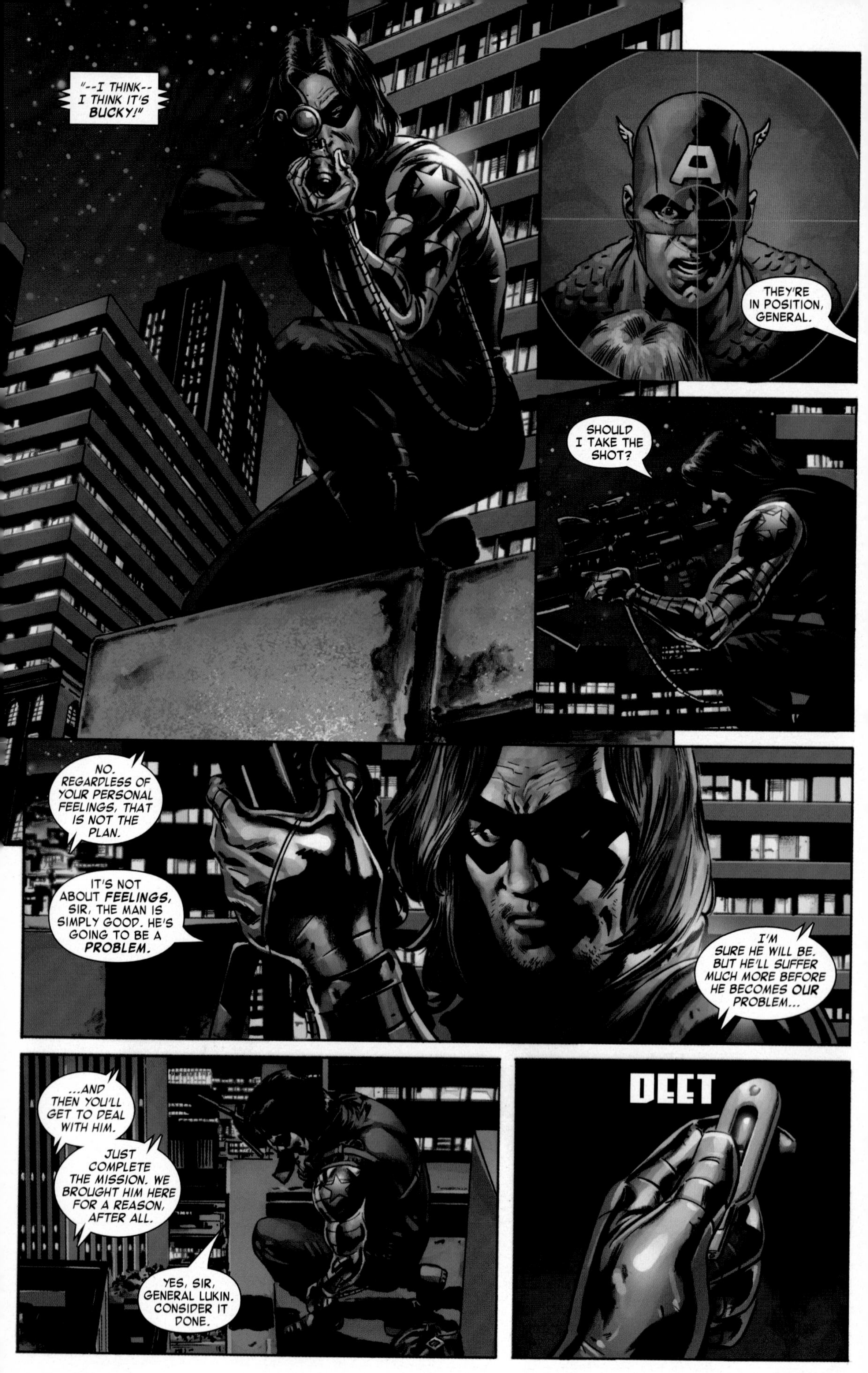
"--I THINK--
I THINK IT'S
BUCKY!"
THEY'RE IN POSITION, GENERAL.
SHOULD I TAKE THE SHOT?
NO. REGARDLESS OF YOUR PERSONAL FEELINGS, THAT IS NOT THE PLAN.
IT'S NOT ABOUT FEELINGS, SIR, THE MAN IS SIMPLY GOOD. HE'S GOING TO BE A PROBLEM.
I'M SURE HE WILL BE. BUT HE'LL SUFFER MUCH MORE BEFORE HE BECOMES OUR PROBLEM...
...AND THEN YOU'LL GET TO DEAL WITH HIM.
JUST COMPLETE THE MISSION. WE BROUGHT HIM HERE FOR A REASON, AFTER ALL.
YES, SIR, GENERAL LUKIN. CONSIDER IT DONE.
DEET

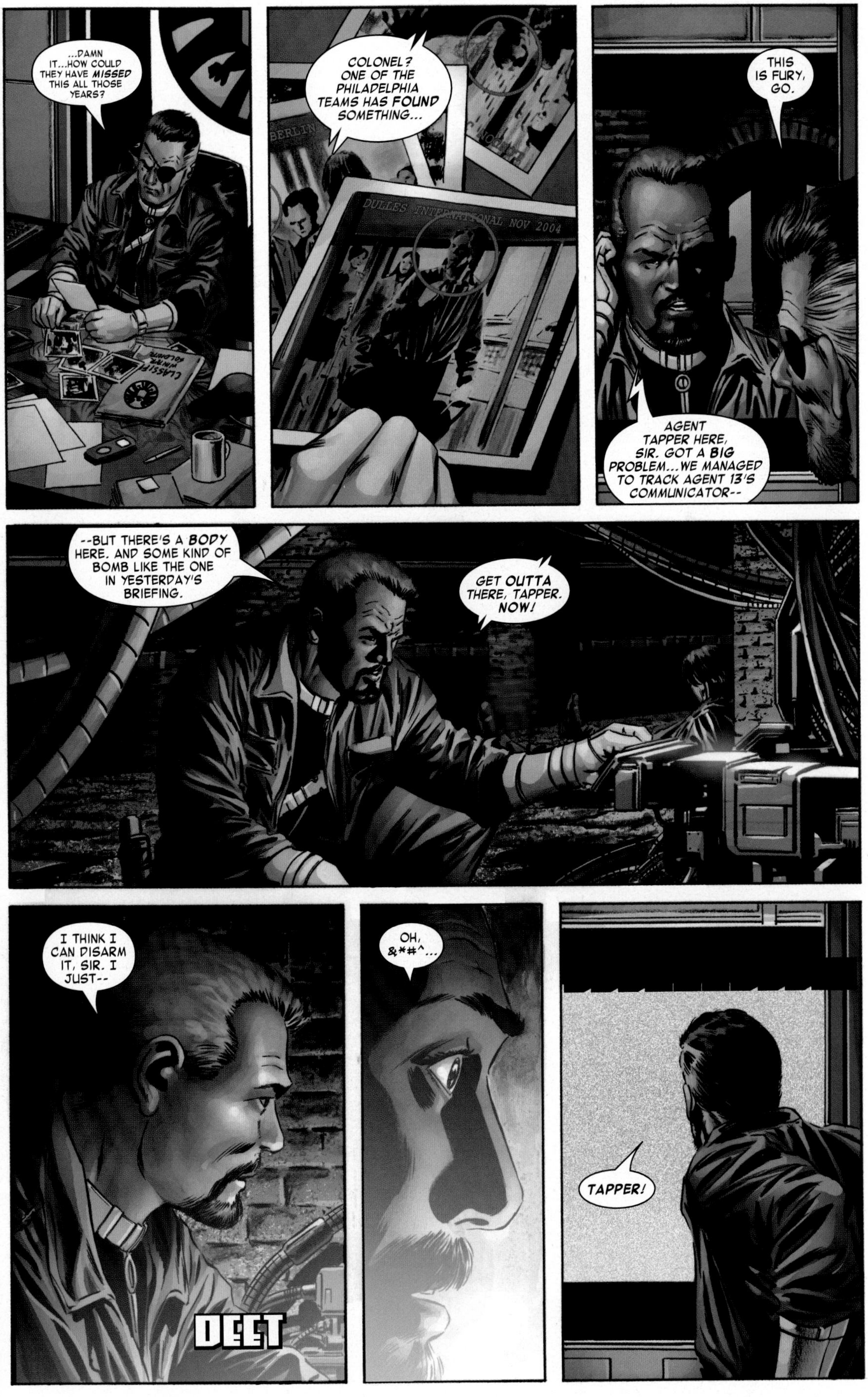
...DAMN IT...HOW COULD THEY HAVE MISSED THIS ALL THOSE YEARS?
COLONEL? ONE OF THE PHILADELPHIA TEAMS HAS FOUND SOMETHING...
BERLIN
DULLES INTERNATIONAL NOV 2004
THIS IS FURY, GO.
AGENT TAPPER HERE, SIR. GOT A BIG PROBLEM...WE MANAGED TO TRACK AGENT 13'S COMMUNICATOR--
--BUT THERE'S A BODY HERE. AND SOME KIND OF BOMB LIKE THE ONE IN YESTERDAY'S BRIEFING.
GET OUTTA THERE, TAPPER. NOW!
I THINK I CAN DISARM IT, SIR. I JUST--
DEET
OH, &*#^...
TAPPER!

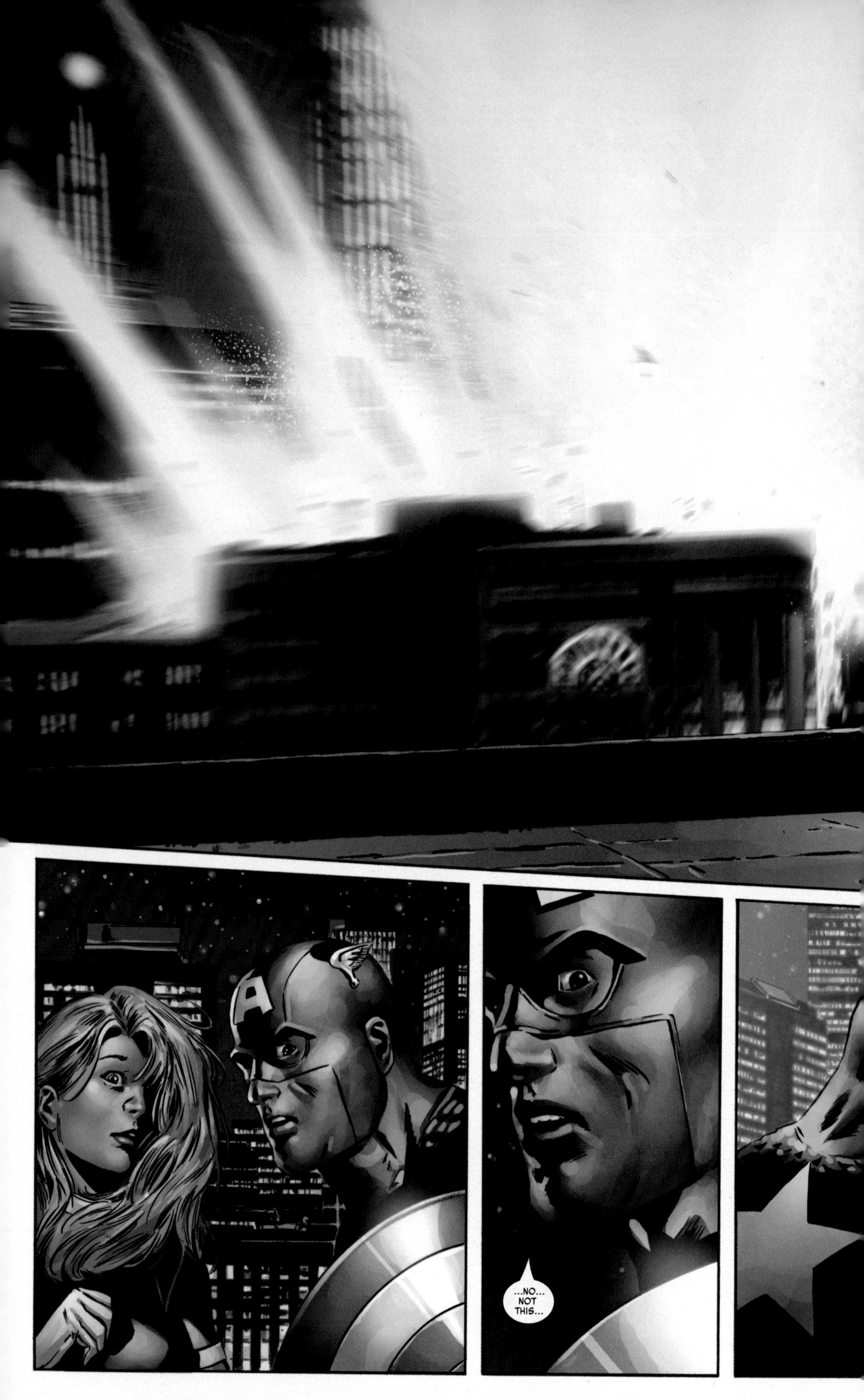
...NO... NOT THIS...

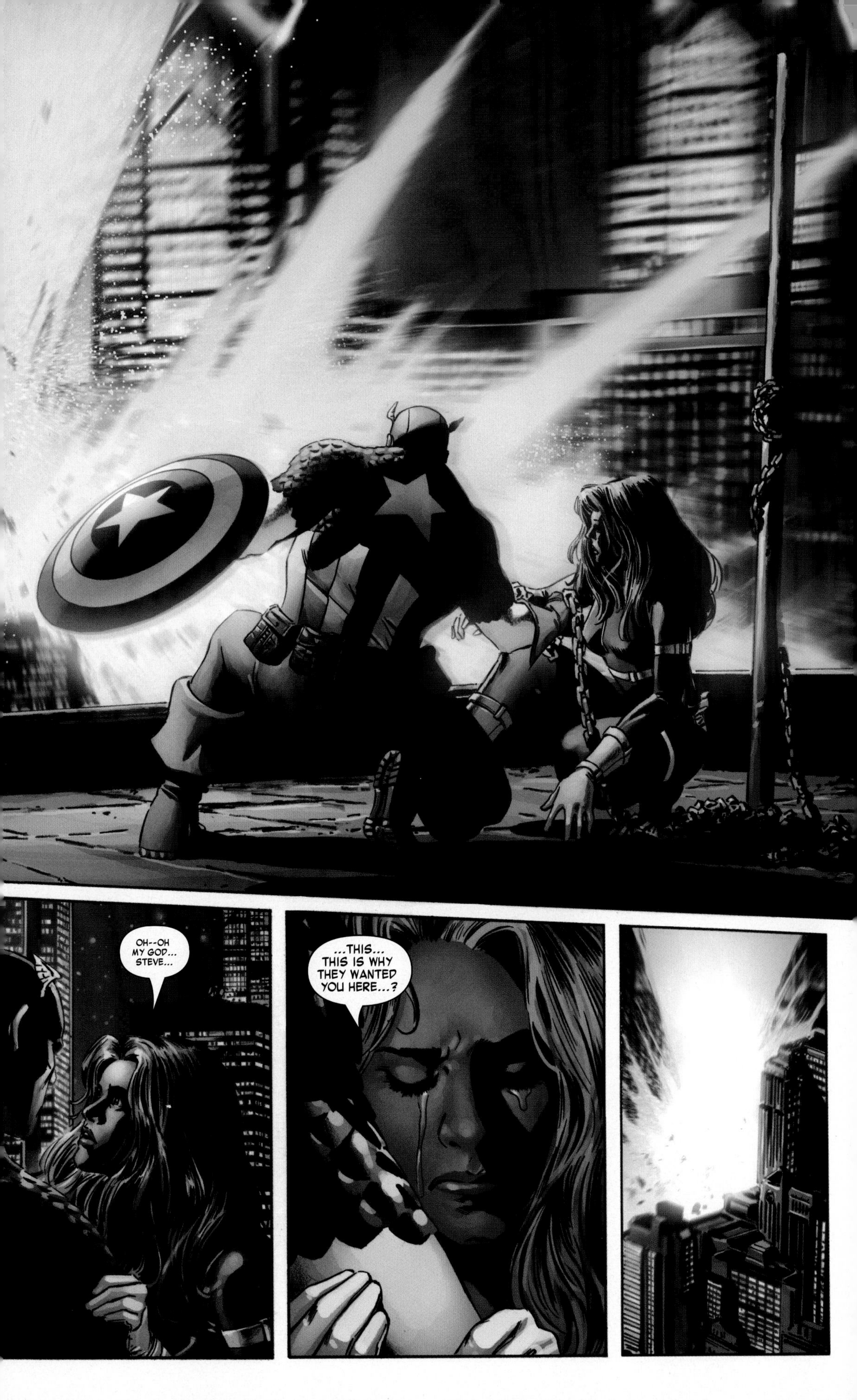
OH--OH MY GOD... STEVE...
...THIS... THIS IS WHY THEY WANTED YOU HERE...?

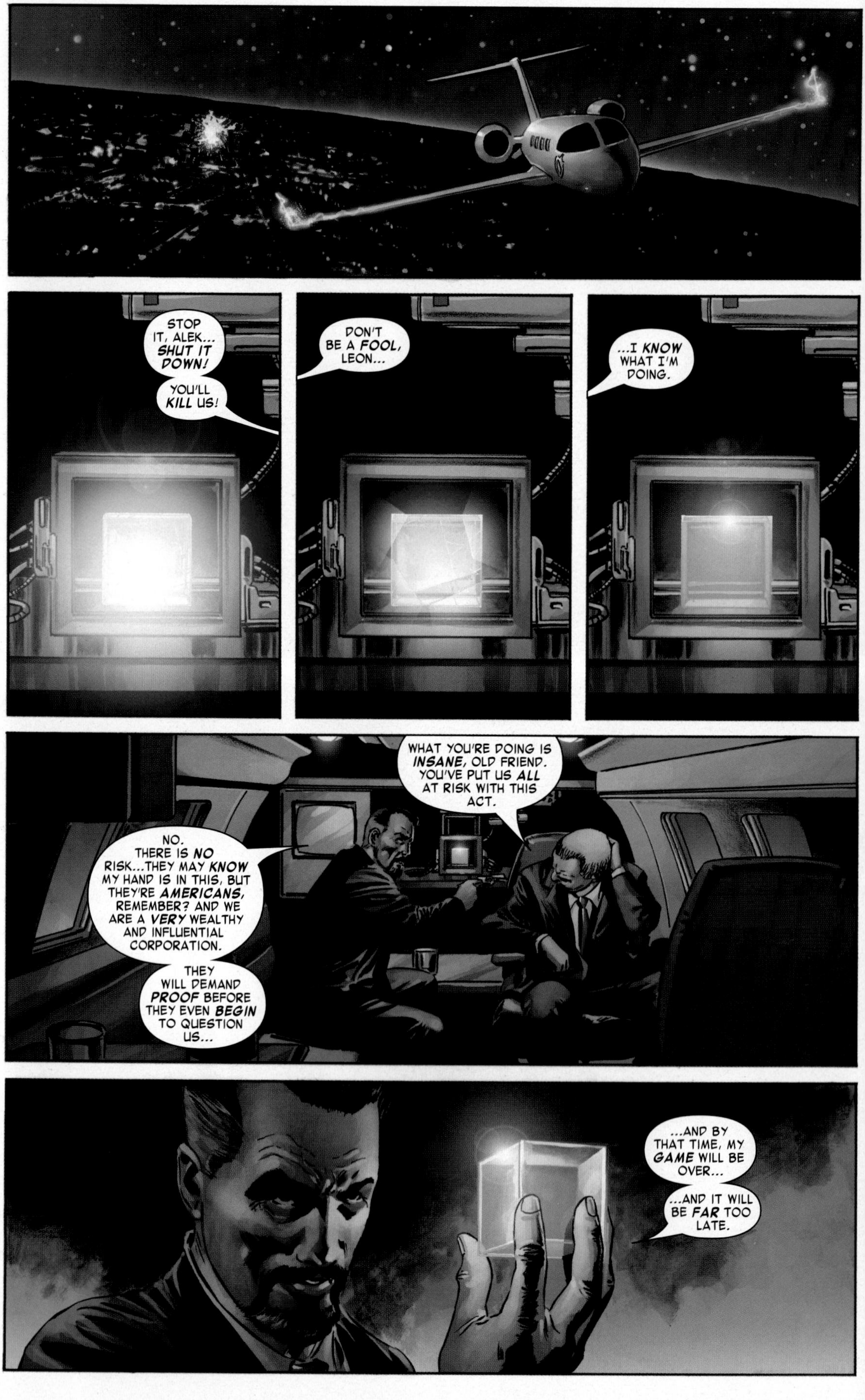

STOP IT, ALEK... SHUT IT DOWN!
YOU'LL KILL US!
DON'T BE A FOOL, LEON...
...I KNOW WHAT I'M DOING.
WHAT YOU'RE DOING IS INSANE, OLD FRIEND. YOU'VE PUT US ALL AT RISK WITH THIS ACT.
NO. THERE IS NO RISK...THEY MAY KNOW MY HAND IS IN THIS, BUT THEY'RE AMERICANS, REMEMBER? AND WE ARE A VERY WEALTHY AND INFLUENTIAL CORPORATION.
THEY WILL DEMAND PROOF BEFORE THEY EVEN BEGIN TO QUESTION US...
...AND BY THAT TIME, MY GAME WILL BE OVER...
...AND IT WILL BE FAR TOO LATE.

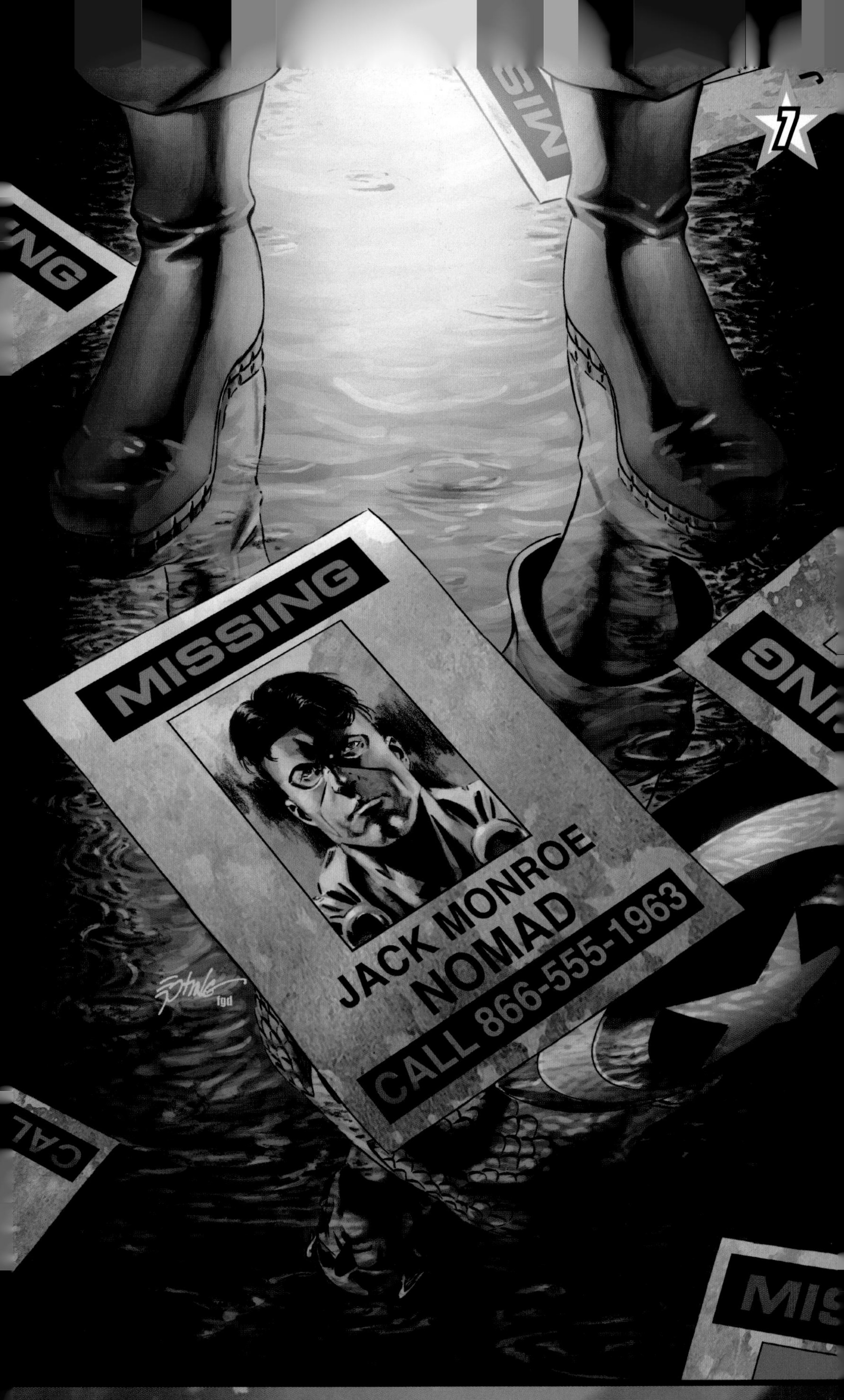
7
MISSING
JACK MONROE
NOMAD
CALL 866-555-1963

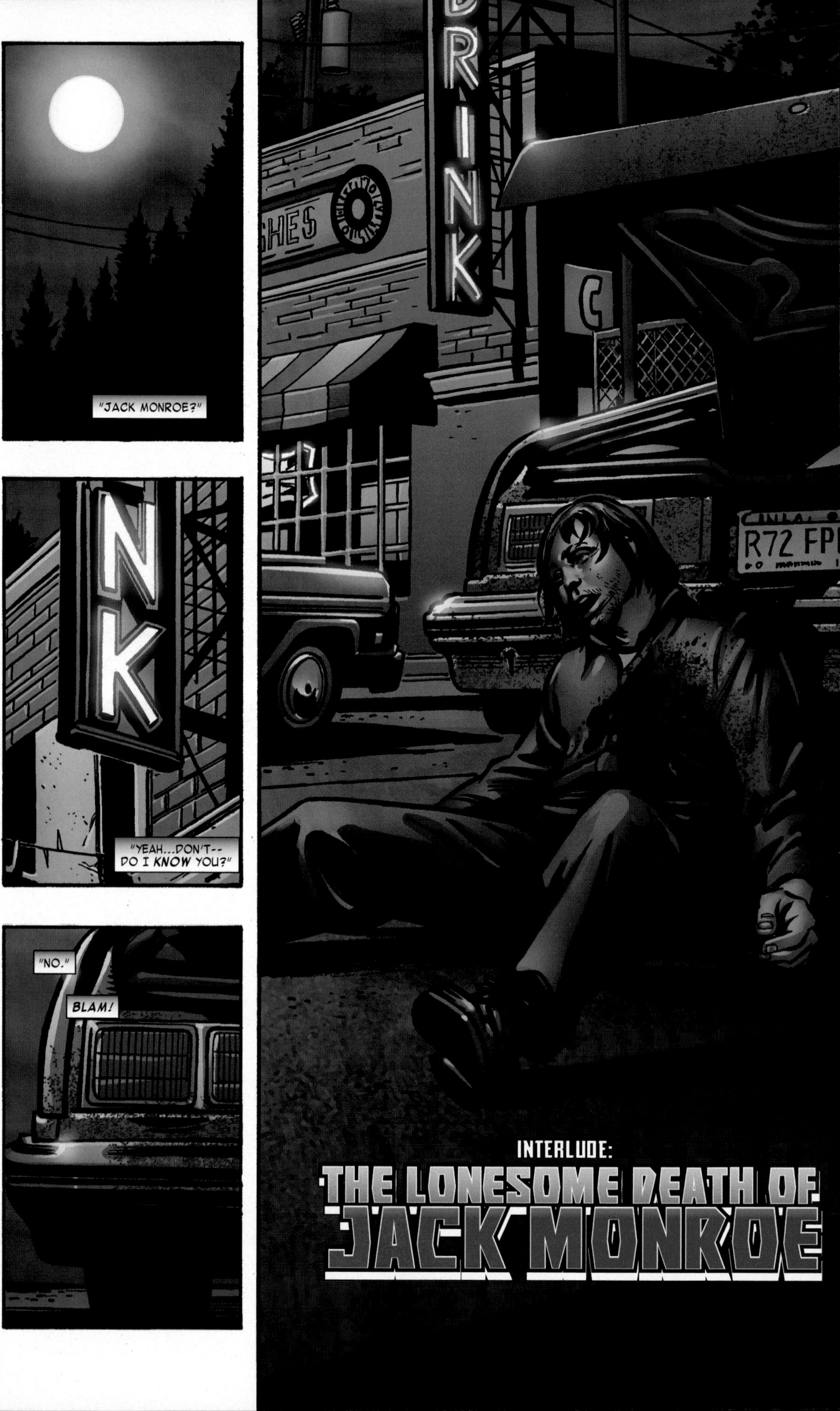
"JACK MONROE?"
"YEAH...DON'T--
DO I KNOW YOU?"
"NO."
BLAM!
DRINK
INTERLUDE:
THE LONESOME DEATH OF
JACK MONROE

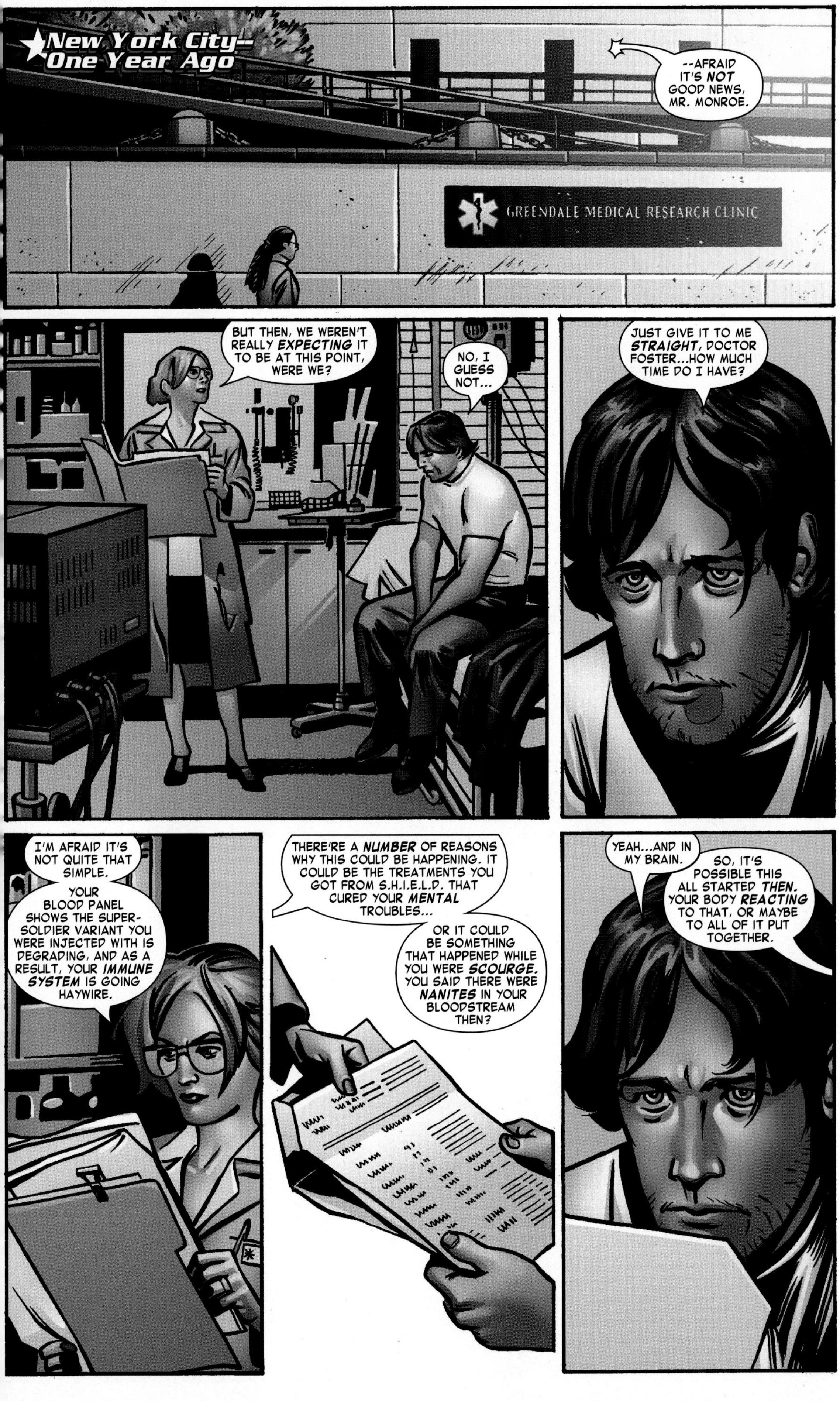
New York City-- One Year Ago
--AFRAID IT'S NOT GOOD NEWS, MR. MONROE.
GREENDALE MEDICAL RESEARCH CLINIC
BUT THEN, WE WEREN'T REALLY EXPECTING IT TO BE AT THIS POINT, WERE WE?
NO, I GUESS NOT...
JUST GIVE IT TO ME STRAIGHT, DOCTOR FOSTER...HOW MUCH TIME DO I HAVE?
I'M AFRAID IT'S NOT QUITE THAT SIMPLE.
YOUR BLOOD PANEL SHOWS THE SUPER-SOLDIER VARIANT YOU WERE INJECTED WITH IS DEGRADING, AND AS A RESULT, YOUR IMMUNE SYSTEM IS GOING HAYWIRE.
THERE'RE A NUMBER OF REASONS WHY THIS COULD BE HAPPENING. IT COULD BE THE TREATMENTS YOU GOT FROM S.H.I.E.L.D. THAT CURED YOUR MENTAL TROUBLES...
OR IT COULD BE SOMETHING THAT HAPPENED WHILE YOU WERE SCOURGE. YOU SAID THERE WERE NANITES IN YOUR BLOODSTREAM THEN?
YEAH...AND IN MY BRAIN.
SO, IT'S POSSIBLE THIS ALL STARTED THEN. YOUR BODY REACTING TO THAT, OR MAYBE TO ALL OF IT PUT TOGETHER.

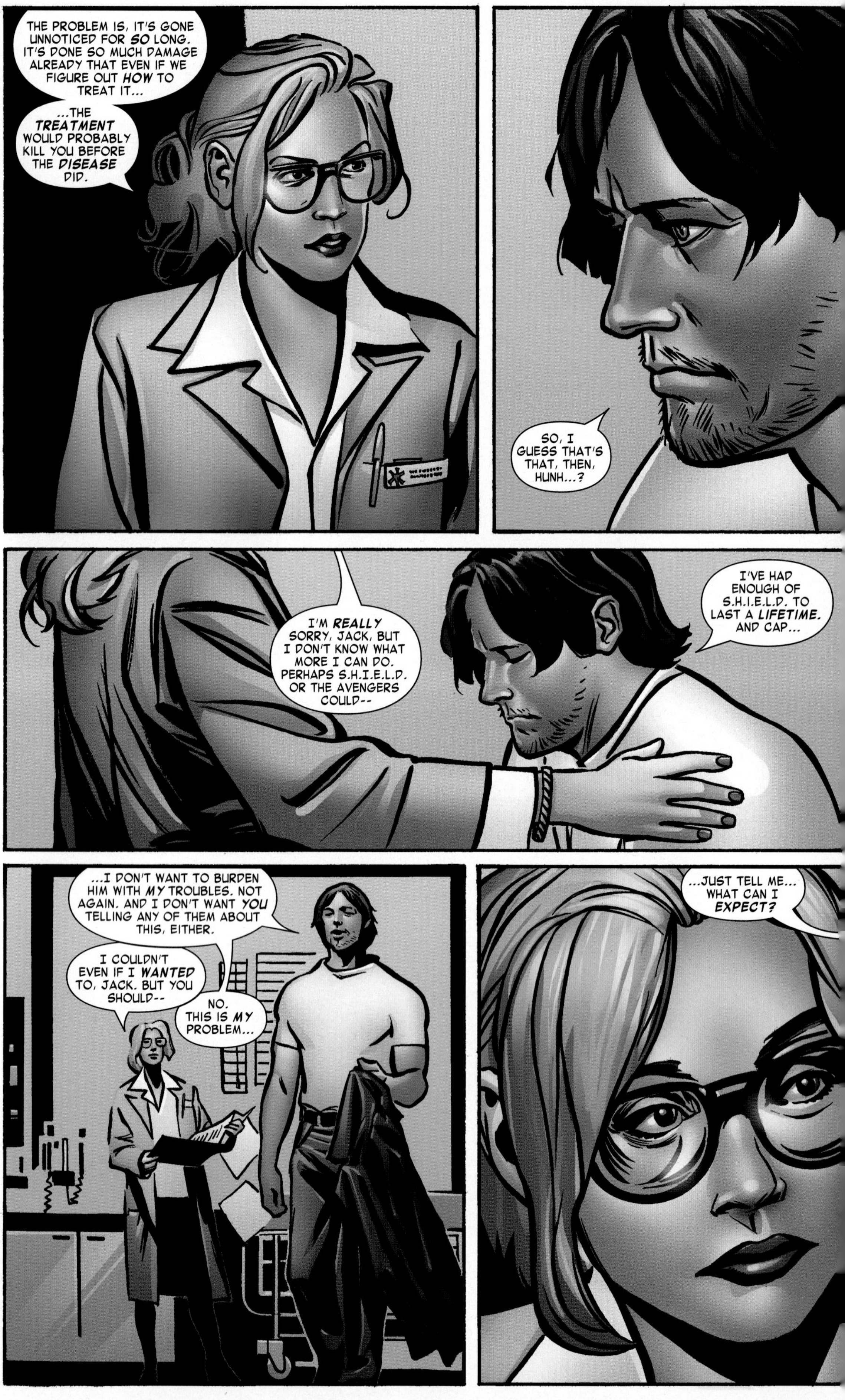
THE PROBLEM IS, IT'S GONE UNNOTICED FOR SO LONG. IT'S DONE SO MUCH DAMAGE ALREADY THAT EVEN IF WE FIGURE OUT HOW TO TREAT IT...
...THE TREATMENT WOULD PROBABLY KILL YOU BEFORE THE DISEASE DID.
SO, I GUESS THAT'S THAT, THEN, HUNH...?
I'M REALLY SORRY, JACK, BUT I DON'T KNOW WHAT MORE I CAN DO. PERHAPS S.H.I.E.L.D. OR THE AVENGERS COULD--
I'VE HAD ENOUGH OF S.H.I.E.L.D. TO LAST A LIFETIME. AND CAP...
...I DON'T WANT TO BURDEN HIM WITH MY TROUBLES. NOT AGAIN. AND I DON'T WANT YOU TELLING ANY OF THEM ABOUT THIS, EITHER.
I COULDN'T EVEN IF I WANTED TO, JACK. BUT YOU SHOULD--
NO. THIS IS MY PROBLEM...
...JUST TELL ME... WHAT CAN I EXPECT?

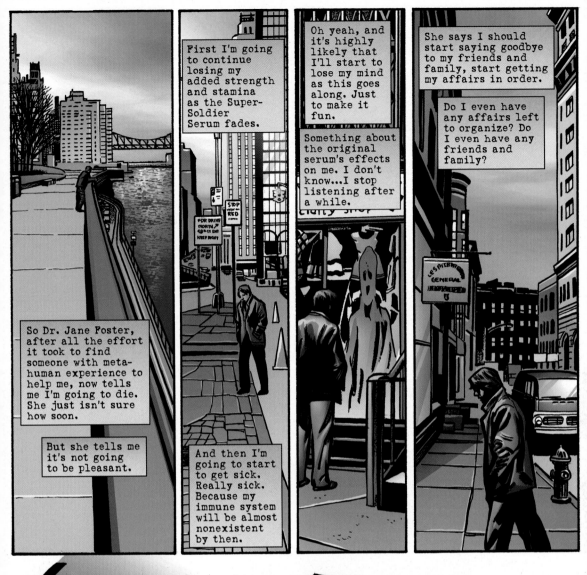

So Dr. Jane Foster, after all the effort it took to find someone with meta-human experience to help me, now tells me I'm going to die. She just isn't sure how soon.

But she tells me it's not going to be pleasant.

First I'm going to continue losing my added strength and stamina as the Super-Soldier Serum fades.

And then I'm going to start to get sick. Really sick. Because my immune system will be almost nonexistent by then.

Oh yeah, and it's highly likely that I'll start to lose my mind as this goes along. Just to make it fun.

Something about the original serum's effects on me. I don't know...I stop listening after a while.

She says I should start saying goodbye to my friends and family, start getting my affairs in order.

Do I even have any affairs left to organize? Do I even have any friends and family?

I suppose the only person I really think of as a friend is Cap...but that's such a twisted history...

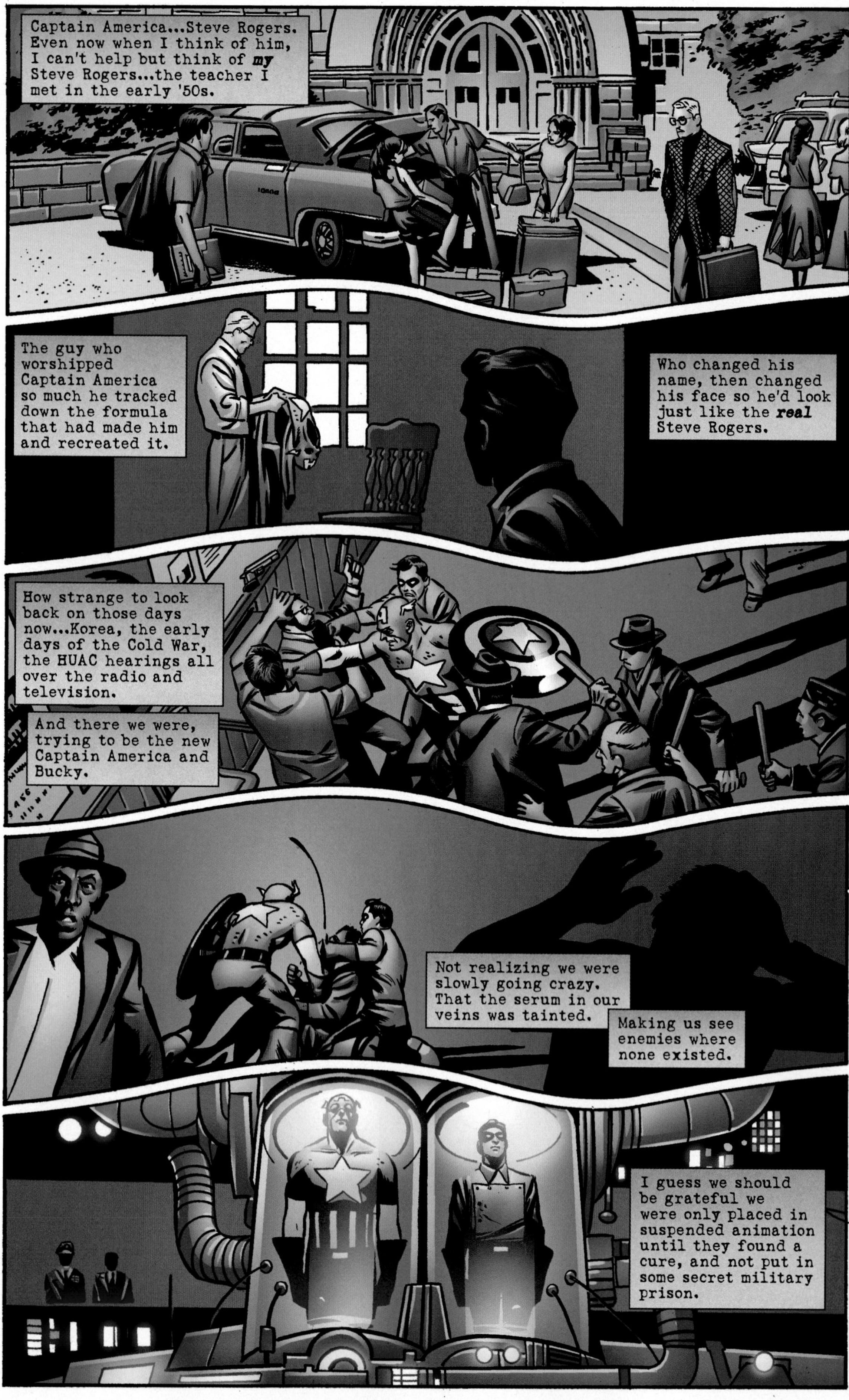
Captain America...Steve Rogers. Even now when I think of him, I can't help but think of *my* Steve Rogers...the teacher I met in the early '50s.
The guy who worshipped Captain America so much he tracked down the formula that had made him and recreated it.
Who changed his name, then changed his face so he'd look just like the *real* Steve Rogers.
How strange to look back on those days now...Korea, the early days of the Cold War, the HUAC hearings all over the radio and television.
And there we were, trying to be the new Captain America and Bucky.
Not realizing we were slowly going crazy. That the serum in our veins was tainted.
Making us see enemies where none existed.
I guess we should be grateful we were only placed in suspended animation until they found a cure, and not put in some secret military prison.

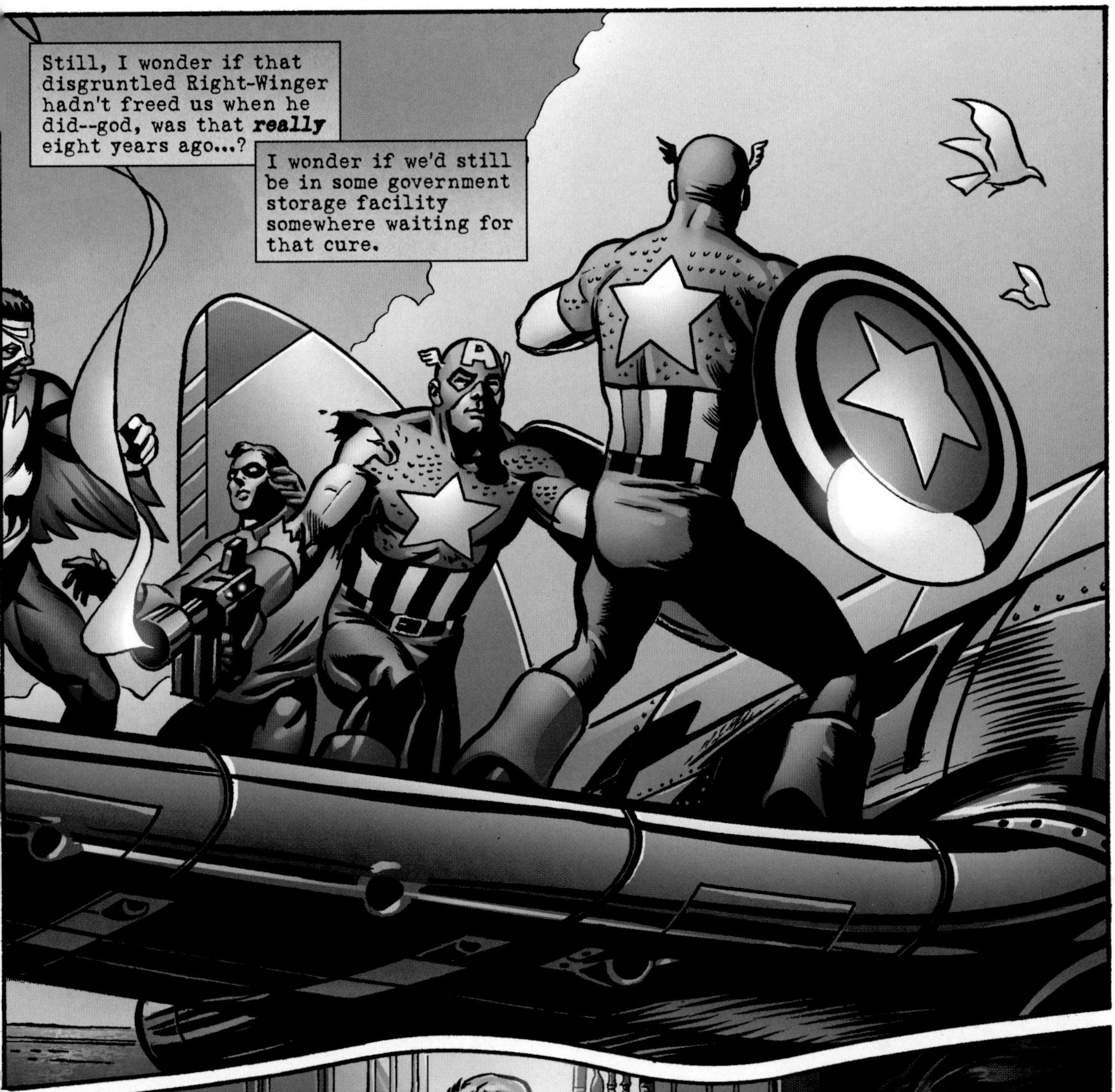
Still, I wonder if that disgruntled Right-Winger hadn't freed us when he did--god, was that **really** eight years ago...?
I wonder if we'd still be in some government storage facility somewhere waiting for that cure.

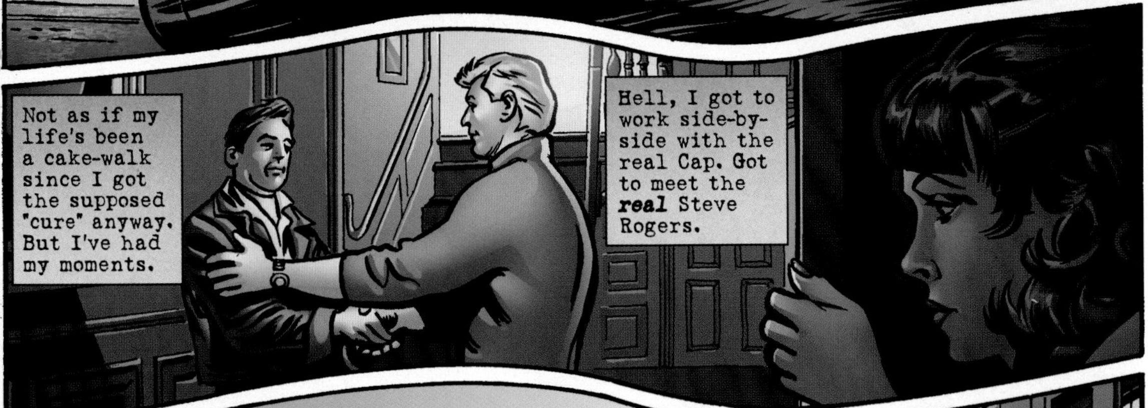
Not as if my life's been a cake-walk since I got the supposed "cure" anyway. But I've had my moments.
Hell, I got to work side-by-side with the real Cap. Got to meet the **real** Steve Rogers.

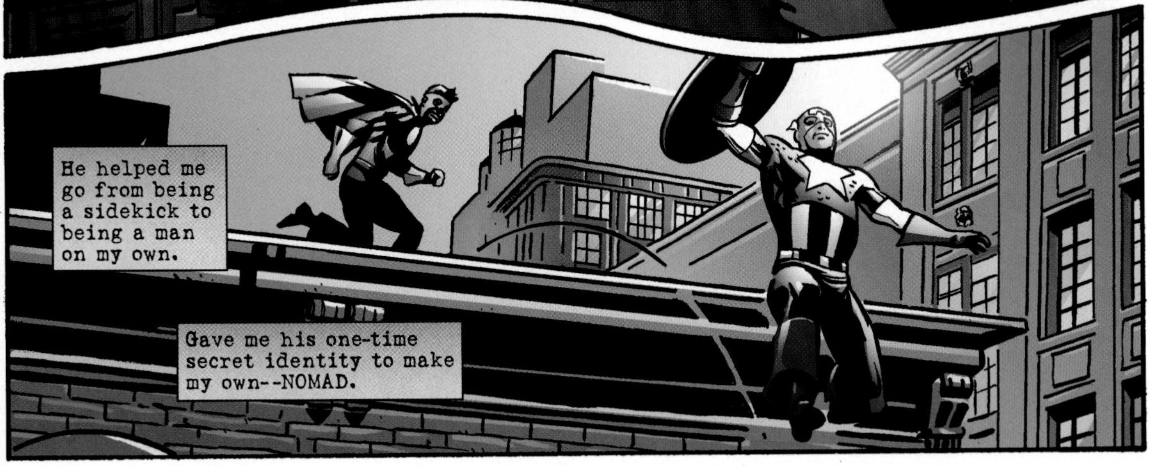
He helped me go from being a sidekick to being a man on my own.
Gave me his one-time secret identity to make my own--NOMAD.

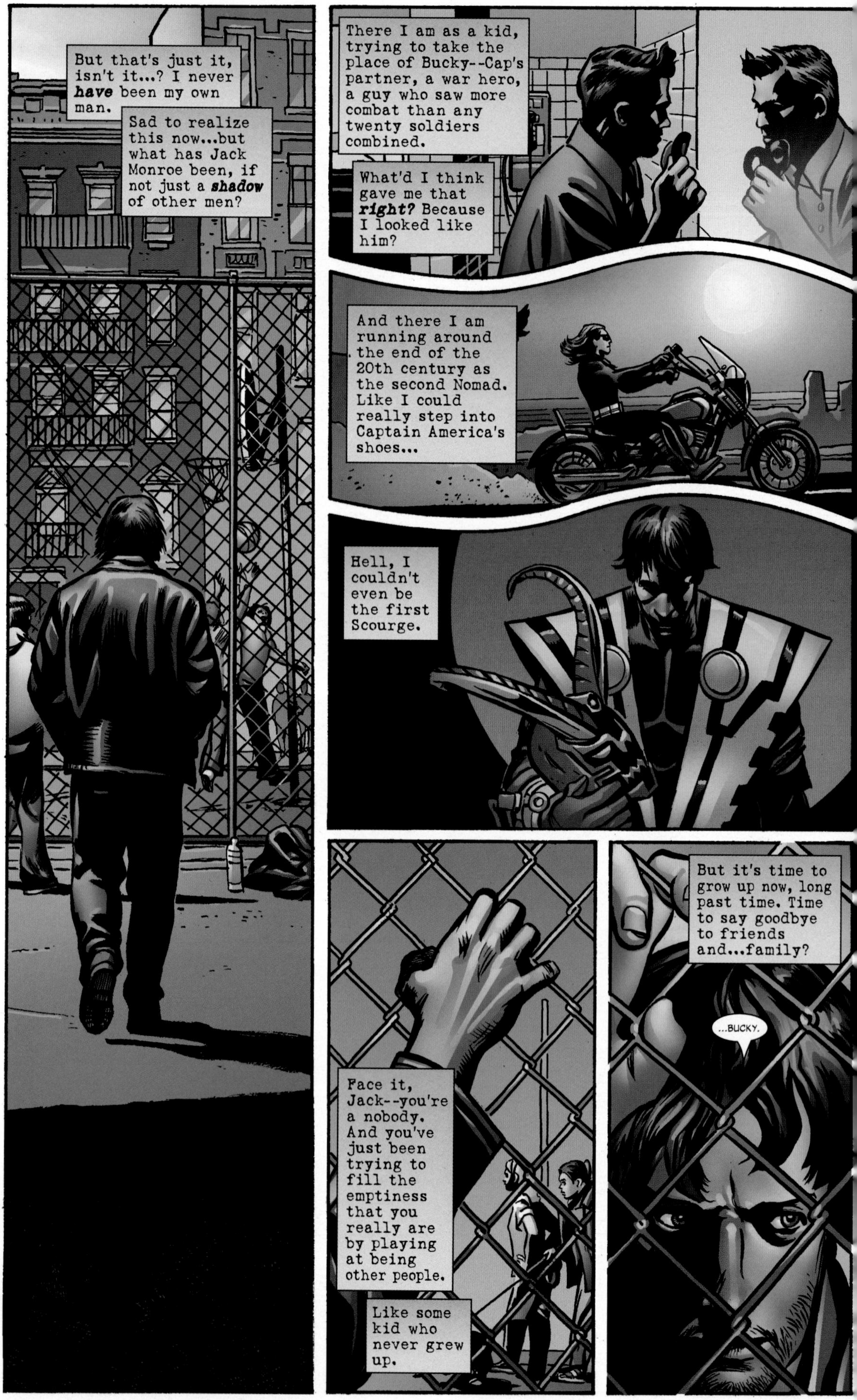
But that's just it, isn't it...? I never **have** been my own man.
Sad to realize this now...but what has Jack Monroe been, if not just a **shadow** of other men?
There I am as a kid, trying to take the place of Bucky--Cap's partner, a war hero, a guy who saw more combat than any twenty soldiers combined.
What'd I think gave me that **right?** Because I looked like him?
And there I am running around the end of the 20th century as the second Nomad. Like I could really step into Captain America's shoes...
Hell, I couldn't even be the first Scourge.
Face it, Jack--you're a nobody. And you've just been trying to fill the emptiness that you really are by playing at being other people.
Like some kid who never grew up.
But it's time to grow up now, long past time. Time to say goodbye to friends and...family?
...BUCKY.

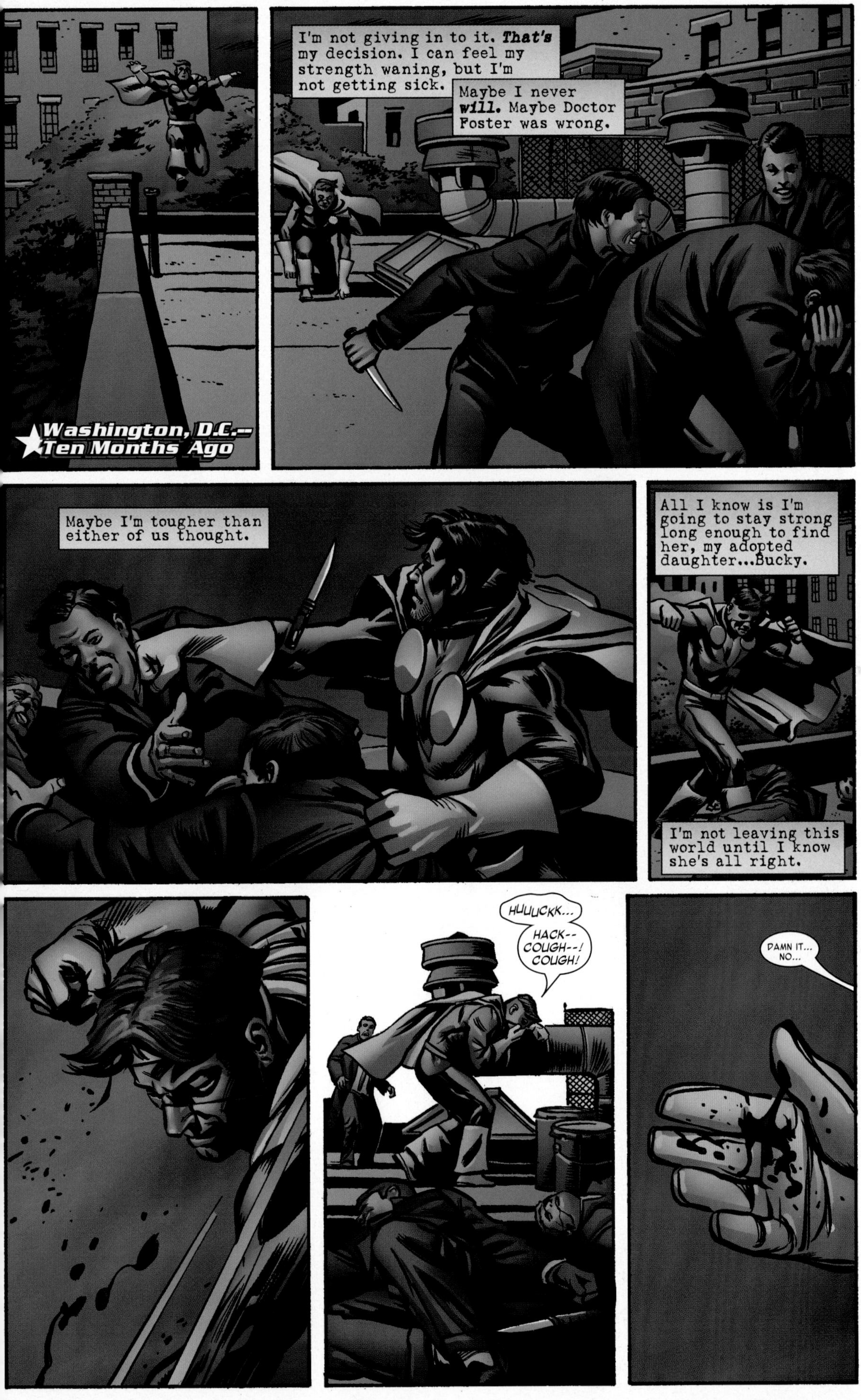
Washington, D.C.--
Ten Months Ago
I'm not giving in to it. That's my decision. I can feel my strength waning, but I'm not getting sick.
Maybe I never will. Maybe Doctor Foster was wrong.
Maybe I'm tougher than either of us thought.
All I know is I'm going to stay strong long enough to find her, my adopted daughter...Bucky.
I'm not leaving this world until I know she's all right.
HUUUCKK...
HACK--COUGH--! COUGH!
DAMN IT... NO...

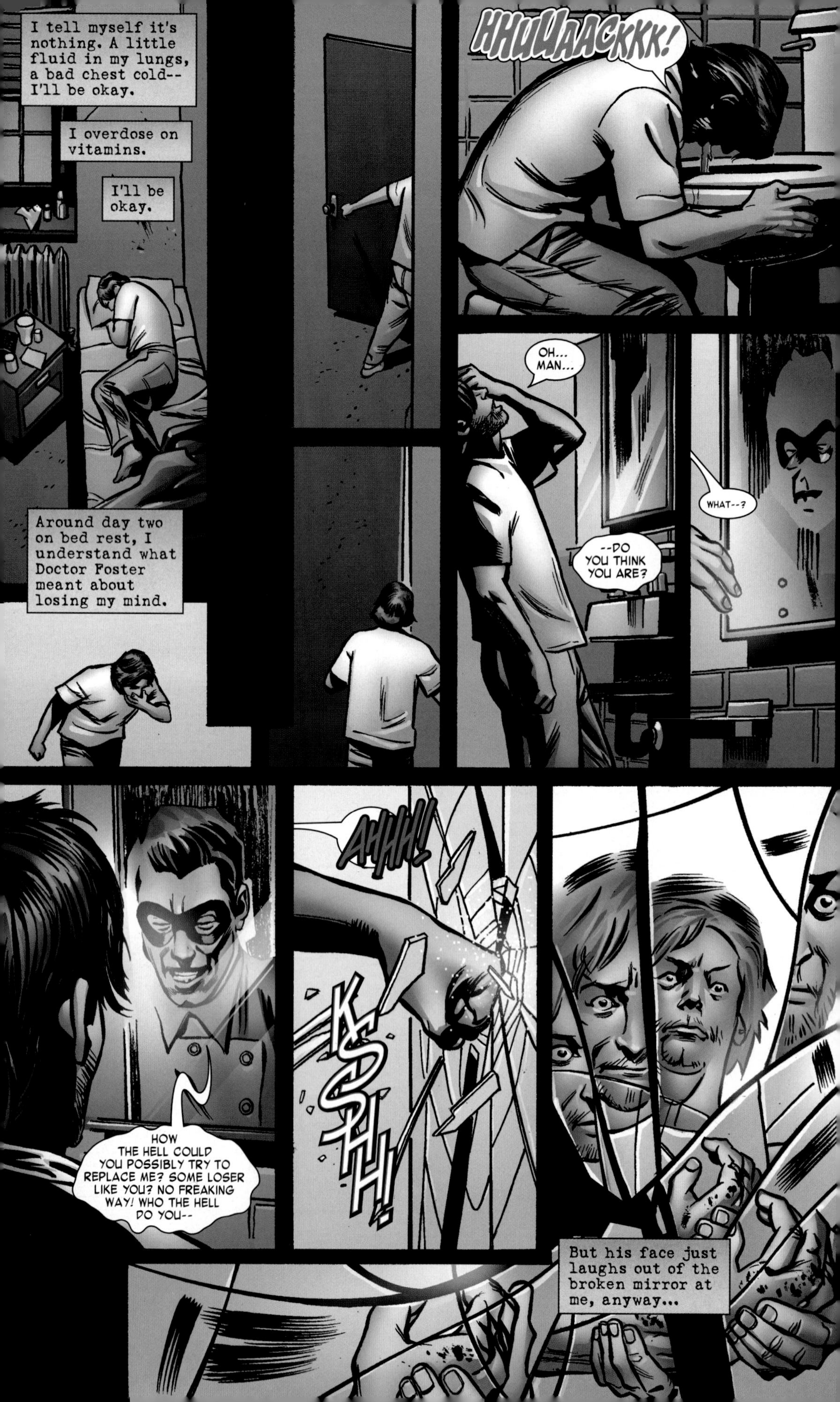

I tell myself it's nothing. A little fluid in my lungs, a bad chest cold-- I'll be okay.
I overdose on vitamins.
I'll be okay.
HHUUAACKKK!
Around day two on bed rest, I understand what Doctor Foster meant about losing my mind.
OH... MAN...
WHAT--?
--DO YOU THINK YOU ARE?
HOW THE HELL COULD YOU POSSIBLY TRY TO REPLACE ME? SOME LOSER LIKE YOU? NO FREAKING WAY! WHO THE HELL DO YOU--
AHHH!
KSHH!
But his face just laughs out of the broken mirror at me, anyway...

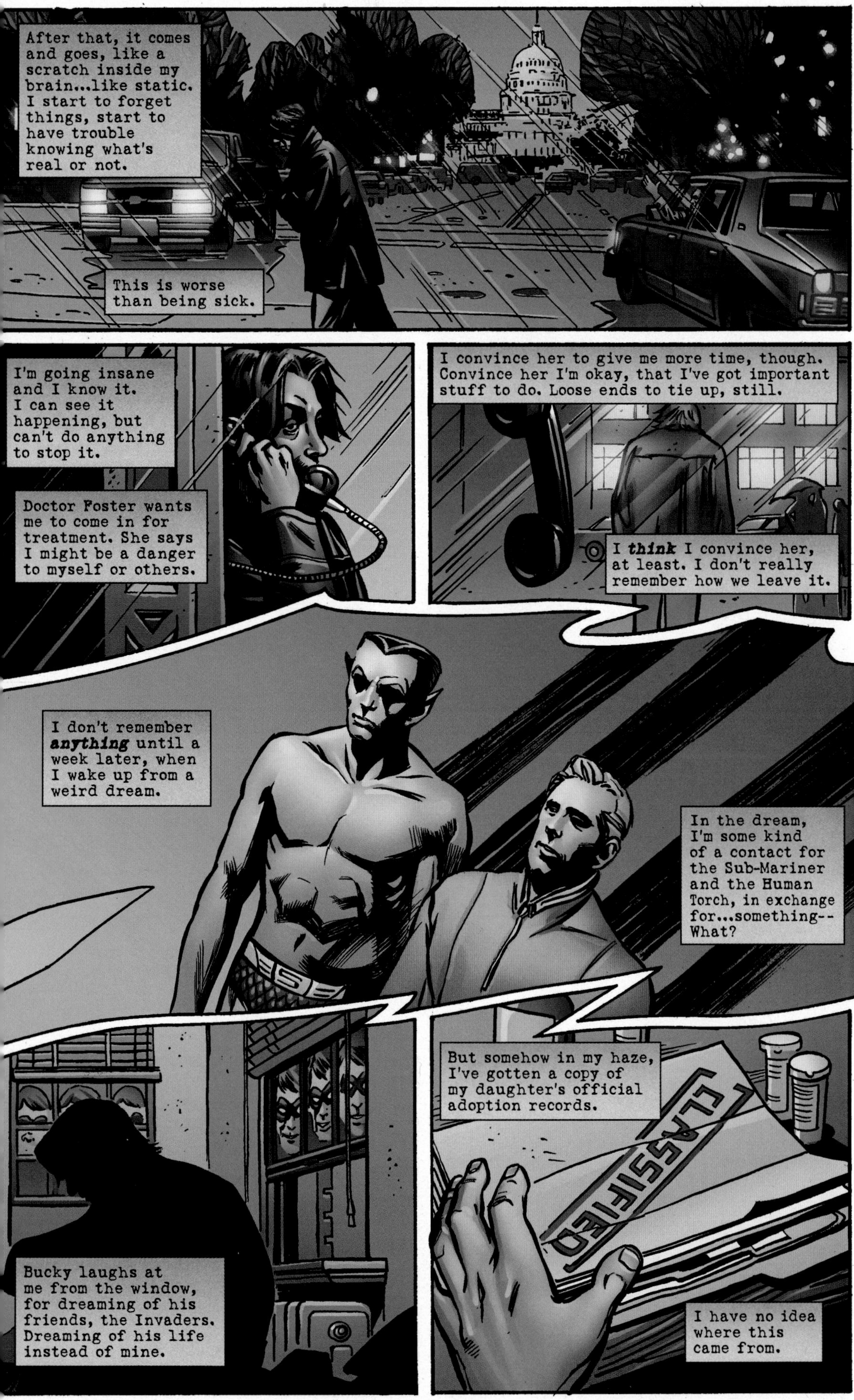
After that, it comes and goes, like a scratch inside my brain...like static. I start to forget things, start to have trouble knowing what's real or not.
This is worse than being sick.
I'm going insane and I know it. I can see it happening, but can't do anything to stop it.
Doctor Foster wants me to come in for treatment. She says I might be a danger to myself or others.
I convince her to give me more time, though. Convince her I'm okay, that I've got important stuff to do. Loose ends to tie up, still.
I *think* I convince her, at least. I don't really remember how we leave it.
I don't remember ***anything*** until a week later, when I wake up from a weird dream.
In the dream, I'm some kind of a contact for the Sub-Mariner and the Human Torch, in exchange for...something-- What?
Bucky laughs at me from the window, for dreaming of his friends, the Invaders. Dreaming of his life instead of mine.
But somehow in my haze, I've gotten a copy of my daughter's official adoption records.
CLASSIFIED
I have no idea where this came from.

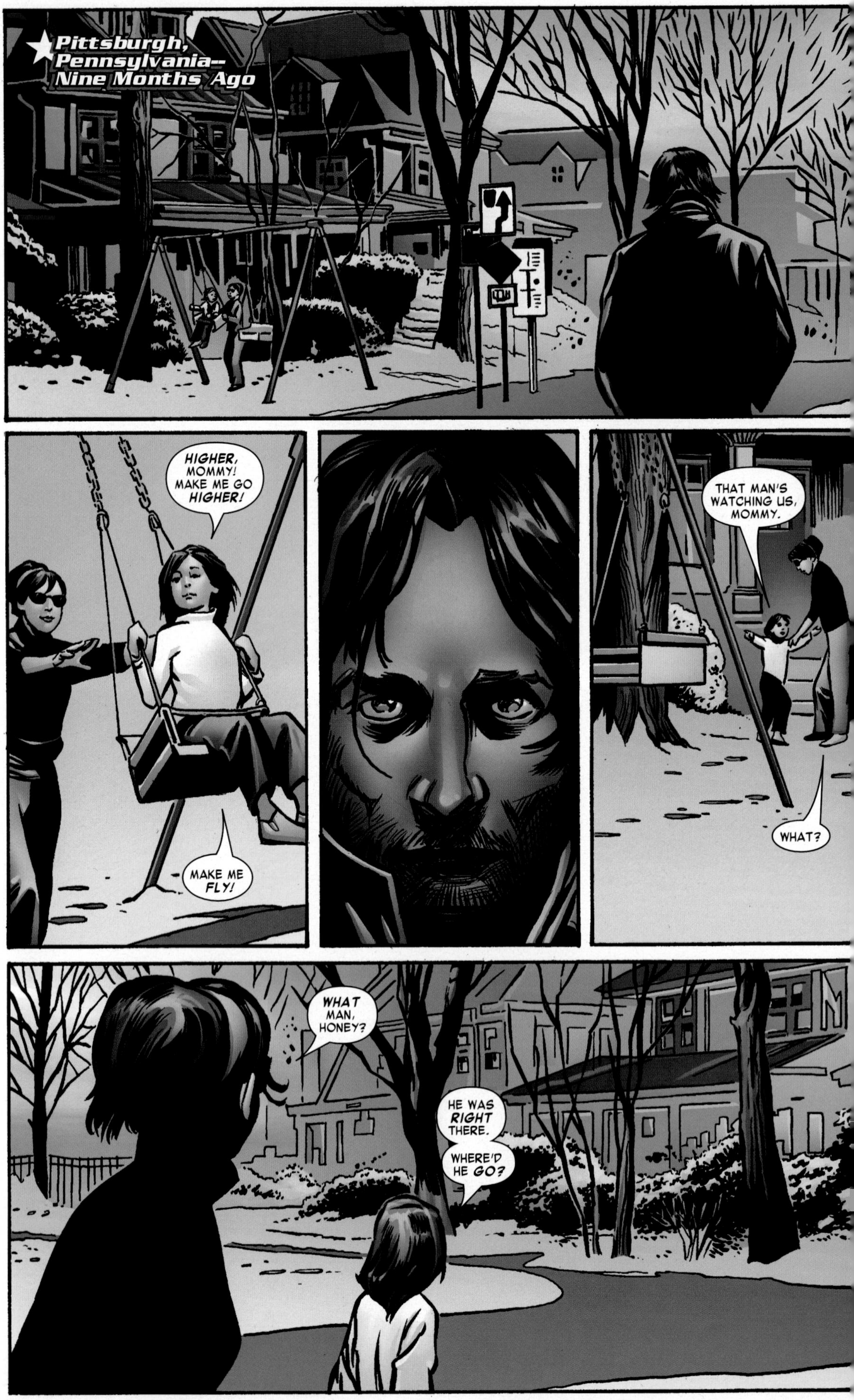

Pittsburgh, Pennsylvania-- Nine Months Ago
HIGHER, MOMMY! MAKE ME GO HIGHER!
MAKE ME FLY!
THAT MAN'S WATCHING US, MOMMY.
WHAT?
WHAT MAN, HONEY?
HE WAS RIGHT THERE.
WHERE'D HE GO?

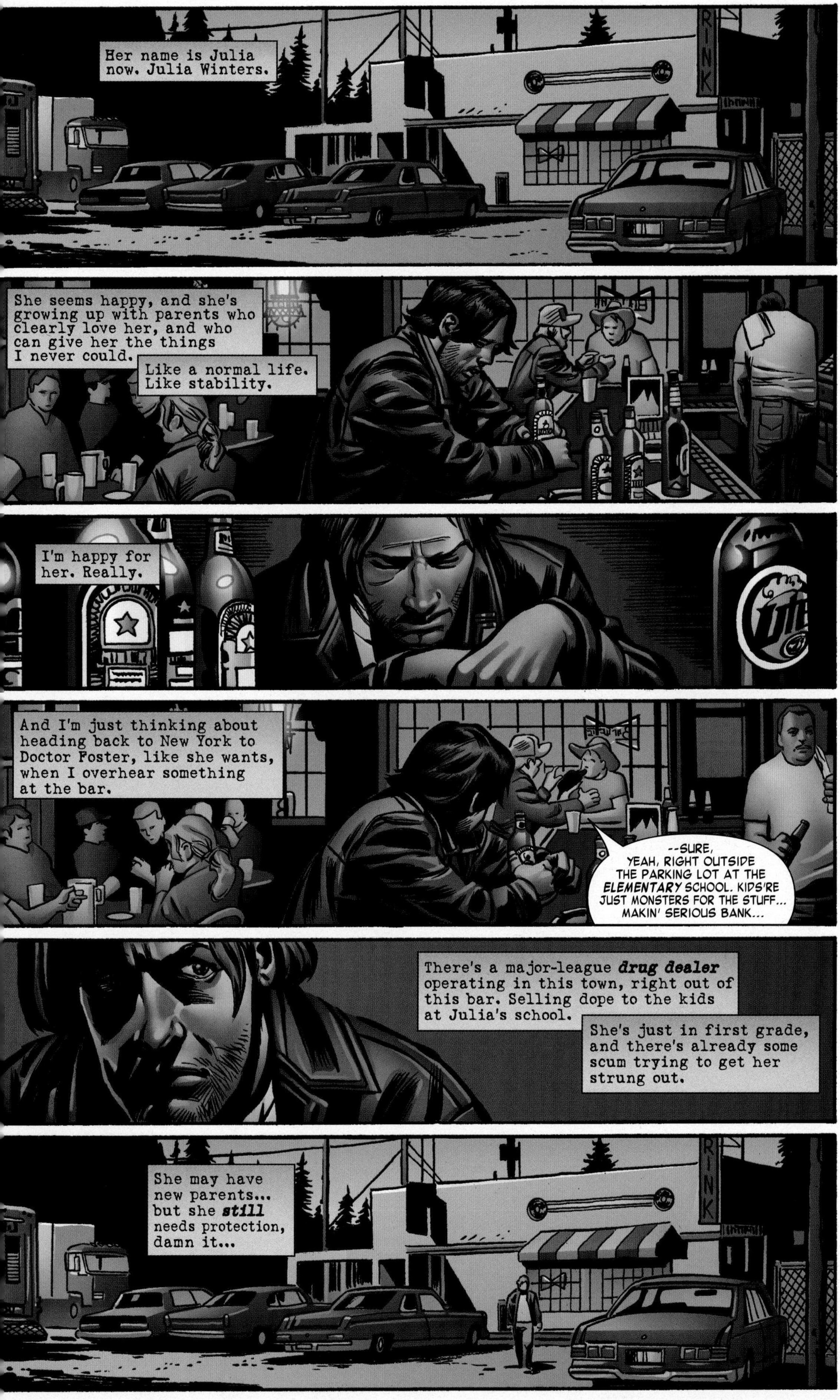
Her name is Julia now. Julia Winters.
She seems happy, and she's growing up with parents who clearly love her, and who can give her the things I never could.
Like a normal life. Like stability.
I'm happy for her. Really.
And I'm just thinking about heading back to New York to Doctor Foster, like she wants, when I overhear something at the bar.
--SURE, YEAH, RIGHT OUTSIDE THE PARKING LOT AT THE ELEMENTARY SCHOOL. KIDS'RE JUST MONSTERS FOR THE STUFF... MAKIN' SERIOUS BANK...
There's a major-league drug dealer operating in this town, right out of this bar. Selling dope to the kids at Julia's school.
She's just in first grade, and there's already some scum trying to get her strung out.
She may have new parents... but she still needs protection, damn it...

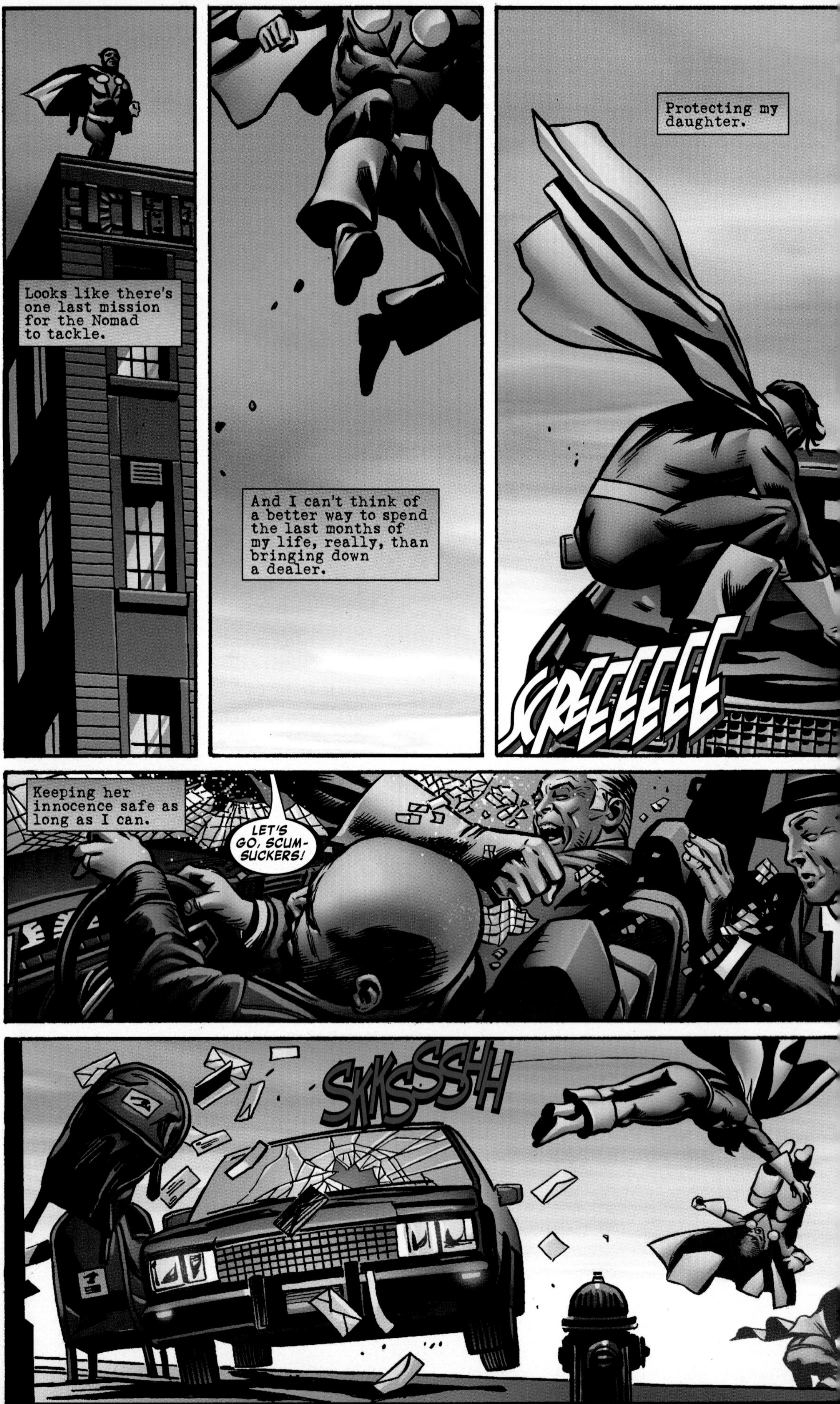
Looks like there's one last mission for the Nomad to tackle.
And I can't think of a better way to spend the last months of my life, really, than bringing down a dealer.
Protecting my daughter.
SCREEEEEE
Keeping her innocence safe as long as I can.
LET'S GO, SCUM-SUCKERS!
SKKSSSHH

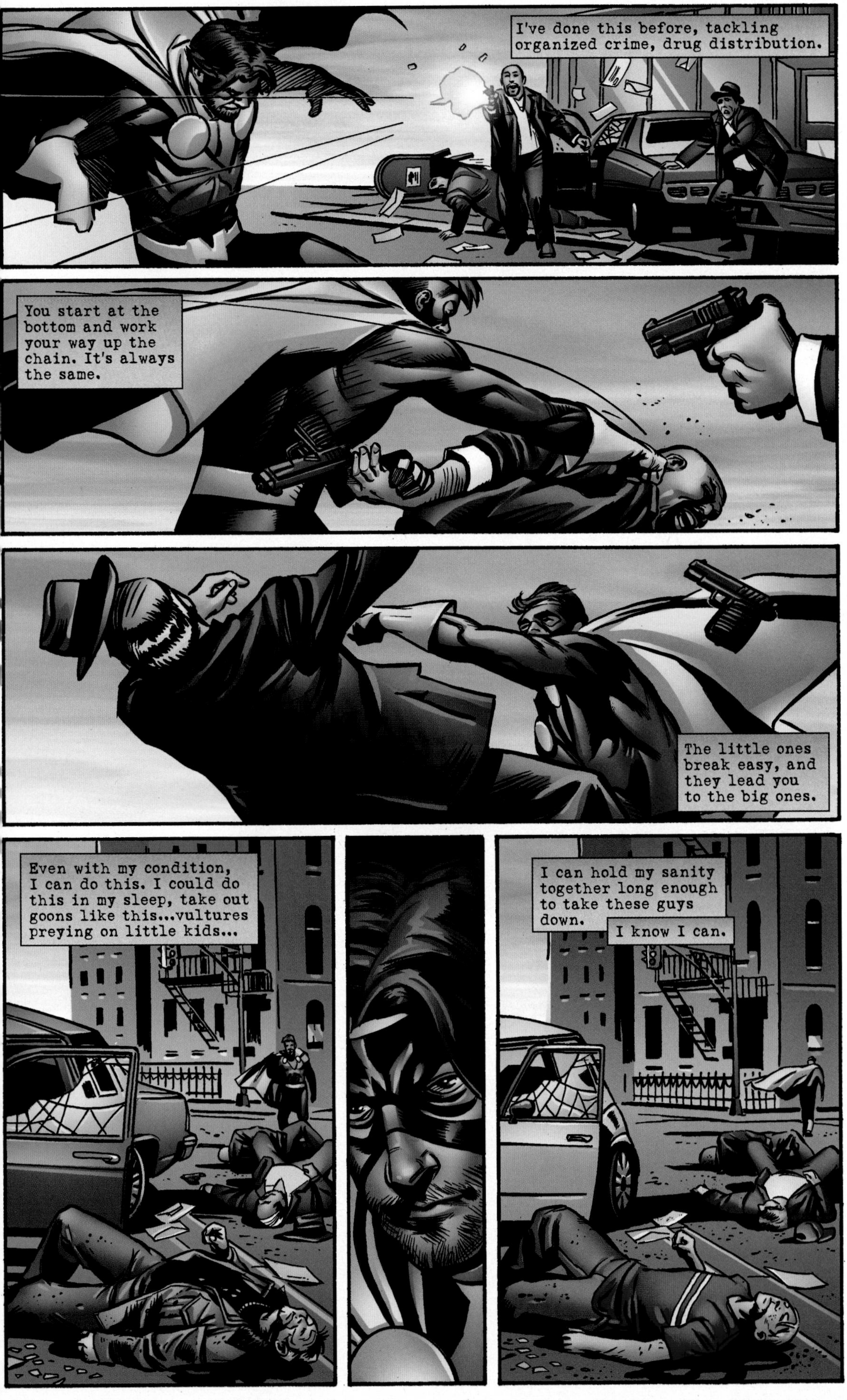

I've done this before, tackling organized crime, drug distribution.
You start at the bottom and work your way up the chain. It's always the same.
The little ones break easy, and they lead you to the big ones.
Even with my condition, I can do this. I could do this in my sleep, take out goons like this...vultures preying on little kids...
I can hold my sanity together long enough to take these guys down.
I know I can.

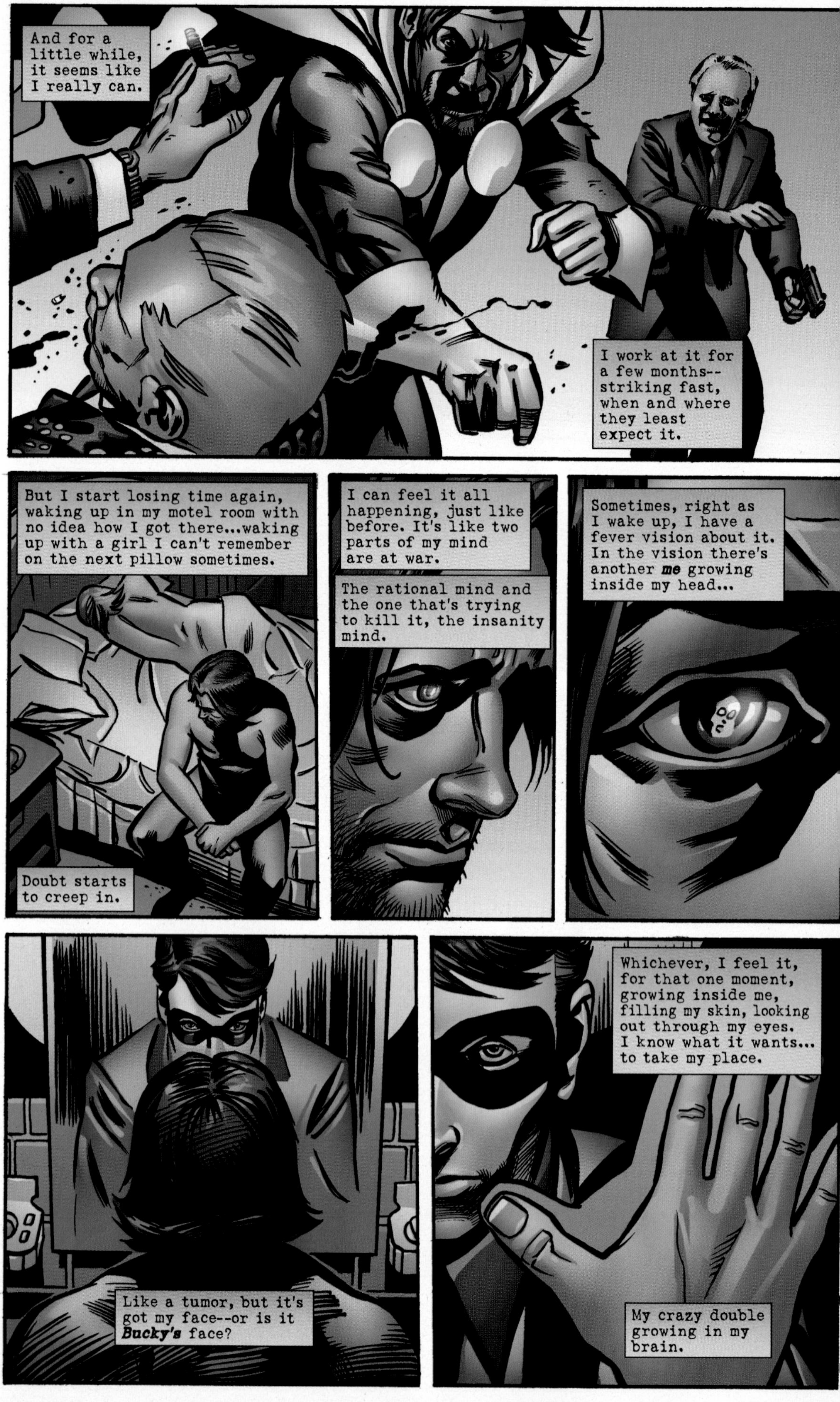
And for a little while, it seems like I really can.
I work at it for a few months--striking fast, when and where they least expect it.
But I start losing time again, waking up in my motel room with no idea how I got there...waking up with a girl I can't remember on the next pillow sometimes.
Doubt starts to creep in.
I can feel it all happening, just like before. It's like two parts of my mind are at war.
The rational mind and the one that's trying to kill it, the insanity mind.
Sometimes, right as I wake up, I have a fever vision about it. In the vision there's another *me* growing inside my head...
Like a tumor, but it's got my face--or is it ***Bucky's*** face?
Whichever, I feel it, for that one moment, growing inside me, filling my skin, looking out through my eyes. I know what it wants... to take my place.
My crazy double growing in my brain.

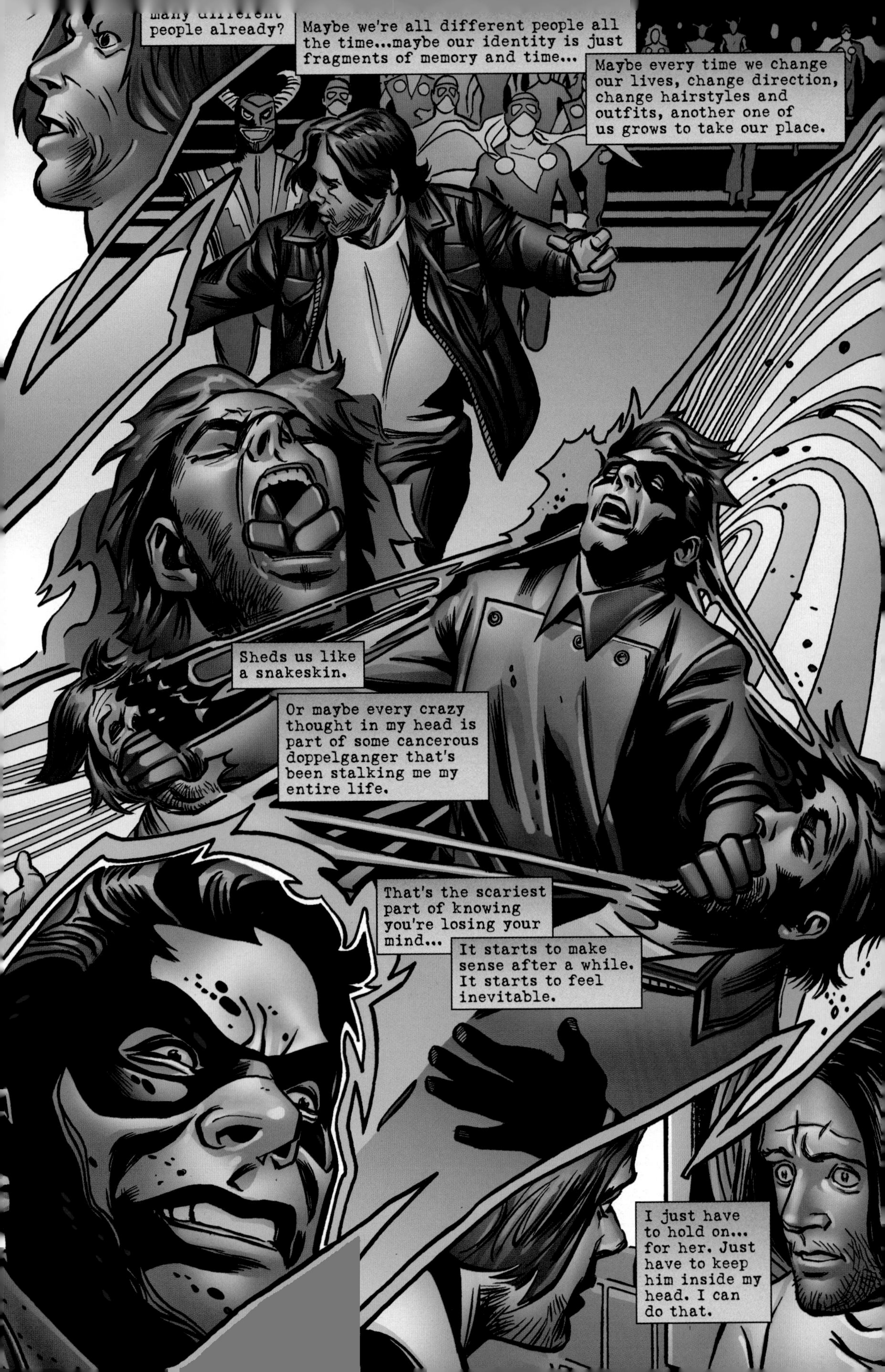

people already?
Maybe we're all different people all the time...maybe our identity is just fragments of memory and time...
Maybe every time we change our lives, change direction, change hairstyles and outfits, another one of us grows to take our place.
Sheds us like a snakeskin.
Or maybe every crazy thought in my head is part of some cancerous doppelganger that's been stalking me my entire life.
That's the scariest part of knowing you're losing your mind...
It starts to make sense after a while. It starts to feel inevitable.
I just have to hold on... for her. Just have to keep him inside my head. I can do that.

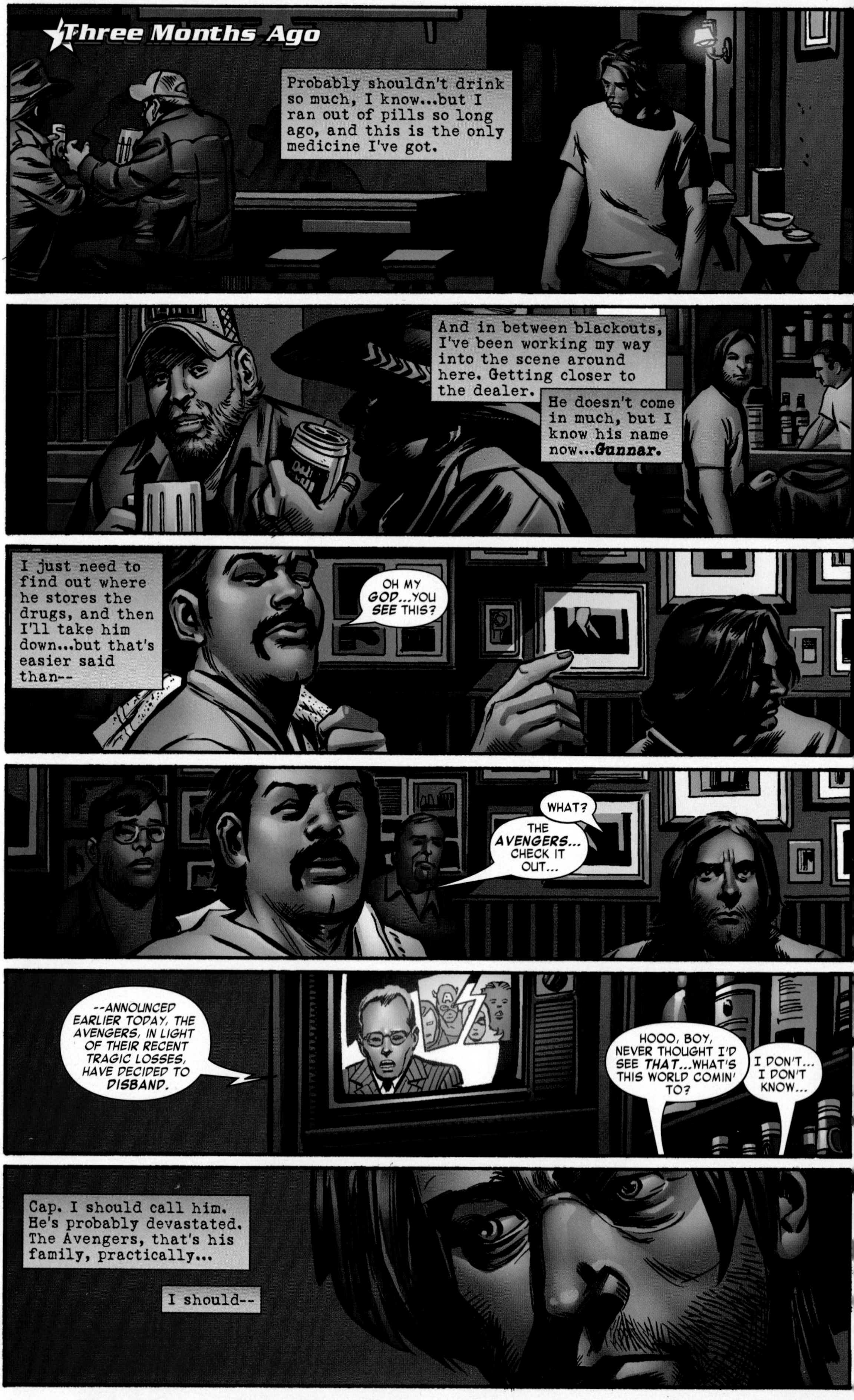
Three Months Ago
Probably shouldn't drink so much, I know...but I ran out of pills so long ago, and this is the only medicine I've got.
And in between blackouts, I've been working my way into the scene around here. Getting closer to the dealer.
He doesn't come in much, but I know his name now...Gunnar.
I just need to find out where he stores the drugs, and then I'll take him down...but that's easier said than--
OH MY GOD...YOU SEE THIS?
WHAT?
THE AVENGERS... CHECK IT OUT...
--ANNOUNCED EARLIER TODAY, THE AVENGERS, IN LIGHT OF THEIR RECENT TRAGIC LOSSES, HAVE DECIDED TO DISBAND.
HOOO, BOY, NEVER THOUGHT I'D SEE THAT...WHAT'S THIS WORLD COMIN' TO?
I DON'T... I DON'T KNOW...
Cap. I should call him. He's probably devastated. The Avengers, that's his family, practically...
I should--

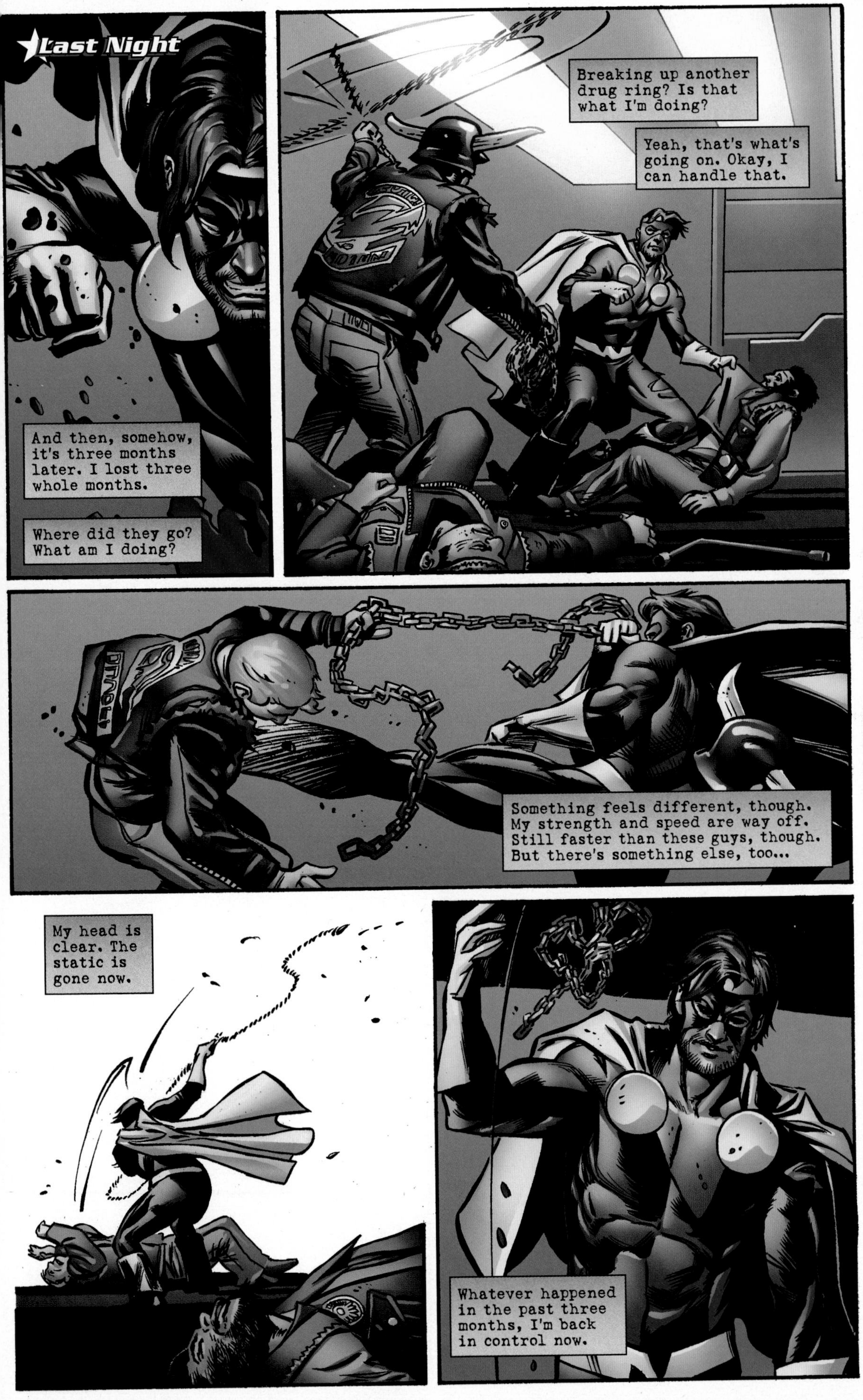
Last Night
And then, somehow, it's three months later. I lost three whole months.
Where did they go? What am I doing?
Breaking up another drug ring? Is that what I'm doing?
Yeah, that's what's going on. Okay, I can handle that.
Something feels different, though. My strength and speed are way off. Still faster than these guys, though. But there's something else, too...
My head is clear. The static is gone now.
Whatever happened in the past three months, I'm back in control now.

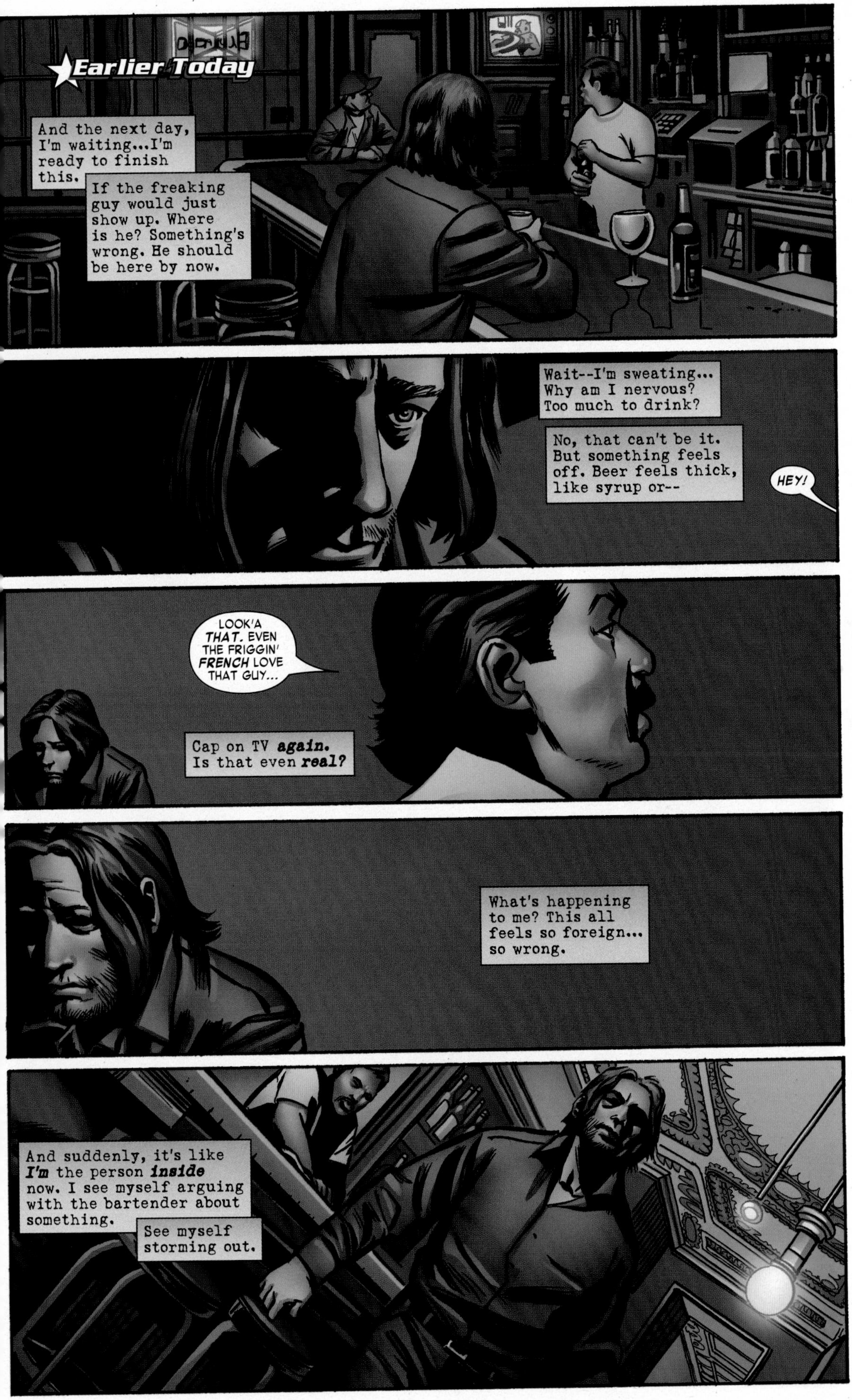

Earlier Today
And the next day, I'm waiting...I'm ready to finish this.
If the freaking guy would just show up. Where is he? Something's wrong. He should be here by now.
Wait--I'm sweating... Why am I nervous? Too much to drink?
No, that can't be it. But something feels off. Beer feels thick, like syrup or--
HEY!
LOOK'A *THAT.* EVEN THE FRIGGIN' *FRENCH* LOVE THAT GUY...
Cap on TV *again.* Is that even *real?*
What's happening to me? This all feels so foreign... so wrong.
And suddenly, it's like *I'm* the person *inside* now. I see myself arguing with the bartender about something.
See myself storming out.

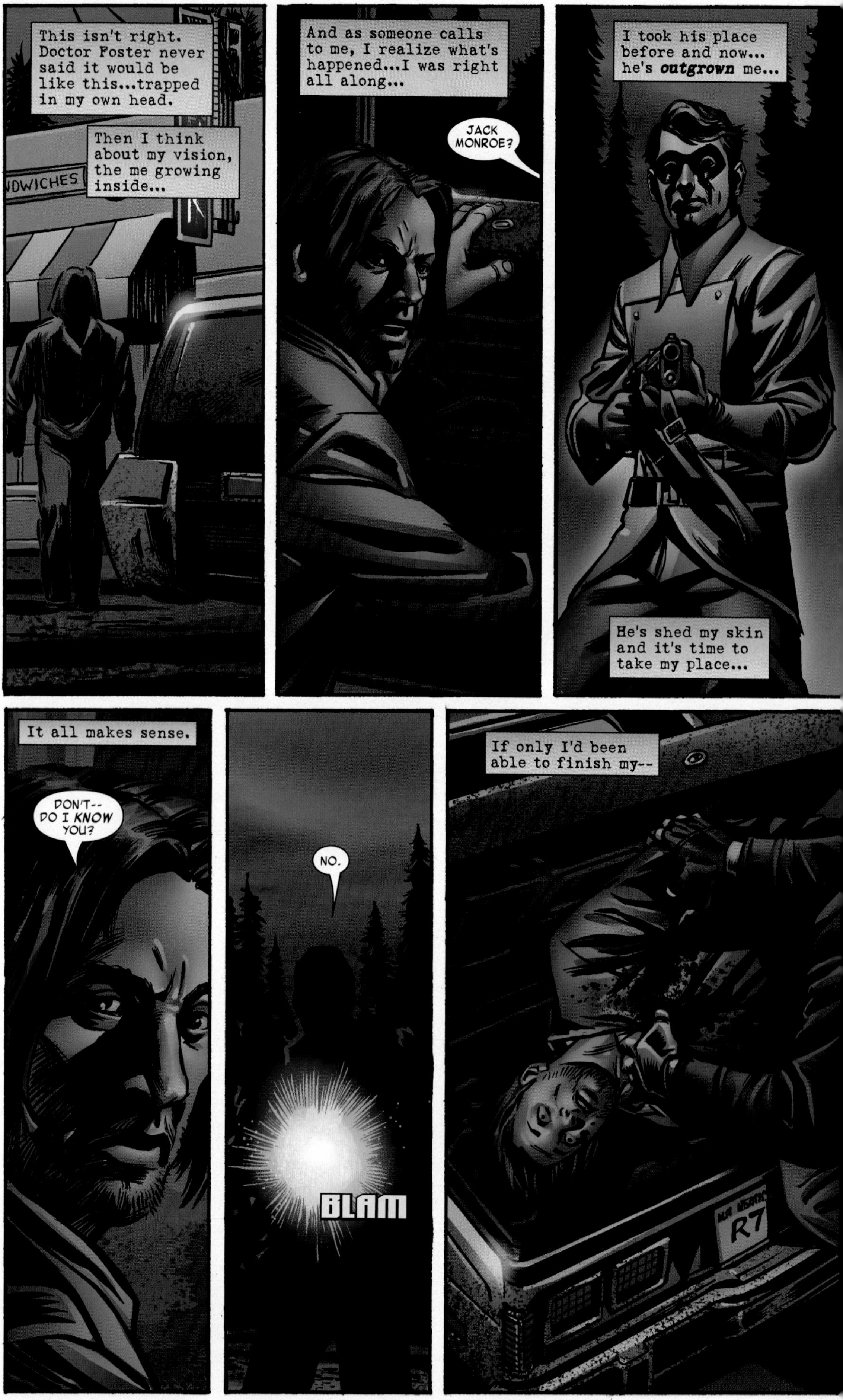
This isn't right. Doctor Foster never said it would be like this...trapped in my own head.
Then I think about my vision, the me growing inside...
NDWICHES
And as someone calls to me, I realize what's happened...I was right all along...
JACK MONROE?
I took his place before and now... he's *outgrown* me...
He's shed my skin and it's time to take my place...
It all makes sense.
DON'T-- DO I *KNOW* YOU?
NO.
BLAM
If only I'd been able to finish my--
R7

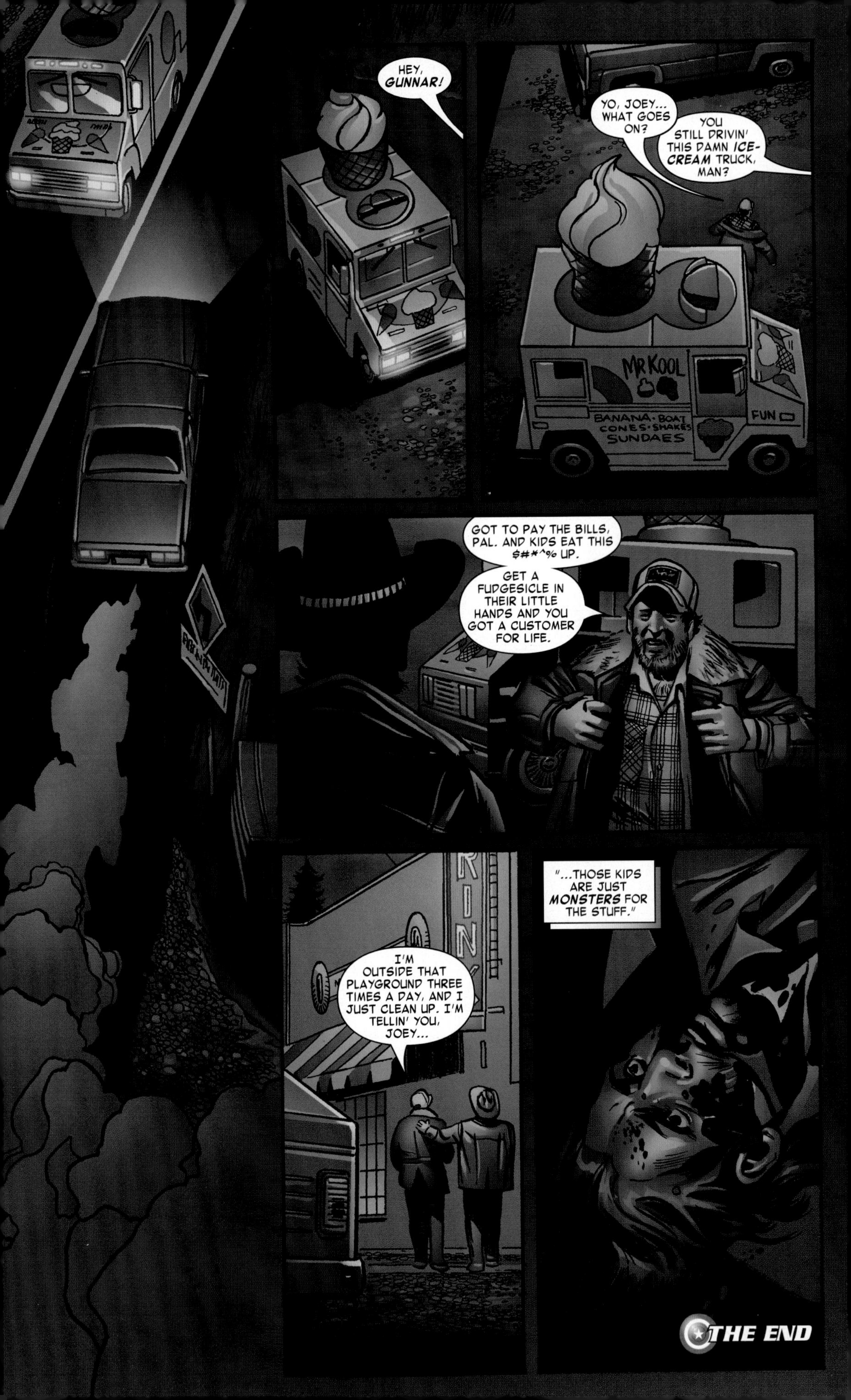
HEY, GUNNAR!
YO, JOEY... WHAT GOES ON?
YOU STILL DRIVIN' THIS DAMN ICE-CREAM TRUCK, MAN?
MR KOOL
BANANA BOAT CONES SHAKES SUNDAES
FUN
GOT TO PAY THE BILLS, PAL. AND KIDS EAT THIS $#*^% UP.
GET A FUDGESICLE IN THEIR LITTLE HANDS AND YOU GOT A CUSTOMER FOR LIFE.
I'M OUTSIDE THAT PLAYGROUND THREE TIMES A DAY, AND I JUST CLEAN UP. I'M TELLIN' YOU, JOEY...
"...THOSE KIDS ARE JUST MONSTERS FOR THE STUFF."
THE END

PROMOTIONAL ART FOR *CAPTAIN AMERICA #1* BY STEVE EPTING

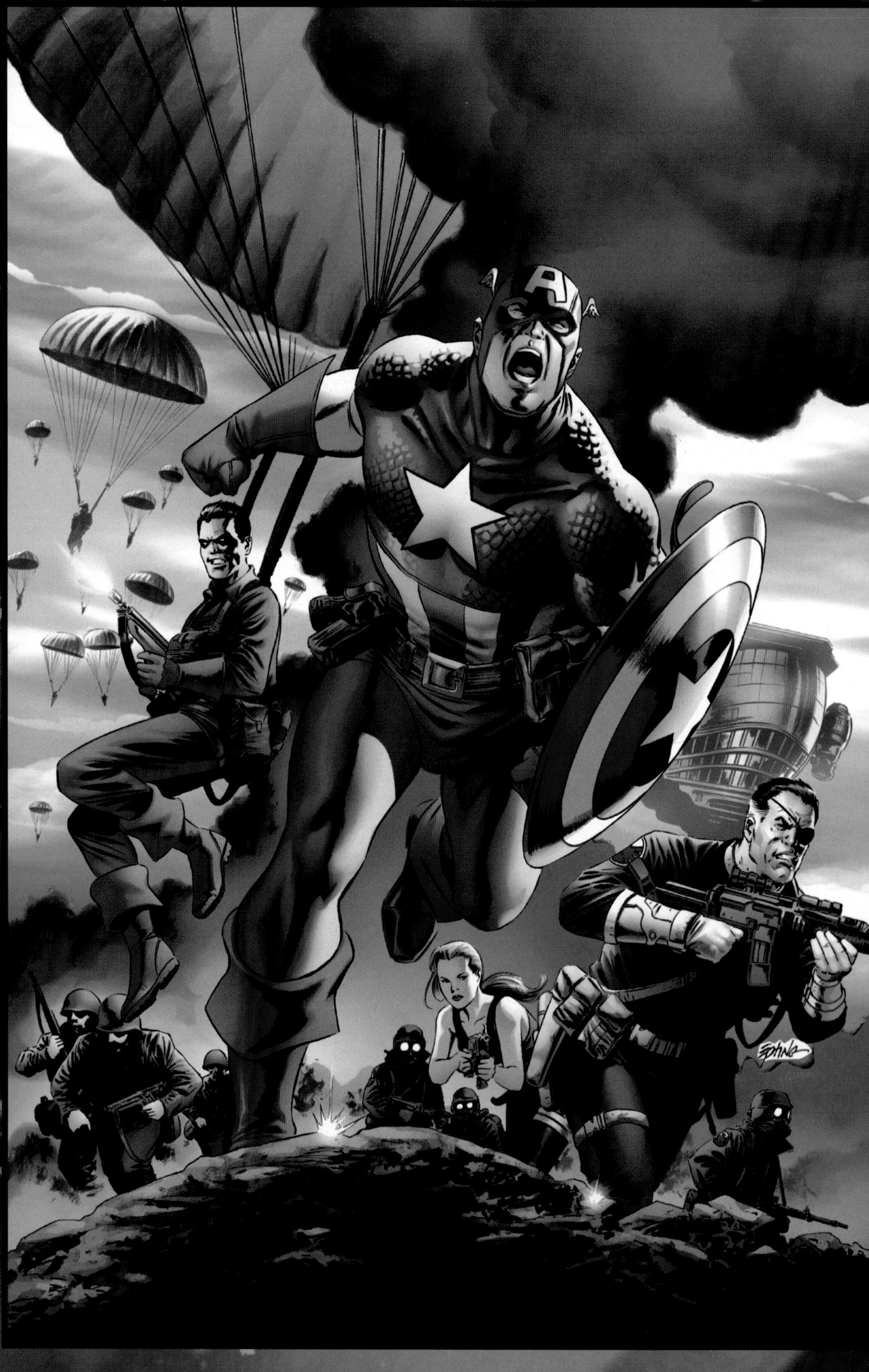

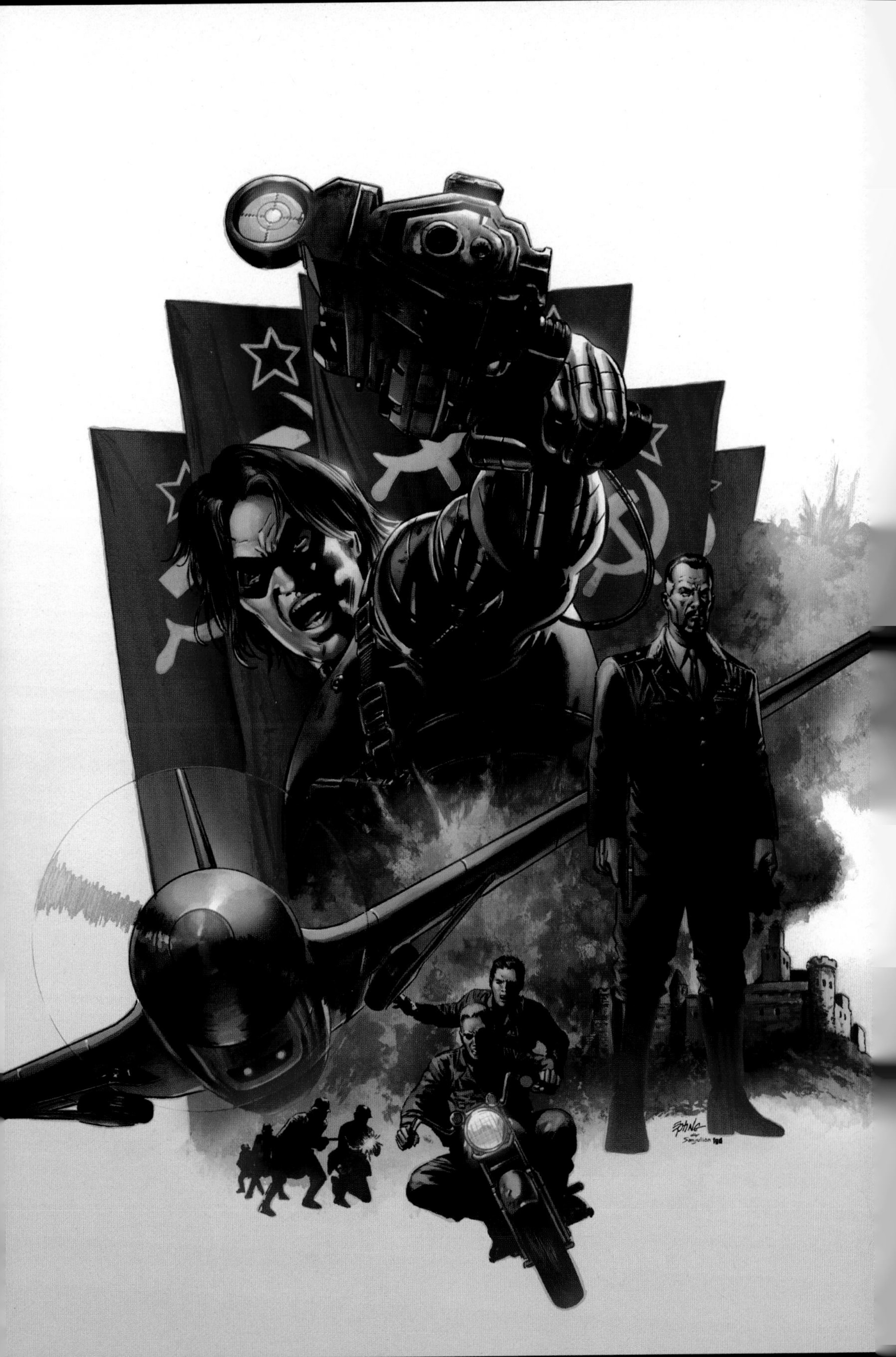

WINTER SOLDIER CONCEPT SKETCHES BY STEVE EPTING

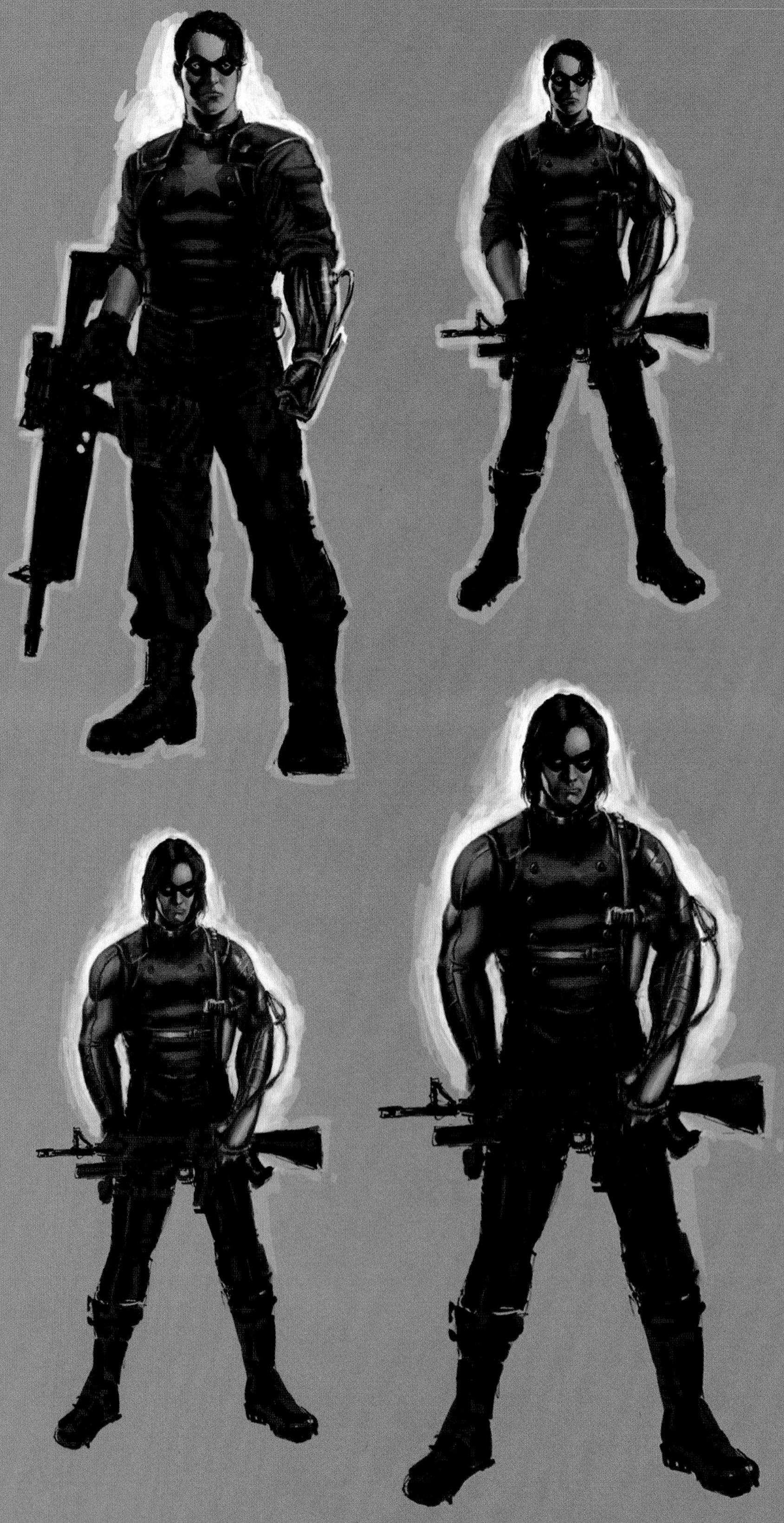

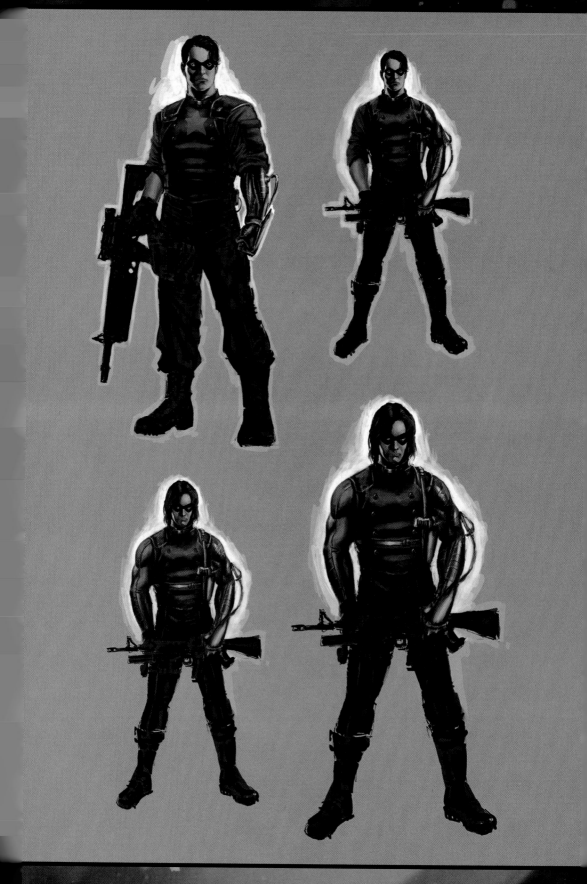